DEVELOPMENTAL CURRICULUM PROJECTS

DEVELOPMENTAL CURRICULUM PROJECTS: DECISION POINTS AND PROCESSES

A Study of Similarities and Differences
in Methods of Producing Developmental Curricula

Hulda Grobman
Professor of Education
New York University

To the memory of Joseph Gross
A reflection of his legacy

FOREWORD

The late 1950's and the 1960's were made more exciting and more meaningful to many people in all aspects of education by the verve and new style of the many curriculum projects. The new approaches to content and to method, carried through in many cases by people new to the game, afforded as a very minimum—and there was much more than the minimum—that breath of fresh air which had been so sorely needed for many years to clear the head and increase the energy of the body called "education." It would be a shame, indeed, if that kind of imagination and exploration were to fail to continue in some measure in American education. However, it would be more of a shame if such a movement were to continue without the benefit of a self-conscious look at its own methods, decision points, constraints, and adaptations.

This book is the first public attempt at a critical overview of those aspects of the curriculum projects of that period. It is true that earlier we had very useful descriptions of the scene. One of the most notable was the report by John I. Goodlad *et al., The Changing School Curriculum.* That treatise not only described a number of the projects but explicated certain problems and issues and offered suggestions for next steps.

This present book adds to the total story by analyzing the processes and decision points of a large number of the notable curriculum-development projects. It helps make clear some of the differences in approach taken by various projects, and it suggests reasons for some of the successes and the failures in certain areas. The treatment ranges in coverage from discussion of financial and organizational constraints to development of aims and purposes, from problems in diffusion to aspects of evaluation. All of this is accomplished through a mixture of good journalism, useful history, and meaningful analysis.

Many of us who have been connected in one way or another with curriculum development in the period under discussion have felt a strong need for this type of approach to the phenomenon. We are fortunate in having the study written by a person who had very real experience with several curriculum projects, who took the time to interview curriculum-project people and peruse the necessary documents, and who has the courage to draw conclusions from personal value judgments. There will be new attempts at reforming curricula and they probably will be of a different order. The story in this book will help them be better projects than they would have been without it.

J. THOMAS HASTINGS
Center for Instructional Research
and Curriculum Evaluation
University of Illinois
Urbana, Illinois

June 1970

PREFACE

This volume is concerned with identifying some of the critical facets of the work of developmental curriculum projects and what seem to be some promising approaches. It reflects knowledge gained from a personal involvement with a number of projects, and background on others obtained from visits, conversations with persons affiliated with such projects, and reading of project materials. It is not an attempt at a census of existing developmental curriculum projects or all possible procedures for implementing projects. And it is not a prescription for new projects and does not attempt to establish a proper set of procedures to be followed.

The conclusions drawn and the suggestions made reflect personal value judgments. The evidence use in arriving at these value judgments is often nonquantified; however, even where documentation of source and quantifiable data exist, citations are not always included. Such omissions are selective and reflect my wish to respect the confidence of many persons with whom I have talked over the last ten years. As groups have been feeling their way in this very new kind of venture, which I call the developmental curriculum project, with no precedents to guide them, they have naturally made some mistakes, some misjudgments, and some inaccurate predictions. To embarrass or hamper such efforts by publicly documenting the persons and groups involved seems far less important than providing information about such mistakes so that others can avoid them; it is especially important to lend support to the strengths of those projects that have produced noteworthy successes.

ACKNOWLEDGEMENTS

For me, there are two kinds of debts a person can incur. One kind is the material one, which can be seen and touched. It may be as small as a cup of sugar, or as large an amount of money as you can borrow. This has to be paid as soon as possible, so that your own good self-image and personal dignity will not be crushed by it.

The other kind of debt is a spiritual one. It is the one that spurs man to be better than he is, and somehow drives him to go beyond the call of need and duty. One should wear this kind of debt as a suit of shining armor. It can never be fully repaid, but you wish that it could be, with such compounded interest that it would go beyond the wealth of Midas.

K. LEE (1968)

The author has many debts that cannot be repaid. Just as there is no such thing as an instant curriculum, there can be no instant book on curriculum projects. In either case, there is a gestation period, a testing of ideas, a working and reworking. And for the most successful ventures, the end result represents ideas from many sources developed into a new end product, a synthesis of many elements.

Many people have contributed the elements included in this synthesis, to the ideas and information underlying the end product. There are too many of them to name. But to all of them I am grateful. Particular mention should be made of the assistance given by the Center for Instructional Research and Curriculum Evaluation of the University of Illinois and the faculty affiliated with CIRCE. For many years, CIRCE has provided gracious hospitality, a sounding board for ideas, and a highly supportive atmosphere, thereby exemplifying the proper role of a university center of learning.

The end product, the synthesis, is the responsibility of the author. The errors of omission and commission are hers alone.

Table of Contents

034491

I

THE DEVELOPMENTAL CURRICULUM PROJECT

BACKGROUND OF DEVELOPMENTAL CURRICULUM PROJECTS

In the United States, education is primarily a local responsibility and is locally controlled. American educators have often contrasted this local control and the resulting opportunity for variability with the French system, which is said to be so rigid that all classes at a given grade level and subject, anywhere in the country, are doing the same thing at the same time. For many years, education books have supported a myth that in America, curriculum is developed in the individual school and classroom, using outside materials largely for guidance or as resource materials to fit into locally created syllabi. Teacher-training courses have included practice in developing such units and putting these units together into semester or year courses. This myth has been presented not only as the optimal method of materials development, but as the actual method used in the schools.

Despite this pride in the variability and flexibility in American public education, the fact is that, until about ten years ago, there has been a high degree of uniformity in schools within the same city or state, and even in schools throughout the country. Courses have been rather closely tied to textbooks that have had relatively few basic changes over the years. Not only have the same subjects been taught at a given grade level, but often, only one or two books were in general use. Thus, some ten years ago, not only were most students taking biology at the tenth grade, but 75 percent of these tenth grade students were using one of two quite similar texts. The same Shakespeare play was being studied by most eleventh grade English students, and a majority of young students were learning to read from one basic reading series. Where more than one book was used in a given subject area at a given grade level, the contents of the various books were very similar.

From one decade to another, changes were largely in the addition of new facts, rather than in basic approach and treatment, and even the new facts were slow in finding their way into the texts. Whether it was the dissecting of frogs in biology, the parsing of sentences in English, or the study of Indians in social studies, the grade level placement, activity, and manner of presentation varied little.

Thus, despite the absence of an official curriculum-standardizing authority, curriculum had been effectively standardized by what A. Grobman (1969) calls "control by the marketplace," by the economics of textbook production and sales. This was a situation in which the dead hand of the past made change difficult, despite periodic investigations of education with resultant recommendations for change by national and scholarly groups in education and other disciplines. In the past, after such recommendations for radical change had been made, the organization of such efforts for change was not developed by any specific individual or group. No single author or publisher could afford to undertake the responsibility and the financial risk of producing radically new materials; if he had, such materials would probably have been unused. The system for training teachers was geared to existing materials rather than to change; college admissions and college admission tests were geared to standard course coverage; and there was a general conservative tenor in most school systems. Thus, radical change, though repeatedly urged, was effectively discouraged.

During the first half of the twentieth century, the rate of change in society had accelerated. There was a shrinking time lag between time of discovery and commercial application of discovery.

> Before WWI, the lag between invention and utilization was 33 years, between WWI and WWII it was 17 years. After WWII it decreased to about 9 years, and if the future can be extrapolated on the basis of the past, by 1970 it will be about five or six years. The transistor was discovered in 1948 and by 1960 95% of all the important equipment and more than 50% of *all* electronic equipment utilized them in place of conventional vacuum tubes.
>
> BENNIS AND SLATER (1968)

In education, the time lag seemed to remain constant. Subjects taught, content of subjects, and method of presentation showed little change.

The University of Illinois Committee on School Mathematics (UICSM)[1] may have been the first group organized to make systematic, radical changes in the curriculum through a developmental process, a trial and error method of preparing materials. UICSM started at the University of Illinois in 1951 as a cooperative effort representing education, mathematics, and engineering, and grew out of a concern with the mathematics competence of incoming engineering students. The initial effort was the improvement of high school mathematics courses to include or improve teaching of some skills found wanting in graduates of Illinois high schools who enter the university. Prior to receiving its first outside grant from the Carnegie Foundation in 1956, UICSM operated on a shoestring budget from the university, a budget which provided some released time for a few staff members and not much else. It

---

[1]Appendix A includes a list of abbreviations and acronyms used in this volume.

produced preliminary classroom materials, systematically tried them out in a few schools, received feedback from teachers and students, rewrote and did further tryouts (McCoy, forthcoming). Thus, the UICSM materials represented a team effort of educators and people from the discipline working on a developmental product with the product reflecting experimental results as the work went along.

Through the 1950's, there was a foment of discontent with public education, which reached a climax with the Russian launching of Sputnik, the world's first space probe. Americans, used to being in the forefront of scientific development, were embarrassed and angry over being outdistanced by the Russians. Education was a handy scapegoat. Consequently, many critics focused on the shortcomings of science and mathematics education in the schools as the cause. Concurrently, there was an interest in a new tactic for producing student materials in science that would permit faster updating of curricula—a developmental approach—and also facilitate a new approach to the subject—an approach more closely approximating the scientist's activities. Federal monies, channeled through the National Science Foundation (NSF), became available for the first time for the producing of high school materials in science and mathematics. Although the idea of federal financing for curriculum work in physics preceded Sputnik by a few weeks, undoubtedly that event stimulated prompt action and increased the amount of funding available. Thus in fall, 1957, the Physical Science Study Committee (PSSC), headed by Dr. Jerrald Zacharias, received its first grant from the NSF to work on materials for a high school physics course.

The purpose of the PSSC materials was to prepare students more effectively for college physics. The approach to the subject matter was to be radically new, and the manner of production of materials was also to be different. (It is not clear whether the UICSM activities in any way influenced the PSSC approach, or whether the PSSC approach, though in many ways similar, was developed independently.) While PSSC was not the first developmental curriculum project, it was the first large-scale, federally financed one. Never before had such sums—over $5 million in the first several years of PSSC—been spent to prepare curriculum materials for a course in one subject area.

PSSC opened a new era of curriculum building and innovation in American education. Closely following were the School Mathematics Study Group (SMSG), Chemistry Education Materials Study (CHEM Study), Chemical Bond Approach (CBA), and the Biological Sciences Curriculum Study (BSCS), all of them financed through NSF funds and using developmental processes in preparing curriculum materials. Initially, NSF funding was limited to science and mathematics education at the senior high school level, but later, public financing through NSF and the U.S. Office of Education (OE) was expanded to other levels of public school as well as preschool and college, and to virtually all subject areas. Private foundations have also been funding similar activities and most recently, such commercial textbook publishers as Rand McNally have supported their own developmental curriculum projects.

There is presently some debate about exactly what constitutes a developmental curriculum project and whether this differs from other curriculum projects. For the purposes of this volume, however, the terms developmental curriculum project and curriculum project are synonymous, and refer to group —in contrast to individual or coauthor —efforts to produce some new kind of curriculum, using experimental tryouts of preliminary materials and collecting feedback from such tryouts to be used for the improvement of the curriculum prior to its release for general distribution.

The earliest developmental curriculum efforts were centered primarily on classroom textbooks for students and guides for instructors to permit effective teaching of these texts. A number of projects have since expanded their interests and approaches (they have been concerned with a very broad interpretation of curriculum) to include any activities relevant to student learnings. Some projects work on student text materials; some work on teacher materials in addition to or in place of student materials; some are concerned with supplemental learning materials; and some are primarily process-oriented, to the extent that no student materials are prepared, but instead, the emphasis is on preparing teachers to operate in certain ways.

Thus, the focus of developmental projects varies widely as does the way they go about their tasks. What they have in common is that the effort is not by an individual author, or one or two coauthors, but is broader; there are experimental tryouts of materials or procedures, and feedback from such tryouts is then used to improve the curriculum before it is made generally available.

Those developmental projects in existence for several years have had an unprecedented success in effecting change in American education. While the results may not have been all that their sponsors may have desired, these projects have made substantive changes in record time. There are currently hundreds of such efforts in the United States and also a growing number in many foreign countries. The speed with which projects are multiplying indicates that this method of preparing curricula will occupy a major place in American education for some time.

The earliest of the NSF projects were located on university campuses. With the exception of BSCS, they were initially part of the university and the director was a university faculty member.[2] They all operated with relatively

---

[2]CHEM Study, although sponsored by the American Chemical Society, was funded primarily through grants to the University of California.

small regular staffs, and used groups of visiting subject-matter specialists and high school teachers for short, intensive writing periods during the summers. Experimental classroom materials were prepared during one summer and, at the end of the summer, teachers were briefed for a few days on the use of the experimental materials. These teachers then used the materials with classes during the ensuing school year, sending comments back to the staff on their successes and failures. The summer following this tryout, the materials were again revised, and for some projects, tried out again experimentally in the schools for another year; a final edition was then prepared and published for general distribution. This constitutes the formative period of project acitivities.

The work of the curriculum projects can be divided into two general periods: the formative period, during which materials are being developed; and the summative period, during which materials have been completed (Scriven, 1967). The initial preparation of experimental materials, the preliminary class-room tryouts, and the revising and additional experimental tryouts typify the formative period. Activities after materials' development is completed consti-tute the summative period. These may include preparation of supplemental materials, teacher training, evaluation of the finished product and its adoption or adaptation for use in schools, and activities related to dissemination of materials in the United States and overseas.

The early projects followed the BSCS and SMSG patterns relatively closely, improving and modifying as they saw fit. Although some of the later groups have indicated that they used the same processes, summer writing conference arrangements, kinds of teacher briefings, etc., actually, there have been wide variations in practice to the point where even those who say they are following the BSCS model are, in fact, doing something quite different without recognizing such differences.

Despite the mushrooming of curriculum projects and their output and numerous descriptions of their materials (Goodlad, 1964; Goodlad, 1966; Lockard, 1968[3]), there has been relatively little attention given the variations in the processes used by such projects, the alternatives such projects have in carrying out their work, and the concomitants of the decisions they make in selecting from among these alternatives.[4] Such background should be useful not only to those studying the process of education but also to persons develop-ing new projects or continuing the work of existing ones.

---

[3]Lockard's annotated listing of science and mathematics projects is an annual series; recent editions have included some "miscellaneous" projects in other fields, including some in sociology, anthropology, geography, and computer science.

[4]Descriptions of some process aspects of several projects are available in project newsletters and in histories of the projects. (See Wooton, 1965; A. Grobman, 1969; McCoy, forthcoming; Merrill and Ridgway, 1969; BSCS *NEWSLETTERS.*)

The importance of such attention to decision points and alternatives reflects the assumption that "Freedom is the existence of alternatives or choice" (Gardner, 1961). That is, an awareness of alternatives improves decision making. And deliberate decision making is preferable to intuitive operations that are free from conscious concern with the making of decisions and the weighing of alternatives.

Each curriculum project makes thousands of decisions. Some decisions are made every day. While some of these decisions are relatively trivial, with little influence on later decisions, others have a far-reaching ripple effect in terms of their impact and in circumscribing future decisions and directions. Thus, some decisions, by their very nature, build further constraints into the system and so delimit the degrees of freedom available to projects after that single decision has been made.

It is not possible to review all decisions made by a project; there are too many. Nor is it possible to consider all the possible ramifications of every decision alternative. This volume will focus on some of the major decisions that existing projects have faced and describe some of the concomitants of these decisions. To do so is not to attempt to arrive at one right or best way of conducting a curriculum project; probably there is no single best way. It is an effort to describe ways that have been used, to clarify the alternatives and the variables involved, and relate them to desired outcomes.

As present projects build further experience, perhaps several patterns will emerge as optimal. However, in the search for such optimal procedures, the developmental process may become systematized and routinized. Such routinizing of the process may eliminate what may have been its greatest asset in terms of curriculum building—flexibility. Thus far, projects have reflected the flexibility of a highly experimental approach where, since no *right* ways were known, each project had to build its own vehicle for operation, and in so doing may have enhanced the end result beyond what would have been possible in a more rigid framework.

As Schon (1967) points out, invention is not a series of orderly steps intelligently directed toward an objective spelled out in advance. Invention may be a nonrational process, building on the unexpected; "it does not usually move in a straight line, according to plan, but takes unexpected twists and turns." Innovation is not entirely a manageable process, and failure may lead to more profitable avenues than initial success. And without room for experimentation and new emergent objectives, we may find that *"plus ça change, plus c'est la même chose."*

A DESCRIPTION OF THREE PROJECTS

To give a better perspective of the activities of developmental curriculum projects, several years of the work of three projects are described below.[5]Using these projects as examples does not imply that they are typical or the best of the projects to date. At this stage of curriculum-project work, there are no typical projects and because of the diversity of existing projects, it is pointless to speculate on which is best. These three projects are chosen because they represent very different kinds of organizations and different approaches to the problem of producing curricula. Each represents a departure in some sense from earlier practice. And the author has had personal experience with each.

Biological Sciences Curriculum Study (BSCS) 1959-63

During the late 1950's the American Institute of Biological Sciences (AIBS), an organization of professional societies in biology, became concerned with the teaching of biology in secondary schools and decided to undertake sponsorship of two programs for improvement. One, a crash program, involved development of a biology course presented in a series of films, which it was hoped would become available quite rapidly, and so provide for immediate improvement. The other provided for a longer-range program for improvement, directed by a new organization created by the AIBS—the Biological Sciences Curriculum Study. A director of the BSCS and a chairman of the Steering Committee were selected by the AIBS Executive Committee, and members of a general policy committee—the BSCS Steering Committee—were also selected by this group. This committee included both research biologists and biology educators, who exercised decision-making powers in setting general policy at meetings which were held two or three times a year.

The mandate given the BSCS was a rather general one, indicating that the necessary steps should be taken to improve the teaching of biology in high school. A modest planning grant was obtained from NSF, and the BSCS opened its office in Boulder, Colorado, in the winter of 1959-60, on the campus of the University of Colorado. (Although the BSCS was on the university campus, it was in no sense officially a part of the university. Rather, it rented facilities on a hospitable campus, as did several other educational organizations.) The initial BSCS staff included the director and one secretary. Later in the spring, an assistant director arrived along with several additional secretaries. And the following fall, another professional staff member was added,

---

[5]More detailed descriptions of process for these and other projects are available in A. Grobman (1969), Wooton (1965), McCoy (forthcoming), Symmes (1969), Joint Council on Economic Education (JCEE) (1969), Merrill and Ridgway (1969), and in the newsletters and annual reports of many of the individual projects.

on a one-year assignment, to prepare a review of biological education and past efforts to improve it.

The BSCS Steering Committee, at one of its early meetings, set up a five-member Executive Committee to act for it between meetings; it also set up a number of working committees. One of them, the Committee on Content of the Curriculum, explored ways of improving biology teaching, and came up with the recommendation that the BSCS prepare units that could be used by teachers to prepare their own courses in biology. Teachers were invited to react to this idea, and their comments were generally unfavorable. The prevailing view of the teachers was that they did not have time to prepare their own courses from collections of units—that they would prefer a complete set of course materials, with the possibility of supplementing or adapting these to fit their own needs. As a result, the BSCS decided to prepare complete course materials.

The view of the various BSCS committees was that biology should be a laboratory science and therefore, course materials should include both text and laboratory materials complementing each other, rather than the traditional pattern, where the laboratory was supplemental to the text. Since most high school students take biology, and the biology course is generally offered at the tenth grade, the decision was made to gear the new BSCS course materials to the tenth grade. It was agreed that while it might be desirable in the long run to make biology a culminating course rather than the introductory science course at the high school level, the Steering Committee felt that the BSCS could best honor its mandate to improve high school biology teaching rapidly by working within the existing framework of biology at the tenth grade level and for the average student. This did not reflect a lack of concern for the gifted student or the slow student, but rather represented what seemed to be the most practical starting point for rapid, overall improvement. Again, this represented a Steering Committee decision.

Suggestions were made to the Steering Committee by various BSCS committees and individual members concerning possible approaches to an up-to-date presentation of biology. Several approaches seemed logical as a vehicle for presenting biology. Three different approaches were selected by the committee as providing valid reflections of the current state of biology, and as lending themselves to presentation at the high school level; the Steering Committee decided to undertake all three approaches or versions at the same time, to determine whether any one was, in fact, superior to the others.

After the decision was made to prepare course materials, the BSCS director consulted with the SMSG and PSSC, where parallel developmental work in high school mathematics and physics had started a year or two earlier.

Typically, materials were being prepared by teams of writers during the summers and then tried out on an experimental basis during a subsequent school year, before they were revised and made generally available. The rationale for the experimental tryouts was that if the programs were truly experimental, no one could be sure of their effectiveness until there were some actual classroom tryouts; if the approach of the new materials was really new, one could not be sure that students could handle the materials and skills involved since no one had tried to teach these to students before.

The BSCS decided to adopt a similar procedure, and during the summer of 1960, a two-month summer writing conference with seventy writers—half of them college biologists, half high school biology teachers—was convened in Boulder to prepare three parallel sets of experimental materials for tenth grade biology. For each set of materials, a supervisor was designated as the person with responsibility for coordinating efforts of the writers working on that set of materials. One person had responsibility for coordinating the laboratory materials for all three of the versions. The seventy participants of the summer writing conference were assigned in pairs—one research biologist and one high school biology teacher—to various writing assignments based on an outline cooperatively developed by the supervisor for that version in consultation with the writers.

Although writers were assigned to one version, there was a borrowing of talent back and forth as a need developed. Also, materials for one version might be used or adapted for other versions as they seemed appropriate. Materials were written and circulated for comments among the writers for that version as well as the other versions. They were then revised and recirculated for further comments, until the final product met with the approval of the supervisor. Writers were housed in adjacent offices so that frequent informal contacts were the rule; and writing teams held frequent meetings to plan and iron out conflicting views. The supervisors of the versions also met regularly to share ideas and problems.

The materials produced for each version included a text, a laboratory manual, and a teacher's guide. A teacher's commentary germane to all three versions was also produced. All materials were in paperback, expendable editions, and were provided at no charge to students and teachers in the experimental program. While examination copies were sold to interested persons, classroom use of the experimental materials was limited to participants in the formal tryout program.

During the 1960-61 school year, some 115 teachers tried out the experimental materials in their classrooms with 13,000 students. These participating teachers were selected to represent geographic clusters in various parts of the country, with at least six teachers in each cluster. This was done to permit the experimental teachers to meet weekly in small groups to discuss their experiences and to send back reports to the BSCS. All teachers using these materials had attended a six-day briefing session in Boulder to prepare them for use of the materials. A further opportunity for orientation to the new materials was provided during the weekly meetings, since each was attended by a college biologist who had been a participant in the summer writing conference, and who was prepared to answer questions concerning unfamiliar content or laboratory procedures.

In addition to the weekly group reports, teachers sent back individual reports of their reactions and classroom experiences using the new materials. Each teacher's classrooms were visited by BSCS staff consultants at least twice during the year. And students were tested on newly developed objective-type tests to reflect the new content and skills of the experimental curriculum. At the same time, other types of reactions to the new materials were obtained. Professional societies in biology, education, and psychology, as well as a number of individual biologists and psychologists, were invited to review the materials and make suggestions.

Data gathered from the various sources were collated and systematized, and the supervisor for each version and several of his writers reviewed this feedback material during the year. The Steering Committee also received summaries of the feedback, and Steering Committee members visited experimental classrooms. The feedback evidence indicated rather clearly that all three versions were appropriate for the intended task; that some teachers preferred one and some another; but that when the teacher used the version he preferred, his students seemed to do as well as students in other versions. Thus, the Steering Committee decided to continue all three of the parallel approaches.

A second summer writing conference was held in Boulder during the summer of 1961, again with half college biologists, half high school teachers. There was considerable overlap in membership with the writing teams of the previous summer, but some changes were made to give greater diversity, some new blood, and some specific expertise needed in various specialities of biology. Again, there were three writing teams, one for each version; for each team there was a supervisor for the text and also one for the laboratory manual, in order to provide a more effective integration of laboratory and text than was possible with one person handling the laboratory materials for all three versions, as had been done the previous summer.

Again, experimental materials for teachers and students were completed during the summer and were tried out in experimental editions during the subsequent school year, 1961-62. This tryout was by 350 teachers, all of whom had had some special training. Most attended a week-long briefing session in Boulder under BSCS auspices, but some had attended NSF summer institutes given by various colleges and universities independent of BSCS direction. While classroom use of materials was still limited, and free copies of the experimental materials were given only to persons in the official evaluation program, classroom sets of books were sold at cost for use in those classes where teachers had had special orientation for the materials through collegiate NSF preparation institutes. Again, data were gathered on the experience of the teachers and their 50,000 students. Additional reviews were obtained from experts. Feedback from these various sources was collated for use in the final writing conferences.

The writing conferences in 1962 were in various locations—one in Palo Alto, one in New York, and one in Boulder. The decision to hold separate writing conferences was based on such considerations as convenience of the writers, availability of compatible surroundings, and proximity to a strong biology library. These writing conferences were smaller and were scheduled for a longer period of time.

For this final polishing task, the supervisors for the three versions felt that the broad variety of backgrounds and experiences needed earlier was no longer as important, and that a smaller team working for a longer time would be more functional. Thus, each team included four or five persons. Each team was assisted by a BSCS staff consultant who had spent the preceding months reading feedback from teachers, visiting classrooms, and talking with students, teachers, and principals. These writing teams worked from February 1962 through the summer of 1962, again revising and putting the finishing touches on the materials.

During the 1962-63 school year, the temporary experimental editions of classroom materials tested the previous year were kept in print so that schools which had been using the books in the previous years could continue using them until the commercial editions became available. Again, schools that had been participating in the evaluation program were provided with free books. Others could purchase these, provided the teachers had special preparation.

Commercial publishers were invited to bid on the BSCS course materials for a commercially distributed edition. Bids were screened by the BSCS Executive Committee, were checked by the AIBS, and the final decision was made by the AIBS with NSF authorization. A different publisher was selected to distribute the final edition of each version, and each of the three publishers assigned an editor to work with the writers at the particular writing conference working on the materials for which he had contracted. The contracts for publishing the BSCS materials specified that the BSCS retained complete control over content.

Contracts for these and other BSCS materials released through commercial channels provided for royalties to be paid to the NSF for return to the United States Treasury, since development had been with public funds channeled through the NSF. Similarly, when the BSCS itself sold experimental editions of materials, funds from such sales were not retained by the BSCS, but were returned to the NSF. The BSCS remained entirely dependent on grants from outside sources for financing all activities in this developmental period, as well as in subsequent years.

During the preparation of the experimental course materials, one of the version supervisors felt that some of the laboratory skills required by his materials might be unfamiliar to the teachers using them, and a written or even pictorial description included in the teacher's manual would not give sufficient background to facilitate mastery of these skills. Thus, he suggested that a series of brief silent films be developed to accompany the materials and illustrate some of these techniques. As a result, the BSCS Techniques Film Series was created.

Concurrently, the BSCS Committee on Laboratory Innovations, with headquarters at the University of Texas, was using a somewhat similar developmental process in the preparation of some six-week laboratory-oriented units which could be used to supplement the BSCS courses. Here, although materials were prepared in experimental editions and tried out in schools before final editions were developed, each unit was assigned to an individual author who worked at his home institution, with materials completed before they were sent to the Texas BSCS laboratory for review, editing, and subsequent field tryouts.

Another committee, the Committee on the Gifted Student, working in Boulder at a summer writing conference, prepared experimental editions of materials that could be used out of class by students who wanted to do some independent research work in biology.

During the period of materials preparation, the BSCS was concerned with keeping the public informed about its work. This reflected a concern with adequate reporting on the use of public funds, a desire to get as much advice as possible from interested and informed persons, and an attempt to prepare the public for the availability of the materials. Since the BSCS mandate was to improve biological education, not simply to produce materials, it was necessary not only to provide adequate materials, but also to have materials that would come into wide use and provide exemplars to others involved in materials preparation in biology; the BSCS felt that its materials would be more acceptable if the potential audience was informed about them in advance.

To reflect these interests, the BSCS undertook a broad public information program, including a *NEWSLETTER* that appeared several times a year and was sent on request to a mailing list that reached over 35,000 persons at one time. Speeches were given at meetings of professional societies of biologists and educators, and the BSCS often had exhibits at such meetings. An Area Consultant Program was established, with consultants designated to cover various regions throughout the country. These area consultants were persons familiar with the BSCS materials, either through participating in a writing conference, using the materials in their high school classrooms, or preparing teachers to use them. The area consultants were available to individuals and groups in their area to provide expert information about the BSCS programs. Thus, a variety of media was used to bring information about the program to interested persons.

As the year-long course materials—the BSCS versions—appeared for general use, other needs were recognized. A second film series—the BSCS *Single Topic Film Series*—was developed by BSCS full-time staff members and individual consultants brought in on each film, as a means of providing supplementary classroom materials. One or two films were made in experimental form, tested, and revised several times before additional films were prepared. As further films were completed, these too were tested in classrooms before the next films were prepared. Since the BSCS conducted no further teacher-preparation activities itself—a decision forced on it by NSF policy—it developed materials to orient people who were doing such training in regular collegiate courses and in institutes and workshops.

Thus, in 1963, the formative phase of the BSCS work on the regular high school biology course for tenth grade was concluded. The BSCS continued to collect limited feedback on the materials, looking ahead to a revision of the materials in a future year. (The revised edition of each of the versions appeared in 1968.) Also, the BSCS turned its attention to other tasks such as the developing materials for slow learners in high school biology, developing a second course in high school biology to follow the tenth grade course, and assisting overseas countries wishing to adapt the BSCS materials for use in their own countries. However, the size of the staff was sharply reduced after the basic tenth grade materials were released for general use.

The BSCS experience is similar to that of other developmental studies in that materials were prepared in experimental format, tested, revised, retested, and again revised before being made generally available. Other characteristics of its operational pattern, while undoubtedly not unique, are by no means universal. There are some salient features in its pattern of organization and operation. The BSCS was established by a professional organization for the sole purpose of working to improve high school biology. It received large-scale funding—some $5 million in its first five years of operation—primarily through the NSF, for specific projects, and it has had no reserves to draw on.

While a great deal of authority was delegated by the parent organization, the precise parameters of the delegation of responsibility and authority were never specifically defined. The director of the BSCS reported both to the parent organization and to his own policy committee, the BSCS Steering Committee. Further, he shared authority with the chairman of the Steering Committee, again without a precise definition of the parameters of authority. While the initial Steering Committee was appointed by the parent organization, it became a self-perpetuating body, since it elected new members to replace those whose terms were expiring.

BSCS materials were released commercially, but the BSCS maintained control over content at all times. Precisely where the ultimate authority for content control rested was never clearly specified. In practice, the supervisor for each version had the final decision. He received advice from many sources, including his writing team, BSCS staff members, the BSCS director and chairman, and the BSCS Steering Committee, as well as the publisher who was to distribute that version. While in many instances this advice was taken, in others it was not, and the decision of the version supervisor prevailed. Although in one or two instances there was some question raised about the wisdom of a decision, there was no important occasion where the version supervisor's decision on content was overridden, or where a supervisor was removed, or where there was a threat of either action being taken.[6] This reflects the high degree of consensus reached by writers prior to preparation of the the final drafts of each edition, since, if there had been widespread disagreement, this would certainly have come to the attention of the director and the Steering Committee members. It also reflects the competence and mutual respect of all the persons involved rather than delegation of absolute power, since certainly, the BSCS would not have been willing to release materials that the director, chairman, or Steering Committee considered entirely inappropriate or substandard.

In large part, BSCS activities were centralized in Boulder, but some activities were carried on in offices at other locations and by personnel in the field. The BSCS operated to a large extent through committee work both in

---

[6]Although there were some changes in version supervisors during the three-year materials' preparation period, this reflected other professional commitments or interests of the supervisors rather than a dissatisfaction on the part of either the BSCS or the version supervisor.

policymaking and in materials preparation. The central office staff was small, and most of the professional staff was on a rotating basis, with appointments for one year.

Very serious efforts were made to involve large numbers of people in all programs and to represent various segments of the interested publics in activities and in decisions, with the result that in its first three years of operation during the preparation of the basic tenth grade materials, more than than 1,000 persons were actively involved in some phase of the BSCS activities. Intensive efforts were also made to keep biologists and educators informed about the work throughout the developmental period, both as a way of feeding ideas into the project and also preparing the target audience in advance of materials release.

In preparing materials, the BSCS gave teachers a choice of approaches rather than providing a single set of materials. The materials prepared represent complete packages, yet provide many options; that is, whatever might be needed for the version chosen by the teacher was made available for both student and teacher. Thus, there are student texts and laboratory manuals which complement each other and teacher guides to both laboratory manual and text. There is general background material for the teacher in the teacher handbook. Objective-type tests are available for testing student achievement in knowledge and skills germane to the course. Supplemental materials are available in the form of additional six-week laboratory units, supplemental laboratory exercises, inquiry-type films for classroom use, supplemental readings in a pamphlet series, films to teach laboratory techniques, research projects for gifted students, suggestions for teachers of gifted students, and background materials for school administrators considering adoption of the program.

Developmental Economic Education Program (DEEP) 1964-69

The Joint Council on Economic Education (JCEE) is a nonprofit educational agency organized in 1949 to promote economic education. At the national level, it consists of a national council with representatives from various segments of the economic community, including business, industry, labor, and education. There is a staff at the council headquarters in New York City. At the state level, there are member councils in many states; and there are similar regional councils at the local level. These councils work with local school systems and colleges and universities as well as with community groups to increase awareness of the need for economic education and to improve such education. National, state, and regional councils also maintain a liaison with Economic Education Centers on a number of college and university campuses.

The national council is in communication with regional and state councils; however, this is a relatively loose association and does not involve coordination of activities. The national council provides information and a variety of services, and acts as a clearinghouse; but it has no real authority over local or state councils. Local, state, and national councils are supported by contributions from individuals and organizations and from private foundations. In recent years, while a major portion of the JCEE budget, particularly for special large-scale projects, has come from private foundations, business and industry are also important contributors. Furthermore, the continued existence of the organization is contingent on the continuing support— nonfinancial as well as financial—of these contributors. Thus, JCEE activities are dependent on funds from a large number of individual annual contributions, and on the approval of a large number of individuals.

In recent years, the Joint Council has sponsored a wide variety of activities to promote education. It has sponsored surveys of economic education and task force reports to establish appropriate guidelines for economic education. It has prepared or cosponsored preparation of teacher materials, bibliographies, film strips, 16 mm. films, and tests; it has encouraged teachers to prepare economic materials for their classrooms; and it has stimulated teacher workshops and institutes in economics.

In 1964, the JCEE initiated a new five-year program, the Developmental Economic Education Program (DEEP), to provide another medium for working with school systems in stimulating economic education. The DEEP program was one of the first broad attempts at developmental curriculum work and concomitant teacher-training efforts on a nationwide basis in the social studies. This program is an integral part of the JCEE activities. The general parameters of the program were established before any of the special central office staff was hired by the JCEE to coordinate DEEP activities for the council.

DEEP staff is hired by the JCEE; all DEEP policies and activities are subject to review by the president of the JCEE, and general policy is subject to review by the national JCEE council. Thus, DEEP is in no sense autonomous; there is no separate DEEP policymaking body or chief executive officer. The DEEP budget is part of the JCEE budget, and DEEP policies and its headquarters staff and their activities are all subject to direct review by the JCEE executive officers.

The DEEP program, which supplemented other existing and new JCEE programs, was intended to stimulate development of economics materials by local school systems for use in those school systems, and training of teachers in economics, again by school systems. In effect, this was an effort to stimulate thirty parallel local efforts in curriculum development and dissemination in public and/or parochial school systems. While it was hoped that once the programs were initiated by school systems, they would operate on a continuing basis, the major thrust by DEEP would be for a three-year period. Each successive year for the three years, ten school systems would become involved in the DEEP program with the official liaison lasting for three years.[7]

During the three-year period of a school system's involvement with DEEP, some limited funds would be given to the system, and various kinds of expertise would be made available through the national, local, and regional councils. To each of three model school systems selected for an intensive effort, $35,000 was granted each year for three years; the remaining twenty-seven pilot school systems received $3,500 for one year, with the remaining years' funding based on arrangements with local affiliated councils, or through special arrangements with the JCEE. In some instances, this supplementary local funding was as much as $70,000; in some, it included virtually no cash but some contribution through provision of consulting services. The advance commitments made by the participating school systems were limited, and even on those general commitments included in the JCEE contract with the participating systems, no attempt was made by the JCEE, beyond general persuasion and encouragement, to require systems to live up to their advance commitments. Some systems went far beyond the initial commitment and allocated significant funds and staff for the project; others did not.

Contacts with the participating school systems were maintained through the superintendent, curriculum supervisors, and through a local DEEP coordinator, appointed by the school system and on its payroll. (In instances where JCEE provided for all or part of the coordinator's salary, the payment was made to the school system and the coordinator remained on the school system payroll.) Some coordinators were assigned to the task full-time; some were assigned part-time, with a concomitant reduction in other responsibilities; and some were expected to handle this work in addition to their other normal assignments. Each participating school system was asked to set up a Community Advisory Committee to assist in the program. Each could call on the services of a JCEE regional economist. (There were several of these regional economists serving various parts of the country; the numbers varied from four to six at different stages of the program.) Also, many had access to Economic Education Centers at nearby collegiate institutions. (*See* Illustration 1.)

The DEEP school systems varied considerably in their initial status on degree of economics teaching in the curriculum. They also varied on the degree

---

[7] A description of the operation and evaluation of one of the more ambitious and successful of the DEEP projects is included in a report of the Contra Costa County, California Department of Education (Contra Costa County Department of Education, 1967).

Illustration 1

THE STRUCTURE OF DEEP IN A SCHOOL SYSTEM

This diagram shows the relationships among each of the parts
which make up the structure of **DEEP.**

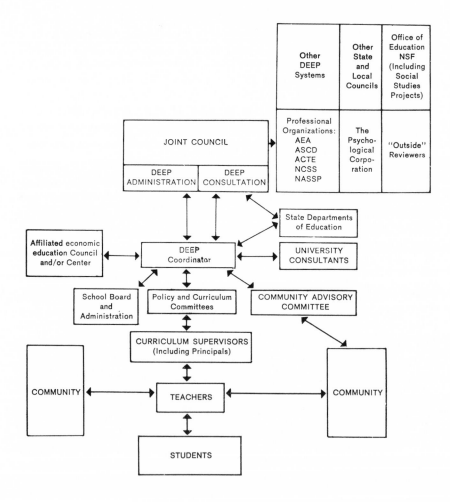

From: John E. Maher, Stowell Symmes, and William D. Green, Chap. 2,
The results of DEEP, in Joint Council on Economic Education, DEEP 1969. New York:
Joint Council on Economic Education, 1969.

of administrative backing for the program; some had strong administrative support for the program, others did not. Some had active curriculum-development projects in other disciplines under way at the time their DEEP activities started; others did not. Some of the systems had a tradition of active curriculum change throughout the system; others were relatively static and highly tradition-oriented. Local financial support for DEEP varied from system to system, with some systems pretty much limited to the council contributions, while others provided staff time, facilities, and funds, and some also obtained supplementary outside grants from other sources to permit a more intensive effort.

Each participating school system made its own decisions, firstly on whether to participate, and secondly on the nature and timing of its activities. Each system appointed its own DEEP coordinator from its existing staff; in most instances, the coordinator was a social studies teacher who was released part-time or full-time from classroom responsibilities to work on DEEP activities. Each also had the services of an economist to advise on its materials.

Each participating system made its own decision on whether to prepare materials, what kinds of materials should be developed, how these should be developed, who should develop them, how they would be tried out, and on the nature and extent of teacher training undertaken. (*See* Illustration 2.) The process for making these decisions varied with school systems and often utilized that system's usual procedure for making curriculum decisions. Here, as elsewhere in the DEEP program, the national, state and local councils could act only in an advisory capacity, backed by a certain degree of prestige which the councils carried.[8]

Some systems developed discrete units in economics for use at a given grade level. Some prepared a series of units for a grade level. Others prepared year-long courses for one or more grade levels. And some prepared coordinated curricula for kindergarten through twelfth grade, while others focused on one or more discrete grade levels. Some focused on teacher preparation, while others focused more on the preparation of student materials. Some systems prepared materials with a clear local orientation, which limited their use to that system; others prepared materials suitable for a wider audience.

In some systems, the coordinator was directly involved in materials preparation; in others, he was not. In some, materials were prepared by a classroom teacher or by groups of classroom teachers; in others, they were

---

[8] It should be noted that the membership of the local councils generally included representation of the major prestigious economic activities in the community: the many banks, industrial, and business establishments, and that a liaison was maintained between local councils and school systems on some basis throughout the program; further, often some of the pilot system DEEP funds came from the local councils.

Illustration 2

THE DEEP NETWORK:

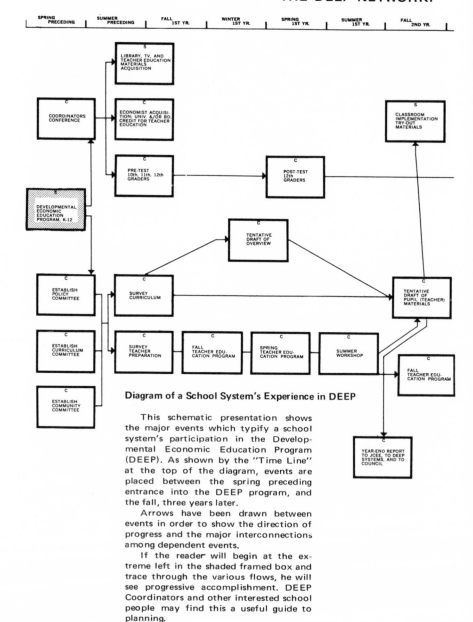

Diagram of a School System's Experience in DEEP

This schematic presentation shows the major events which typify a school system's participation in the Developmental Economic Education Program (DEEP). As shown by the "Time Line" at the top of the diagram, events are placed between the spring preceding entrance into the DEEP program, and the fall, three years later.

Arrows have been drawn between events in order to show the direction of progress and the major interconnections among dependent events.

If the reader will begin at the extreme left in the shaded framed box and trace through the various flows, he will see progressive accomplishment. DEEP Coordinators and other interested school people may find this a useful guide to planning.

S=START   C=COMPLETE

Illustration 2 Continued

Illustrating a single system's schedule

of significant events and major interconnections

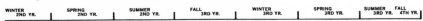

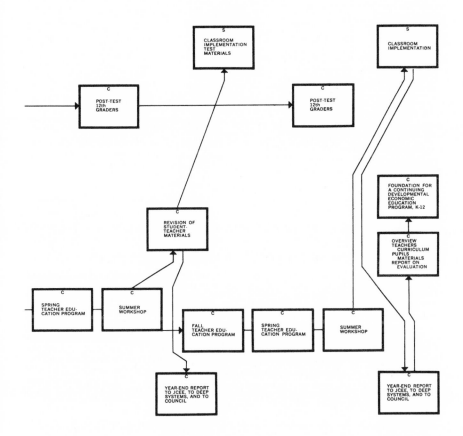

Source: Joint Council on Economic Education, DEEP '67, A progress report on the Developmental Economic Education Program.

prepared by economists, with or without collaboration with classroom teachers. While each participating school system had an economist to serve as a local consultant, there was considerable variation in the frequency and extent to which these economists were used.

Quality control at the local level varied in timing, nature, and extent. In some cases, materials were reviewed by economists and/or teachers frequently during the course of preparation; in others, the review did not take place until large segments or an entire unit or course was virtually completed. Further, the extent of systematic tryout of experimental materials and feedback for the purpose of revising materials varied from frequent experimental tryouts with open feedback channels to tryouts of materials in relatively final form with little opportunity for honest reaction by users.

Quality control by the JCEE was advisory and operated on an intermittent rather than on a day-to-day basis. Materials were reviewed from time to time by the local economist-consultant, by visitors from the JCEE office once or twice a year, and at the JCEE headquarters whenever a local project submitted them and requested review. Thus, for some projects, there were more frequent reviews than for other projects.

Some projects welcomed the JCEE advice and followed it; others did not. The decision here rested with the school systems, and individual systems did what they thought best, at times against the specific advice of the JCEE staff. While the JCEE encouraged quality control through its promise to disseminate exemplary materials, it had no mechanism for preventing distribution within the sponsoring system, or outside the sponsoring system, of nonexemplary materials produced under the aegis of the DEEP program and carrying a JCEE identification.

As part of their initial contracts with the JCEE, all participating school systems were committed to initiating or extending teacher-training activities in economics. Some participating school systems initiated teacher training comparable to the usual collegiate introductory courses in economics; some modified these as the instructor—often an economics professor from a nearby institution—felt necessary or desirable for the participating classroom teachers. And some geared the teacher training specifically to the materials being prepared for use in that system, and made the teacher training part of a plan for disseminating locally prepared materials into the system. For some, the teacher preparation was offered for college credit or for in-service credit; for others, no credit was given. For some, teachers were paid to attend; for others, they were not.

The JCEE evaluation of its DEEP project focused largely on process, rather than on student achievement of specific objectives or skills in economics.

Although many excellent materials were prepared by participating school systems, perhaps the major outcome of the first five years of the project was the development of some guidelines for curriculum change in economics, to be suggested in the future to school systems interested in developing curricula, training programs, and dissemination of economics materials.[9] For the DEEP participating school systems, evaluation varied from some sophisticated, relatively comprehensive evaluation programs to virtually no systematic evaluation efforts.

The process used by the JCEE in its developmental curriculum project was characterized by certain features. The sponsor, the JCEE, is a continuing multiactivity organization that is dependent on annual contributions from individuals, organizations, and private foundations. Although general budget approval is given by the council, there are relatively few constraints on the types of expenditure that JCEE may make, and there is considerable flexibility in reallocating funds, given the approval of the JCEE president.

The JCEE has a history of acting as a clearinghouse and decentralizing many activities through state and local councils. The developmental project was delimited in advance in size (thirty systems), in the period of support to school systems (from one to three years), and in the relatively modest level of support for a large, diverse project, with most of the JCEE financial resources for the support guaranteed before the initiation of the project.

Materials were developed by local personnel rather than at a central location, and there was local determination of the nature and scope of the materials. There was a diversity of types of student materials prepared (texts, supplementary readings, teacher guides, films, filmstrips, TV programs, charts, acetate overlays, educational games, evaluation instruments) and supplementary activities (such as teacher-preparation institutes and development of teacher-preparation materials) in the program.

The sponsor, the JCEE, and its special staff to coordinate the program, had little control over selection of activities and personnel working on local planning and materials development. Its quality control mechanisms operated at infrequent intervals, largely during site visits or by mail, when the participating school system requested a review, rather than on a day-to-day basis. Thus, the programs depended on local initiative, local know-how, and local staff, and the materials developed were indigenous.

The role of the central office was to give some financial support, to coordinate efforts insofar as possible (given limited authority), to act as a clearinghouse for information, to provide library materials, and to disseminate

---

[9] Symmes (1969) summarizes the suggested guidelines, based on the experiences of the thirty DEEP school systems.

exemplars developed by local systems. Its control mechanisms were some relatively small grants, the influence of the prestige of the JCEE and the local councils, publicity, and the opportunity of some participants to attend national DEEP meetings.

The DEEP program was based on several assumptions. Curriculum diversity is desirable. Curriculum improvement is a local concern. Some outside stimulus and resources are needed if economics education is to be expanded at the local level. Local school personnel—primarily teachers—can develop and evaluate materials. Local systems know how to plan for materials development and dissemination. Once materials are prepared, they will be used by the system sponsoring their preparation. Teacher training is a major facet of curriculum-improvement efforts. Community involvement is essential in change. And major curriculum development and dissemination can be accomplished in three years with relatively small funds and limited personnel.

During the course of its program, the JCEE learned that some of these assumptions were valid and others were not. Some school systems were better geared to curriculum development and change than others. For some, the JCEE contribution served as seed money, and stimulated far greater local contributions; for others, it did not. Despite some dramatic successes in terms of quality of new materials prepared under the DEEP aegis, numbers of teachers trained in economics, and students actually using the new materials profitably, it became obvious that some circumstances were more compatible with the effective development and dissemination of materials and teacher preparation, and that certain procedures for materials development and implementation were more appropriate than others. Thus, to a considerable extent, the DEEP project changed its focus to an exploration of various processes for curriculum development and dissemination and to the development of effective prototypes for such curriculum development and change.

Interaction of Matter and Energy (IME) 1964-69

During the late 1950's, several of the teachers in the science department of Yuba City Union High School in California began the development of some laboratory-oriented student materials for their ninth grade classes in physical science because they were dissatisfied with the classroom materials that were then available. The new materials were developed as time permitted, and were fed into the classes as they were prepared. From year to year, the materials were improved and supplemented, but these units formed only part of the course materials.

When the BSCS began the preparation of materials for tenth grade biology in 1960, the chairman of the Yuba City Union High School science department was invited to spend the year at Boulder as a staff consultant, to visit schools using BSCS materials, and to review feedback coming from teachers, students, and other sources. Later, he was invited to act as chairman of the BSCS writing team developing the second course in biology. He then served as associate director of BSCS, while on leave from his school system. During this same period, several other teachers from the Yuba City science department were involved in various phases of BSCS activities, including participating in writing conferences, using BSCS materials in their tenth grade classrooms, and serving as staff members for collegiate teacher-preparation institutes and as area consultants. These teachers became more aware of the need for stronger ninth grade science materials to precede BSCS biology and lead into it, materials with an inquiry orientation and focusing on the laboratory. They were enthusiastic proponents of the developmental approach in the preparation of materials, but they were also aware of the problems of financing such activities with public funds.

In 1963 or 1964, through informal contacts with people from the Yuba City school, Rand McNally, one of the commercial publishers selected to publish BSCS materials, heard about the ninth grade science materials that had been developed earlier and expressed interest. At that time, there was little being done on junior high school science courses through developmental curriculum projects, though many science educators recognized this need and deplored the lack of activity. A number of publishers were looking for new materials for these grades, and Rand McNally, in addition to trying to fill this gap at the junior high school level, was enthusiastic about the developmental process that had been used by BSCS, about the laboratory-oriented approach to school science, and about the competence of many of the people who had worked with the BSCS.

As a result, when the Yuba City science department chairman left the BSCS late in 1965 to return to his school system, Rand McNally arranged with him and several of his co-workers to act as sponsor for a small-scale developmental curriculum project based in Yuba City to refine further the materials that had already been developed there, and to build these into a year-long course in physical science for the ninth grade.

This was a highly unusual arrangement at the time, and the agreement between the writers and Rand McNally differed from the usual author-publisher arrangements. Rand McNally was providing basic funds for a three-year effort to build developmental materials based on the BSCS model of materials preparation and experimental tryout. It also followed the BSCS model in terms of allocation of responsibility for content with the authors, and responsibility for format decisions with the publisher. (In both the BSCS and IME arrangements, this did not preclude consultations between authors and publishers on both format and content.) Thus, Rand McNally gave an advance guarantee to subsidize developmental activities for materials, and to release these materials after they were completed, while relinquishing control over the content of these materials.

The writing was to be done by a four-man writing team, including the three high school teachers involved in developing the initial materials some years earlier, and one research scientist who had been on various BSCS writing teams earlier. The project chairman (the former chairman of the Yuba City science department) directed negotiations with Rand McNally and generally supervised the project. The project office was set up in his home, and he devoted half of his time during the school year to the project, and the remainder to supervisory responsibilities with the local school system.

While some of the sponsor's funding was specified in advance, the precise amount and activities were not rigidly established, and as the project developed successfully, some new activities and consultant services were added as they appeared desirable. Beyond some basic developmental funds, the principal authors worked on a royalty basis; other consultants and writing associates were brought in from time to time on an honorarium basis for specific services.

As was the case with the BSCS, the project chairman was to have the final authority over the content decisions. He had responsibility for coordinating activities, and his was the final review of manuscripts. It was agreed that the materials would be highly laboratory-oriented, geared for use at the ninth grade with average students in school settings where laboratory facilities might be minimal. The experimental materials were titled *Interaction of Matter and Energy*, and the project came to be called IME.

Contract negotiations between the writers and Rand McNally were completed in the early winter of 1965-66, and in the spring of 1966, after some hasty consultations with teachers and school systems in various parts of the country, forty teachers and their 5,000 students tried out the classroom materials prepared by the authors prior to that time. These materials were provided free by the project.

Lining up the experimental teachers for this first tryout was difficult, not only because of the limited time available for negotiations, but also because, in a sense, the project was suspect. Schools did not expect textbook publishers to sponsor real developmental projects, and they tended to regard the request to try out materials as a promotional device to sell books, rather than as a genuine attempt to get information to improve materials. While this problem diminished as the project became better known and as experimental materials became available, this was a problem in some phases of the program to some extent throughout the developmental period.

For the spring, 1966 tryout, the materials were received in the participating experimental schools in March, and were inserted for eight or ten weeks into whatever course materials the classroom teacher happened to be using. There were no special briefings for teachers; and there were no tests to use with the materials. This tryout was admittedly very tentative, and it was recognized that the results would provide only very general direction. But even this was thought worth obtaining before any intensive attempt was made to revise and build on the embryo course materials. Teachers were asked for their reactions in some detail, and these teacher reactions guided the revisions and work on additional materials.

During the summer of 1966, a four-man summer writing conference in Yuba City produced much of the materials for the 1966-67 tryout, with the remainder being completed during the fall. Because of the staggered completion of various parts of the materials, they were issued in three volumes, as were the explanatory materials for the teacher. The volumes were paperbound and expendable, and were provided free to participating schools.

During 1966-67, some 200 teachers and about 14,000 students field tested the second experimental edition of IME, which had become a year-long course based on the nucleus used the previous spring, with the addition of new materials. In preparation for this classroom trial of materials, teachers were asked to attend a two-day briefing on the use of the materials. IME scheduled these in thirteen different cities late in August, and paid the expenses of those teachers attending.

During the year, teachers were again asked to react to the materials based on their classroom experience. Feedback from the teachers was reviewed by the IME chairman, and then sent to the writer who would be concerned with refining that particular portion of the materials. Some special IME tests to cover the materials were prepared by the writers, and student performance on these tests was analyzed to determine the extent to which students were mastering desired knowledge and skills. The editors and authors did some limited classroom visiting, but the manpower and budget for this were severely limited. Fortunately, some of the writers were using the materials in their own classrooms, and other teachers in their schools were also using them.

Two other feedback activities were initiated in preparation for the revision work of the 1967 summer writing conference. At the start of the summer of 1967, five classroom teachers from various parts of the country, who had used the materials both years of the experimental tryouts, met for several days with the writers to react and to suggest. They were asked specifically what went wrong and how this might be corrected. Also, five eminent research scientists and science educators prepared written critiques of the materials and also served as consultants at a two-day meeting with the writers to react to various aspects of the materials, to criticize, and to make suggestions.

Summer, 1967, marked another writing conference with the same writers. These writers did two things: first, they made a few modifications in the 1966-67 experimental edition of IME, for the materials that were to be used in experimental editions in the 1967-68 school year, pending availability of the regular commercial edition of IME in fall, 1968; second, they did the bulk of the preparation of this 1968 edition, completing the last parts of the students' materials and the accompanying teacher manual during the fall and winter.

Since the student materials for this final edition were to go to press during the winter of 1967-68, not too much teacher feedback during that school year could be built into the student materials; however, since the teacher materials did not go to press till spring or summer, teacher feedback was still useful. Also, teachers were asked to focus on providing feedback on the classroom tests, which were given greater attention during the 1967-68 year. Outside consultants worked on test preparation and editing, and more systematic statistical analyses of test results were made, for purposes of improving later editions of the tests, and describing the course and its outcomes for the target population that would be considering the materials for use.

During the summer of 1967, an additional 300 teachers attended IME two-day briefing sessions held at twenty different locations; again, these were organized by IME, and teacher expenses were paid. Since the project no longer needed extensive feedback, free student books for the 1967-68 school year were provided only for the students of the original forty teachers who had tested materials in the first pilot experiment; others could purchase these revised experimental editions at cost. In either case, sets of tests were provided with the materials. By June, 1968, the end of the field testing period for experimental materials, some 500 teachers had taught the course to 55,000 students.

In 1967, a project newsletter was initiated to keep teachers participating in field tests informed of the progress of the project, and also to begin to inform a wider audience. Also, a system of area consultants was set up, modeled on that of the BSCS, so that informed persons were available to speak on IME, to answer questions about the programs, and to give help to teachers and systems interested in considering the program. The area consultants were selected from the group of teachers who had already used IME. They were successful IME teachers who could talk about the program and answer questions from their own experience.

In the fall of 1968, the regular edition of IME materials became available. These included student materials, a rather complete teacher handbook which contained both teacher and student materials interleaved, and a set of six tests to accompany the materials. In addition, equipment for the course was available from the publisher, either as separate items or in complete classroom kits. This equipment and the kits were made available as a convenience, since the teacher material included directions for constructing the required equipment.

As the work on the experimental editions of IME progressed successfully, Rand McNally and the project chairman decided to initiate the preparation of developmental materials for a seventh or eighth grade life science course on much the same basis. Later, it was hoped, the group would prepare a junior high school earth science course.[10] The developmental project was retitled the *Interaction Science Curriculum Project* to include this broadened scope, and work on the biology course materials was started in spring, 1968, following the same pattern used for IME. The first writing conference on *Interaction of Man and Biosphere* (IMB)—the new eighth grade course materials—was held in summer, 1968, followed by experimental classroom testing in 1968-69. The writing conference staff changed to reflect the change in subject area covered, but remained small and included research scientists as well as science teachers.[11]

The IME project was characterized by certain features. All funding was from a single commercial source, a publishing house. The total budget was comparatively modest, and the writing teams were smaller than had been the case on many other parallel projects. Because of the sponsorship, the process to be used in the ultimate release of the materials—through a publisher specified in advance—was predetermined. Content control rested with the writers; format control with the publisher.

There is a clear reflection of the influence of the BSCS throughout the project, reflecting the earlier close involvement of the sponsor and the writers with the BSCS. Insofar as the budget permitted, the project tried to use the BSCS process for materials development as a prototype, including use of writing teams, representation of both high school and college scientists on the writing and review teams, and experimental classroom trials of materials, with feedback from several sources systematized. It differed in magnitude of operations and in method of payment for writers' services. There were fewer writers, smaller tryouts, and less ambitious evaluative activities. The principal IME authors received royalties rather than salary or honoraria.

---

[10] While the authors would like to see the biology course taught at the seventh grade and earth science at the eighth grade, as a practical matter since junior high schools vary greatly in their grade level placement of biology and earth science, these are being written so that either can be used at the seventh or the eighth grade, and one is not a prerequisite for the other.

[11] The regular edition of IMB appeared in fall, 1970, and the first experimental edition of the earth science course also appeared in fall, 1970.

Because concomitant teacher preparation was not being offered through publicly financed institutes, as was the case with NSF-supported curriculum projects, the teacher preparation in face-to-face encounters was more limited, and the teacher manual was far more detailed. Fewer supplemental materials were prepared. This was a reflection of the more limited resources of the project, and the more limited facilities available in the ninth grade. It also reflected the need for a less complex and more leisurely approach appropriate for the lower grade.

Since IME was sponsored by a book publisher, it faced some early problems of credibility and acceptance not encountered to the same degree by projects financed from public sources or foundations. There was an initial skepticism that a publisher would be supporting the preparation of materials through a genuine developmental process. Teacher training was not handled through publicly financed or publicly subsidized institutes and courses. And the project probably had fewer of the opportunities afforded other kinds of developmental projects, such as presenting reports of its activities through articles in professional journals and at speeches at professional meetings, PTA's, and civic organizations.

* * *

BSCS, DEEP, and IME differ in many ways. Some of the differences are minor, but a number of them are highly significant. They differ in the source and amount of funding, in their primary goal, in the kinds of materials prepared, and in the responsibility for policymaking and for decision making. They differ in the involvement of scholars and educators, in the way in which materials were prepared, and in the way they were released. And they differ in their impact on education at the target grade level.

Clearly, there is no single pattern to developmental curriculum work, and probably, there should be no single pattern. The very diversity of the approaches used by projects in the past may constitute a major strength of the developmental method of preparing materials. However, much of the diversity to date has been unplanned and unsystematic, and some of it has been ineffective. Often, developmental projects have not made a clear and systematic choice with a knowledge of available alternatives, perhaps because the alternatives have not been clear. Sometimes, projects have made choices without recognition of the ramifications of the decision. The identification of some of the major decision points and the avenues open for dealing with the problems that arise in developmental curriculum work may throw light on past project work, as well as facilitate systematic consideration of choices for future projects.

II

SITUATIONAL AND ADMINISTRATIVE
CONSTRAINTS ON DEVELOPMENTAL PROJECTS

Regardless of the decisions concerning materials development, the outcomes of a project appear to be strongly affected by the time and place of its initiation, by the source of funding, by the nature of the organizational structure and its relation to a parent organization, and by the personnel involved.

SITUATIONAL CONSTRAINTS ON CURRICULUM PROJECTS

There are a number of external constraints on curriculum projects related to timeliness. Clearly, the climate of the moment may facilitate or preclude the success of a given change effort. An idea that is acceptable at one time may be completely unacceptable, even though equally appropriate, at another time. An idea that is not of interest to the profession, to a funder, or to the schools in one decade may be highly attractive in another.

For example, radical curriculum change was not highly attractive to schools until the 1960's. True, prior to this, some schools did experiment, but those that did represented a relatively small minority of schools. Most experiments were not radically different, but represented only minor adjustments in content or timing, and most involved only a small portion of the school curriculum.

Thus, in the 1930's, a school might be considered relatively daring if it adopted a core curriculum, which combined English and social studies in one block of time, with an integration of subject matter, while leaving the rest of the school day unchanged. A few college of education laboratory and demonstration schools tried new approaches to education. But for the most part, neither public school authorities nor school patrons seemed to want drastic change. While they talked about better education, this was largely a matter of doing more of the same thing, rather than attempting a complete overhaul of the system or any parts of it. There was a pervasive don't-rock-the-boat atmosphere, in which the truly innovative was suspect. The time was not ripe for change, even though critics of education had repeatedly and clearly documented the need for major revisions.

The fate of the Eight-Year Study,[1] the most comprehensive study of its kind prior to World War II, is illustrative of this atmosphere. Although the findings of this massive follow-up study (carried out from 1933 to 1941) of collegiate success of students exposed to experimental curricula in high school appeared to indicate that traditional college preparatory curricula were not uniquely appropriate for students going on to college, virtually no change resulted in the high school curriculum as a result of these findings. While there was some criticism of the research techniques used, failure of the Eight-Year Study to stimulate change in high school programs probably reflects a resistance to change, rather than a reaction based on such criticisms.[2]

During the World War II years, a primary preoccupation in education was keeping the schools operating in the face of shortages of teachers and facilities, and of the rapid shifts of population, reflecting the expansion of defense industries in communities throughout the country. For the 1950's, the education focus was on handling increasing enrollments and catching up with the capital construction and repairs, delayed because of the war. There was relatively little done to change the curriculum.

In contrast, change has now become fashionable. Today, those who want to develop new curricula are operating in a climate favorable for radical change. Yet, even in this generally favorable climate, there are situational factors facilitating one kind of change rather than another equally sound and justifiable kind. For example, in the late 1950's and early 1960's, the focus of attention was on science and mathematics education at the senior high school level. Other large-scale developmental projects could not be financed.

The first federal funds for developmental curriculum work became available through the NSF in the late 1950's. During the mid-1950's, the NSF saw as the most practical way of fulfilling its charge—to increase the nation's scientific research potential—the implementation of programs at the senior high school level in science and mathematics, both for teacher training and for development of course materials. Under its mandate, perhaps the NSF interpretation of its mission need not have been limited to the areas of science and mathematics. But those at the NSF who planned the course-improvement program, did not feel it proper to go beyond these areas of clear responsibility. Also, the tenor of public opinion in the country was such that science and mathematics were clear and urgent concerns.

Apparently, a number of factors were involved in the NSF decision to focus course-improvement work exclusively on the high school level. First, there was strong criticism of the senior high school teaching by persons in the

---

[1] Aiken (1942) and Chamberlin *et al.* (1942) are among the volumes describing this study.
[2] These criticisms are summarized in Wallen and Travers (1963).

disciplines. These people—most of them teaching at the college level—were not equally critical of collegiate teaching. Further, outside criticism of collegiate teaching was often answered by citing the lack of adequate high school preparation of students. Second, the recruitment of students into sciences and mathematics seemed to be more a precollege rather than a college problem, since career choices and attitudes towards subjects are often built before college. The NSF programs were limited to the senior high school level rather than including all grades, since the senior high school appeared to provide a more practical point of attack than the junior high school and elementary levels. There is greater consensus at the senior high school level as to what subjects should be taught, and when these should be taught, and also the populations are of a more manageable size, and the teachers are better prepared in the specific disciplines.

Thus, NSF budget provisions for curriculum development were initially couched in terms of the senior high school, and the disciplines of science and mathematics only. The Office of Education, the only other logical existing federal agency to propose curriculum-development work in the other subject areas and grade levels, apparently did not take an active initiative at this time. And so, the only public funds initially available for curriculum work were through the NSF. At the same time, considerable private foundation money became available for educational television (ETV). And projects involving ETV could obtain funds where some equally reasonable ideas were lost or delayed simply through lack of funding.

In the late 1960's poverty programs and programs involving hardware (learning machines) and software (materials to be used with these machines) were readily financed. At the same time, some areas receiving funds earlier encountered difficulties in obtaining new or continuing funding.

Research and Development Centers (R and D Centers) and Regional Laboratories, initiated under Office of Education designation and funding in the mid-1960's, appear to provide an appropriate and attractive setting for developmental projects. Multipurpose, nonprofit educational corporations established during the 1960's have also become an accepted part of the educational development picture. Such corporations are a relatively recent development.

A project that could obtain a million dollars in 1968 might not have obtained even a small grant in 1960. Conversely, ideas that received several millions in 1960 might not be able to obtain even a tenth that in 1968, because of changes in national concern, the competition for funding among the growing number of developmental projects, changes in the interests of the funding agencies, and changes in the general availability of funds resulting from the Vietnam War.

Unfortunately, even worthwhile projects cannot continue if not well financed, regardless of the commitment on the part of project sponsors. While some projects do operate on minimal budgets—on budgets that may be one-quarter or one-fifth those of other projects apparently doing similar work—the kinds of tasks involved in the developmental process take hard cash, rather than merely time and supplies scrounged from other jobs.

Funding is not the only problem related to timing. A project that may be highly successful in the 1960's could have failed miserably in the 1950's because the audience for the proposed innovation was not ready for it. A project concerned with introducing the role of the Negro in eighth grade or eleventh grade American history, or exploring the implications of race on such facets of biological inheritance as intelligence in tenth grade biology, might have failed in the 1950's or early 1960's.

Even if such efforts had been financed and if excellent materials had been produced, such materials would probably have had few adoptions by schools. In fact, curriculum projects interested in developing such treatments might even have had difficulty finding representative school systems willing to use them experimentally during the developmental period. Yet, just a few years later, these subjects became of great interest not only to legislative bodies and funding sources, but also to schools actively seeking such materials.

At any given time, those projects that are able to couch their interests in terms of a current public concern or current educational fad will be more likely to be able to fund their work; those that cannot may never get started, or if they are initiated, they may die from lack of continuing financial support. Thus, opportunism may be the only road to survival for a given project. For example, when one group was asked why its project had *gifted students* in its title when the materials produced seemed eminently suited to the average student, it replied that the legislature was enthusiastic about education for the gifted and had appropriated money for this purpose; there were no developmental or research funds available from the state for work with average students. The educators in this project had simply couched their request in terms of the gifted, and while the materials they produced were certainly useful and appropriate for the gifted, they could have been produced with little modification under the aegis of a group concerned with the average student.

Other facets of situational constraints on developmental projects are the relative age of the project movement and the prior activity in the pertinent subject area. It is easy to criticize PSSC for real or imagined shortcomings, but the job of PSSC as the first large-scale curriculum study was far different from those of later studies that could utilize past PSSC experience in planning their strategies.

Many such early projects have been generous in sharing their experience with later groups, including in this sharing not only what has worked well, but also in discussing limitations of ideas that were not particularly successful, and in exploring some of the problems encountered with these. The later projects were also able to observe for themselves the limitations in earlier efforts, and what projects participants or users of materials complained about, and they have been able to utilize this background in their own planning. Thus, a project working in the late 1960's is in a different situation concerning precedents than one starting eight or ten years earlier.

Project operation is also different when the project in question is the first in its discipline or grade level—the first in junior high school science, in elementary school social studies, or in senior high school mathematics. The first group to suggest teaching evolution to tenth graders in biology, to teach set theory in elementary school mathematics, or to teach economics in first and second grade is in a far different situation than the second or third such project in the subject area and grade level. For example, given the impact on the American public of SMSG's new math for elementary school, parents and schools are far less resistant to what might seem to be impossible or inappropriate ideas in the teaching of mathematics than was the case ten years ago.

Another constraint on projects is the availability of teacher-training resources. In the late 1950's, the OE and NSF inaugurated large-scale, publicly financed teacher-training opportunities. Prior to that time, it was virtually impossible to effect nationwide change in curricula involving materials or techniques not part of the educational background of most teachers, unless such changes were simple enough to be explained in a rather brief teacher manual which would accompany the materials.

Without special instruction, a science teacher with no college biochemistry cannot effectively teach a high school biology course oriented to biochemistry; a history teacher with no economics background cannot effectively teach a senior course in economics; and an elementary school teacher with no college mathematics (and perhaps only two years of high school mathematics) cannot effectively teach number theory. Providing the teacher with a college text in the subject is impractical. Even if the teacher had the time and motivation to master the subject in this way, it is questionable that the kind of mastery needed for teaching at his grade level would be acquired.

While some school systems did have in-service education programs, many did not; and the relatively few in-service programs in existence were often relatively short term and underfinanced, thereby precluding needed resources and released time for proper training. Once the possibility of retraining teachers on a large scale was developed in the late 1950's, through grants from NSF,

OE, and state departments of education, curriculum change of different dimensions became feasible.

In reviewing the early curriculum projects, it is tempting to be critical of their strategies and purposes, of their attack on the secondary school curricula in isolation from the curricula of the preceding school years, of their concern with science and mathematics to the exclusion of the social sciences and humanities, or of their concern with materials rather than with implementation techniques. Yet, the situation in which these projects operated often precluded broader concerns. That this was shortsighted is now obvious; but for such projects as PSSC, SMSG, BSCS, in the early years of their operation, the only alternative to acceptance of the narrow parameters established by the funders was to do absolutely nothing—to prepare no curricula.

As the parameters of the situation changed, the decisions available to projects changed. Projects can help change the existing parameters by continuing to insist that these are inadequate, by creating patterns of successful innovation that encourage further experimentation, and by educating their various publics. But this takes time, and if a project wishes to survive and be financed through this period, it must accept existing parameters, at least in the short run.

Thus, one of the concerns in establishing a developmental program is an assessment of the situational factors that set parameters. Unfortunately, in the past, this assessment may have been overly conservative. Some things have not been tried because of a misjudgment in assessing the situation. For ex - ample, at times controversial subjects have not appeared in textbooks because of a judgment that the public would not accept them. In many areas, teachers had reported that it is not possible to include discussion of human reproduction in a high school biology class, because the community would not allow this; in some cases this assessment was based on the recollection of the firing of a teacher thirty-five years earlier for including such material in his course. Yet, when parents in the same community were asked if they fa - vored such teaching, they were often overwhelmingly enthusiastic about the idea.

To go too fast for the situation, to be too far out-of-step with the times can defeat a project. However, to accept the past assessment of the situation, or to fail to attempt to change an existing situation may preclude meaningful improvement in education.

FUNDING CONSTRAINTS ON CURRICULUM PROJECTS

Unfortunately, while availability of funds does not guarantee a quality outcome in developmental curriculum work, adequate funding is a prerequisite. By its very nature, the developmental curriculum process is more expensive than are conventional methods of preparing new materials. In contrast to the individual author, or two or three coauthors, who write a textbook after regular working hours or during summer vacations, the developmental project requires a larger staff of writers, a year-round operation, experimental editions of materials for trial use in the classroom, and visits to observe this use, even if no other activities are conducted. Thus, where conventional materials might require only the time of the author and the cost of typing, the developmental curriculum requires advance cash outlays far greater than the usual textbook publisher's advance on royalties to individual authors.

The amount of funding required for project work varies. While some projects operate on as little as $25,000 a year, and others need $1 million a year, all need some kind of subsidy during the developmental period, and such funding requires a grant or advance of funds. To obtain these funds, a prospectus is prepared, the nature of the prospectus varying with the funding source.

The neophyte might expect to prepare a proposal requesting funds from a given funding source, submit it before an announced deadline, and then expect to receive either a negative or positive response, or a request for a modification in the request by a previously announced date. He would then anticipate receiving the funds requested, and being able to spend them in the manner proposed in his fund request and subsequently approved by the funder. If his project were to cover several years, he might expect that after the first grant is made and he carried out the program previously proposed with a high degree of success, subsequent grants would follow almost automatically. He might also anticipate that as unexpected developments in his program occurred, he could shift funds from one activity or category to another, in order to accomplish the same goals more effectively. All these expectations are logical and reasonable. But project funding rarely proceeds in such a manner.

Funding sources work in different ways, and the eccentricities of their requirements and ways of handling grants circumscribe the freedom of the developmental project in ways beyond the control of the project. The same amount of money over a three-year period obtained from one source may permit a far more effective operation than is possible when the funding is from another source. Thus, the amount of funds available is not the sole constraint. Further constraints arise from the source of funding, the time when funds become available, the strings attached to the funds, and the funding uncertainties. Those who have not had direct experience obtaining outside funding generally have little appreciation of the problems involved, and of the restrictions on project activities as a result of the kind of funding obtained.

The funding source may be public or private. Funds may be granted for several years at a time, or for only a few months. The proposal requesting funds may be detailed, or couched in general terms. The grant may be flexible, or restricted to the minutiae of the initial proposal. The grant may be made well in advance of the grant period and for a logical work period, or it may be a last-minute grant for a period that does not fit in with the work calendar of the project; or it may be one of a series of continuing grants promised for the same work; or it may be a discrete, short-term grant with no guarantee or even promise of continuity after the initial period, even though the initial period was intended to produce only a beginning, preliminary product, rather than a complete one.

The periods for which grants are made depends, in part, on whether the grantor is private or public, and if public, which government agency is involved. There are a number of sources of public funds for developmental project work, including the various OE programs, the NSF, state departments of education, and local school systems. Or funding may be private, from a research fund of a university, foundation, or business.

Such sources as the Carnegie Foundation or Ford Foundation may make grants for a period of several years, and although money is paid out on a yearly basis and reports may be requested annually, there may be an advance commitment for the entire developmental period, or for a period of several years. Publishers supporting developmental work also contract for periods of several years.

However, federal agencies often are precluded by law from making firm commitments beyond the appropriations for the fiscal year. In such cases, grants cannot be made for more than one year, and there is no guarantee or even tacit commitment that funding will continue. Often, federal grants are made for even shorter periods, with a single project needing four or five separate grants to continue its work on a single curriculum through a single year. To some extent, this reflects the granting agency's uncertainties about its own budgetary allotment from Congress, but this does not account for all the uncertainty in the grant awards to projects. Thus, planning for operations is made highly tentative by uncertainties about funding from one year to the next, and even from one month to the next—a situation that is highly inappropriate, given the long-term nature of developmental curriculum work.[3]

This short-term grant system is not only a barrier to effective planning, but the time involved in modification of budgets can become nightmarish when a budget prepared for a twelve-month period, at the suggestion of the funder, is later subdivided, at the funder's request, into a three-month budget, a budget

---

[3]Boffey (1968) describes the kinds of crises that may result from cutbacks of NSF funding to a large institution. The situation is even more critical for smaller organizations with few or no reserves; some of these have had even larger cutbacks before or even after initial budget approval and allocation of funds.

for the succeeding five months, and then one for the following four months. This budget revision may be required by the funder weeks after a firm decision on the year-long budget had been promised. Furthermore, when a project has received several concurrent grants to cover different phases of its current activities, each grant may be for a different budget period.

While these examples may sound extreme, they are not unique. Many projects funded from federal sources have faced such situations. A. Grobman (1969) reports:

> Although some indecision is within comprehension, the very lengthy period of NSF indecision seemed to be beyond such limits and they certainly have affected the BSCS program adversely. Not only have certain policy decisions been repeatedly postponed in issues of sponsorship, copyrights, and revisions, but a more direct impact has been the last-minute awarding of grants for brief and uneven periods, which have mitigated against well-organized planning on the part of the BSCS. For example, of the ten major proposals made by the BSCS to the NSF for funding of its program, only four have resulted in grants of approximately the same scope and period as proposed. The remaining six proposals were responded to by ten different grants awarded for extremely variable periods. During its ten-year history, the BSCS has had to operate, at one time or another, with two-month, four-month, five-month, six-month, eight-month, twelve-month and fifteen-month budget periods . . . .

Funding is further complicated by the number of separate grants required to develop a single curriculum effectively. Some agencies make broad-based, multipurpose grants, while others make individual grants for each separate but related activity. Thus, according to Harvard Project Physics (HPP), its carefully coordinated, long-range, teacher-preparation program, covering seven facets of teacher training over a five-year period, would require thirty-five different proposals, one for each facet of the program, for each of the five years.

A conservative estimate of the top-level executive time required for preparation of each proposal, for discussions of the proposal within the project and with the funding agency, and for negotiations with the funders, would be one to two weeks, and if prior experience is indicative of future trends, the time required would probably be longer. Thus, a year or more of the time of a top professional might be involved in obtaining funding for a single, multifaceted teacher-training program, after the program had been carefully planned by project staff. And this is only one part of the developmental project's program on a single set of curriculum materials.

When multiple grants are needed by a project, either for continuing a program over a period of several years, or for carrying on several activities simultaneously, it can be difficult to maintain continuity of contact with the funding agency personnel, since some granting agencies have little stability in organization, personnel, and requirements. The OE, for example, has been characterized by frequent reorganizations and high personnel turnover.

The particular individual or division of OE handling the proposals for one project may be different in different years, and often, there are changes during the time a single proposal is being considered. For example, within a twelve-month period, there were three successive different contact people for a single OE-financed project. None of these contact people had any background in the OE grant procedure, in developmental curriculum work, or in the area of education in which the project was working. Not only do people change, but regulations also change frequently. Within a few months, the proposal format and the requirements and deadlines may change.

Separate grant requests submitted at the same time for concurrent, complementary activities may be channeled through different people and different divisions of the funding agency. And the reviewers for one request may be unaware of or unfamiliar with the others. The public granting agencies customarily have individuals outside the agency review proposals individually or as a panel. Thus, for an ongoing project, each new proposal may be reviewed by persons unfamiliar with the background and previous activities of the project and with other projected project plans, and the project has no opportunity to confer with the reviewers, to answer questions, correct misunderstandings, and counter objections.

The reviewers are also pressed for time in their consideration of each project, since they may be asked to review twenty or thirty voluminous proposals at one time. These reviewers often serve without renumeration beyond travel expenses to panel meetings; and even these expense payments may be less than the actual cost to the reviewer, since the payment often is on a flat per diem, rather than on a cost basis. Under such circumstances, it is not surprising that the review process is not entirely satisfactory from the standpoint of the project, the granting agency, or the reviewers.

Project funding may be so tightly budgeted that there is no leeway for planning of future activities. While some limited planning grants may be available, even the groundwork needed before a planning grant proposal can be prepared requires considerable resources. Some project funding is too de-limited in the activities approved to permit the use of staff time and funds for such advance program planning, if the project is to live up to the grant restrictions implicitly. Also, there is the question of how projects are to survive in the period between grants. For ongoing, multipurpose projects, the problem is less serious. JCEE, DEEP, or EDC (Educational Development Center, Incorporated), have other sources of interim funds, and the overhead funds they receive from previous grants can also be used for some advance planning.

For other projects—UICSM or BSCS, for example—overhead funds go to the sponsoring institution. They are not available to the project. The project's sole source of funds is grants; and unless a special planning grant is available, there are no funds for planning.

Such projects may borrow a little time from other of the project's grant-supported activities. However, in times of fund shortages, the amount of time that can be borrowed is very limited, and no funds may be borrowed for conferences and consultations. And so, for the most part, planning is done by the available staff working on its own time and imposing on friends for free consulting services. On a one-time basis, this may be practical; but over the years, it is an inefficient way of carrying on operations and a great burden on the staff and on those who try to retain the staff.

Some funders make grants for periods that fit the logic of project operations; others do not. The latter procedure is particularly burdensome when there is no firm commitment that follow-up grants will be forthcoming. Because projects generally use academic personnel on leave for a school year, and also work with school systems in trying out materials during the school year from September to June, a fiscal year starting in July or September may fit their operations better than a calendar year. In any event, projects need information on the monies that will become available well in advance of the start of the school period to permit effective continuous operations; yet this information is often not available. A project building a year-long history course to be tried experimentally in the schools during a school year starting in September, 1969, and continuing through June, 1970, may not know until late in December of 1969 that it has funds to continue the second half of the year's tryout of materials, or that it can continue to pay project staff hired for the duration of the school year to supervise this tryout.

It may also be necessary for the project to make firm commitments to staff and schools before funds have been granted to cover costs of some activities. Project staff often must be hired on an academic-year basis, since either they are on leave of absence for the school year, or will be going back into academic work after leaving the project and so will accept only contracts which terminate at the end of the school year. Yet grants may be made for a calendar year, without reserves to cover costs of services contracted for beyond the grant period.

For grants made on a fiscal year basis starting July 1, the project may receive notification of award of the grant late in June, or even July, despite the fact that it had to make firm commitments to schools the preceding spring that classroom materials would be provided the following fall if testing of materials is to be carried out during that school year. A grant may be awarded in June to cover a summer writing conference to be held that July and August, when arrangements to hire the writing conference participants had to be made the preceding winter. Of ten major NSF grants to the BSCS between 1959 and 1967, six were awarded less than a month prior to the scheduled starting date of the grant; two of these six were awarded during the month preceding the effective date, and four were awarded after the scheduled starting date (A. Grobman, 1969).

Thus, projects operating on public funds spend much of their time cliff-hanging while waiting for funds, and they lose much time negotiating for funds. Few seem exempt from these pressures. The problem is not necessarily the late submission of fund requests by projects; timing of grant awards is not necessarily related to the amount of advance time needed for consideration of the request, or to the necessary lead time needed by the project for planning before the start of the award period. Promises of decision dates are not predictive of the date of the actual decision. A decision on one project proposal was received fifteen months after the proposal was submitted, despite an initial promise of a decision within ninety days, and in a situation where the activities under consideration could only have been implemented if they had started immediately following this ninety-day period.[4]

Multifunction projects which have several activities carried on at one time, or projects that are part of a going operation such as a university or large research organization, may have more flexibility and backup guarantees of employment for their staff than those that are single function, having no financial reserves, and no way of providing funds or alternative employment for their staff. For example, a Regional Laboratory with a dozen or more different projects may be able to shift personnel from one project to another if grants are delayed. A unipurpose project—such as BSCS—cannot.

Some projects can borrow funds while awaiting promised grants; others cannot. At one time, HPP was without a grant contract for seven months. Although it did have an OE letter of intent, it had no money to pay its mounting bills. While it had no cash reserves, it was able to borrow money from the Harvard Corporation at 6 percent interest. An independent curriculum study, or one sponsored by a professional organization, probably would not have had this source for borrowing, and even for HPP, the borrowing was expensive. When the grant was finally received, the interest took more than half of the funds allowed for overhead costs for the seven-month period.

---

[4]Some of the uncertainty reflects fiscal uncertainties of the NSF, OE, or state and local education departments, pending Congressional or state legislative action on appropriations measures. But, regardless of the cause, the result is an inefficient, less-than-optimal operating situation for developmental projects working on public funds.

Given the late receipt of information on grants, and the operation of many projects without grant authorizations for several months, it is difficult to think of any publicly funded project that has not had to make firm commitments beyond the funds it has on hand, in order to carry out an effective program. On some occasions, when it is not possible for the project to go beyond the funds on hand, the entire program may be delayed, or some necessary activities may be deleted or postponed to a time when they are less useful than would have been the case had they been carried out on schedule. While outsiders are often justified in criticizing developmental programs in terms of a rational approach to curriculum or economical operation, such criticism may be unjustified in terms of what is possible and practical, given the complexities and uncertainties of the funding structure in which the project operates.

Even after funds from a public source are granted, there may be cutbacks arising either from legislative mandate—as for example, during a legislative economy drive—or because other higher priority demands on agency funds preclude implementation of previously planned programs. Even receipt of funds for a calendar quarter does not always mean these can be spent during that quarter. One month after the receipt of funds for a calendar quarter, the project may learn that the money will have to cover a four- or five-month period rather than the three-month period for which funds were initially granted, or that some percentage of the funds already granted and in hand may not be spent; this has been the experience of many projects several times during the Vietnam War. If the project has planned ahead and made personnel and other commitments, it may have no way of honoring these. Yet, it can hardly operate rationally and effectively without advance commitments.

Another type of limitation on use of public funds reflects the legitimate concern of public granting agencies about the extent to which public funds should be used to finance dissemination of materials it has helped finance. The specter of federal control of education is raised if the federal government first finances preparation of materials and then finances promotion of their use; and there is no clear boundary between necessary public information programs— to report to the public on the use of public funds and to keep potential users informed of the progress on materials—and promotional activities which are in the nature of advertising.

Certainly, public funds should not be used for outright promotional activities. Yet, unless the public knows about materials, and unless teachers are trained to use them, funds for developmental activities may be largely wasted. Furthermore, study after study of the change process in education indicate that desirable and lasting change does not occur simply because of the availability of better ways of doing things or of better materials. Change requires more than an awareness of the innovation and the ability of teachers to use it. The building of strategies for change is also an important element in effecting desirable, lasting change. (Bennis, 1966; Bennis, Benne, and Chin, 1969; Rogers, 1962; Carlson, *et al.,* 1965.) Without concern for the way materials can best be introduced into school systems, the development of materials may be largely an academic exercise.

Projects financed with public funds are more limited in their activities relevant to diffusion than are those funded from private sources. For example, after the formative period in development of curriculum materials, the BSCS was largely limited in its teacher-training efforts to working with persons in colleges, universities, and school systems who were responsible for teacher training, rather than executing the teacher training itself. Yet, some public funds were available to the colleges and universities and to school systems for such training. IME funding constraints on teacher training reflect the problem of keeping within a budget compatible with a commercial profitmaking enterprise. As a result, rather detailed teacher materials were prepared, and these were supplemented for a short time by brief (two-day) teacher training financed by the publisher with only limited teacher-training activity in colleges and universities.

Neither BSCS nor IME could explore the problems of dissemination within the school system in great depth –BSCS,because it might seem improper to use federal funds to promote dissemination of materials prepared with public funds, and the IME, because of cost considerations necessary to a commercial enterprise. In contrast, the JCEE project was able to focus considerable attention on the process of dissemination, on how to bring about change in schools and to stimulate actual adoption of materials. Its grant from the Ford Foundation had few constraints, and the individual contributors to the JCEE were directly concerned with dissemination, wanted to stimulate adoption as widely as possible, and wanted funds directed to this end.

While the public granting agencies and foundations deny any desire to control the products being developed, the very nature of the process of obtaining grants may clearly modify what is possible, may preclude certain types of operations and may, in fact, dictate the kinds of materials produced, even where the funder has no such desire. For example, there may be some general regulations that funds may be spent only for certain purposes. Or certain budget categories may be cut or eliminated in budget reviews. Here, the deletion of an item by the funder may be specific; at other times, it may be indirect, through some such off-the-record comment as, "If the item for equipment design were eliminated, we might look with more favor on the proposal."

Thus, for several years, one project repeatedly included an item for teacher-training films in its proposed budget, and this item was systematically deleted. This deletion directly influenced the teacher-training effectiveness of the project, since the project did not carry out any other teacher-training activities directly, and, although there were many NSF teacher-training institutes preparing teachers for this curriculum, the project had no direct relation to or control over them. Yet, many critics of the project said that the project's materials were ineffective because of poor implementation by teachers.

Funders may also influence the activities of projects by restrictions on travel, or on the amount that may be paid to consultants, or on who may be paid as a consultant. For example, for some funding, a project may not pay a consulting fee to any member of the faculty of the college institution through which the grant is channeled. This may mean that local personnel cannot be used on a consulting basis at all. Or when last-minute cuts are made in a grant, the project may be forced to honor certain commitments already made, when, if it had a real choice, these are the activities that would be cut.

For some kinds of developmental activities, it is still difficult to find any funding source. For example, for some NSF-financed developmental projects, requests to the NSF for funds for various kinds of evaluation work have been refused with the comment that the activity is more properly the concern of the OE. However, when OE has been approached the reaction is that science and mathematics are the areas of NSF concern, and OE should not compete with NSF in providing funds for science and mathematics education. Also, OE has been reluctant to provide funds for evaluating materials produced under funding by another agency. In effect, such OE funding for evaluation might be considered a review or judgment of another agency. Or one division of NSF may feel that a particular teacher-training activity is the prerogative of another NSF division. The second division may feel it does not have that authority. And the activity may never be funded simply because of a confusion over authority rather than on the basis of the merits of the proposed activity.

There is a problem of budget rigidity for some funding. While some funders request only general guidelines for budget categories, others demand highly specific advance blueprints.

Detailed budgeting involves problems of predicting an uncertain future far in advance. While some projects outline their advance activities in detail, the majority are emergent in the sense that they are operating with so many unknowns that highly specific advance planning would be meaningless, and could be most unfortunate in committing a project to an idea or activity that does not work out.

For some public funding, the budget –for example, 1968—must be submitted by October, 1967; thus, in September of 1967, when the project is just starting its preliminary pilot tests for feasibility of experimental materials, it may be completing details of its budget for the large-scale field testing for revised materials from September, 1968 through June, 1969. If the group is really pioneering in a new approach to education, if it is really exploring the unknown, it cannot be sure the pilot test will work. How, then, can it sensibly plan the details of expanding the experiment, when it may be that a further year of pilot field tests will be indicated? On the other hand, to wait for results of the pilot test before budgeting in detail the next activity would mean a delay of one year between the pilot test and revision work and field testing of revised materials, since the classroom trial of a year-long curriculum must start in September, at the start of the school year, and the pilot testing would not have been completed until June.

A funder's approach to budget detail is not necessarily consistent or logical. Detailed specifications may be requested for one budget category and not another, or for one year and not for another. Thus, in one year a large and undifferentiated figure for evaluation activities may be unquestioned and the next year a smaller request may be returned for details on scheduling, size and composition of experimental sample, statistical treatments to be used, etc. Coupled with the requirements of great detail may be stringent regulations concerning shifting of funds from one budget category to another after funds have been awarded. Such regulations can make later changes in the budget so difficult and time-consuming as to be impractical. Where funds come from several sources within the same agency—for example, the Curriculum Improvement Division and the Institute Division of the NSF, or the different title programs of the OE—such transfer of funds from one grant source to another is precluded.

Constraints resulting from funding vary with different funding sources, and they change over time. The requirements of an OE grant from one division may be far different and far more detailed than those from another division of OE. The National Institutes of Health (NIH) grant stipulations and arrangements are different and far less troublesome than those of OE or NSF. In the early days of NSF funding of developmental projects, there were far less rigid parameters than was the case later, perhaps because when the process of developmental curriculum work was new, no one knew what questions to ask. Yet, a number of persons connected with the earlier NSF projects feel that those projects could never have accomplished as much as they did as rapidly as they did, had the constraints of funding been what they later became. Some persons now feel they can accomplish more with a smaller grant—perhaps from a private foundation or private publisher—when this imposes fewer constraints.

Given the uncertainties and complexities of public funding, why do projects turn to public rather than private sources for funding? The funds from private foundations appear to offer the most flexibility with the least red tape. However, competition for these limited funds is keen and foundations are not equally interested in all areas of curriculum development, so that a given project, or some part of it, may not fit into the foundation's area of concern. Further, the private foundations have been understandably reluctant to provide support for science and mathematics curriculum activities because they feel that the NSF is taking care of these. Yet, in many instances, the NSF does not consider the particular activity in science and mathematics to be part of its responsibility.

Recently, a number of textbook publishers and commercial educational combines have financed developmental work. This avenue may offer less leeway to the developmental work than does public funding since, obviously materials prepared under the auspices of a commercial publisher must give promise of selling well to be worth his backing. This raises various questions of quality control in terms of the extent to which compromises will be necessary to make materials more attractive commercially. That is: Will the educator or the sales manager be more influential in determining the directions the materials will take? Will publishers risk production of highly experimental materials? Who will control content? And will projects and project writers be able to resist the lure of high royalties?

It is too early to determine how these publisher-financed projects will fare, how long publishers will be willing to subsidize developmental work, and whether this will permit a viable relationship between the curriculum producer and the funding source. A number of the people now working on developmental projects funded by commercial publishers have been key people in earlier publicly funded, highly successful, developmental projects. For them, perhaps the degree of freedom in developing materials will be greater than would be the case for a person whose reputation in developmental curriculum work is more limited. At any rate, to date there is no basis for concluding that such privately sponsored projects will be less creative or more constrained than those financed through public or foundation sources. However, it seems unlikely that a publisher would support highly experimental, large-scale developmental activities, given the financial risk involved in these. Yet, some highly competent and respected people are now working on developmental projects financed by publishers, and some seem reasonably satisfied with the relationship. While private financing will probably not replace public financing of developmental work, if the present activities of publishers are successful, it seems likely that such activities will be greatly expanded.

There are necessarily some constraints involved in all funding. Whether the monies are public, from private foundations, or from commercial enterprises, no one is willing, or should be willing, to give money away with no accountability for the expenditures. While excessive constraints can defeat the very purpose of the funding, and make the implementation of an imaginative developmental curriculum project impossible, the very general mandate of some private funders—amounting to an injunction to "go and do good"—on a number of occasions has resulted in wastefulness, ineffectiveness, and carrying an activity beyond the point of diminishing returns.

The fine balance between accountability for funds and necessary flexibility for efficiency of operations has rarely been achieved in the funding of developmental projects of the last decade. Unfortunately, the imbalance—an imbalance highly detrimental to developmental work—seems to be growing with the passage of time. Increasingly, educational decisions seem to be made for noneducational reasons, and, granted the fact that records must be kept and there must be an accounting for

> ... the original purposes of the federal grant programs are endangered by having too many of the rules written by accountants. Although scientists and accountants, in and out of government, are aware of the other's point of view, they consider scientific activities and the grants that support them from fundamentally different vantage points. The scientific interest is primarily in the purposes for which funds are granted and in the accomplishments made possible by grants. The accounting interest is primarily in seeing that the accounts balance accurately and that there is a proper piece of paper on file to justify each expense item. The danger ... is the obvious one that the form will be given more weight than the substance.
>
> WOLFLE (1967)

AGE AND LIFE-SPAN OF THE ORGANIZATION

Some curriculum projects become new parts of an existing organization, and others represent new organizations set up for the specific and sole purpose of effecting the curriculum project. When an organization has been newly created for a specific developmental activity—for example, a new developmental project in sociology or anthropology—it may be freer from some of the constraints of an ongoing organization in terms of starting fresh, being free of precedents and previous staff commitments, and of the expectations traditional in the existing organization. Earth Sciences Curriculum Project (ESCP) and Sociological Resources for Secondary Schools (SRSS), for example, did not start out with existing organizational norms, but had to create their own, and so they may have been freer to experiment and improvise and select appropriate staff, rather than accepting existing arrangements, prior staff commitments, and a traditional or customary way of doing things. Thus, they may have had fewer initial constraints than would be faced in a similar activity developed in an established Regional Laboratory or R and D Center.

Such freedom to start a new organization has its price. Routinizing of management and housekeeping concerns can be time-consuming and can result in inefficient or ineffective ways of carrying on activities. The new organization may have fewer in-house resources to draw on. It may need its own business office, purchasing arrangements, shipping arrangements, proposal writers, and office management staff. While these are peripheral to the preparation of developmental materials, they are nonetheless vital to the success of a project; yet, often the kinds of people most interested in and concerned with developmental work are untrained and impatient with the detail of housekeeping arrangements requisite to an effective operation. Where a business office or administrative management officer of the university, school system, Regional Laboratory, or R and D Center can take over such housekeeping detail, the academicians and educators are freed for curricular concerns.

There may also be more staff flexibility in the affiliation with an existing multipurpose agency, since staff members can transfer from one project to another and back as the demands of the work schedule call for a particular skill. But this advantage may carry a concomitant disadvantage, in that the developmental activity may be saddled with a staff member to whom an earlier commitment has been made, perhaps for a very different purpose, when a new person would be more appropriate. It may also be burdened with regulations which have been established for other activities—regulations concerning purchasing, use of personnel, staff promotion policy, staff travel, decision making, budgeting—that may be less appropriate for the developmental activity.

Projects that have successfully completed one developmental curriculum task can easily phase into another, taking advantage of the expertise gained in the previous developmental work. Some projects or project organizations continue beyond their initial foci and develop relatively permanent organizations. Some go on to different ventures in the same subject area. Others pursue work in new and sometimes quite unrelated disciplines. Some projects deliberately decide to continue either with the same or with other work. Some make the decision by default; they go on without a deliberate decision on whether to continue, how long to continue, and why to continue, and they may accumulate new grants and even new functions without systematic advance planning.

In the past, some projects seem to have continued beyond the point of diminishing returns. Others have been cut off before optimal returns were possible. Should existing projects stop after a few years, or continue with the same work or with new work? What are the advantages of each course? For those that stop, what is an optimal stopping point? The question of project life-span involves some basic issues in terms of efficiency, effectiveness, and long-range desirability.

Some projects come to a halt through lack of continued funding. The problem may be that the organization previously granting funds has changed its interests; several private foundations provide funds in a given field as seed money, to stimulate interest and a beginning effort, and after the effort is under way, they turn their interests to other fields. The projects involved may have come to a logical stopping place, since they are forewarned by the foundation of a cutoff date. However, they may have had false hopes about continued foundation financing, or unrealized hopes of being able to obtain funding from other sources.

There are also projects that are cut off by the funder because the funder has experienced a reduction of funds and can no longer make grants, or because the funder is dissatisfied with the results, or because the funder feels that his available resources can be better used elsewhere. In this last case, which reflects a degree of dissatisfaction with results produced, there is a question of how much time should be allowed for a developmental project to prove itself.

There is no such thing as an instant curriculum; developmental curricula take longer to complete than do curricula prepared in a traditional manner. Furthermore, if the project is to be optimally productive, it must have a chance to experiment, to take a chance on new, unproven techniques, techniques which may not work. If a project faces a threat of dissolution after a year or two if the preliminary products do not work out as anticipated, genuine experimentation is precluded.

How long should a funder or sponsor wait for results? One project director has suggested that one reasonable index of progress is that some materials should be completed and ready for general release within four years of initiation of the venture. Given the timetables of projects to date, this would seem to provide one reasonable bench mark. However, there have been projects that obviously should have been stopped sooner, that clearly have not made appropriate progress. Should initial funding commit a funder for four years? Obviously, this does not make sense. Yet, alternative criteria are not clear.

When is it justifiable to withdraw support? This question is rarely discussed openly, and sometimes is avoided entirely by the funders when they diminish support to a token amount, so that the question does not have to be faced. Certainly, various funders must have considered this problem and made decisions, but the bases for specific decisions or the criteria used in making such decisions are generally not public information.

For other projects, the matter of life-span is a choice of the project or sponsoring agency. The BSCS and PSSC decided to stay in business, and both were able to obtain further funding. The BSCS stayed with biology at the secondary school level, the PSSC expanded into Educational Services, Incorporated (ESI) and then to Educational Development Center, Incorporated (EDC) and undertook a wide range of activities in curriculum at various grade levels and subject areas. The project initiators of ESSP (Elementary-School Science Project) working in astronomy, deliberately ceased operation when the initial work was completed. CHEM Study made a decision to phase out more gradually. And SSCP (School Science Curriculum Project) was phased out through failure to receive continued funding even though a natural closure point had not been reached. Why does one project decide to stop and another decide to continue? A major factor seems to be the personal interests of the people involved.

The initiators of ESSP had felt that the astronomy taught in the schools was trivial and not representative of the field and of the investigatory styles of the field, and they decided to prepare elementary materials to correct these shortcomings. The group worked several years building materials in summer writing conferences and trying them out during the year. When project initiators felt that the initial aims had been reached, they discontinued the project. They had no desire to develop new aims, to work in fields other than astronomy, or at grade levels other than the elementary school years. Project personnel evidently had interests other than developmental curriculum work to which they wanted to return. The project had no large staff, and so it had no long-term commitments to staff members. There was no large-scale sponsoring organization with broader goals, and so there was no organizational pressure to go beyond a relatively narrow grade span or limited subject focus as might be the case for projects sponsored by such groups as the American Association for the Advancement of Science (AAAS) or the American Historical Association (AHA).

Probably several factors contributed toward the BSCS decision to continue beyond completion of its initial task. This initial task was the rapid improvement of biology education at the secondary school level, which was interpreted as indicating that the first job was to reach as many students as possible as quickly as possible. Thus, work was initially undertaken at the grade level where biology was generally taught—the tenth grade—where three-quarters of the students at grade level take biology, and the target audience for the initial thrust was the average student. The BSCS deferred consideration of such other groups as the lower-ability student and the student who takes a second high school course in biology.

After the initial job was well in hand, and those working with the BSCS —staff and policy committee members—felt well satisfied with their accomplishments, with the organization that had been built up, and with the method that had been used to build materials, the BSCS Steering Committee considered the question of whether to continue or to stop, whether to go on to other aspects of high school biology or to leave the remainder of the job to others. The committee decided to go on to curricula for the lower-ability student and the student who takes a second high school biology course. Attention was also turned to teacher preparation and to assisting overseas countries wishing to adapt materials for use in their countries. By the time some of these additional tasks were well in hand, the initial tenth grade materials needed revision.

Thus, it became increasingly clear that curriculum improvement is a continuing function, even if limited to one discipline and one school level— the high school. Although the content of other biology books was reflecting the new emphases used by BSCS biology, it also became clear that these competing volumes were not finishing the task. And no other project had been set up to do this.

As activities on the original BSCS versions were completed, the BSCS staff was reduced in size; but this did not constitute a serious problem, since most professional staff members were on one-year or shorter term appointments. Thus, the nature and magnitude of the activities changed, but the operation continued, and apparently will continue for some time, since although the BSCS versions are now in a revised commercial edition, provisions have been made for a second revision a few years hence.

CHEM Study phased out after general release of its materials. According to Merrill and Ridgway (1969), the group perceived itself as a temporary task force rather than as a permanent organization, and felt that long-term continuing activity "might have the unfortunate effect of deterring other individuals and groups from creating new materials for commercial publication." CHEM Study expressed a concern with "terminating its activities and at the same time stimulating the development of other new materials" in high school chemistry; it tried to do this through its provision for revisions of CHEM Study materials by authorized commercial publishers.[5]

What are the gains and losses when a successful project decides to stop? Having built up considerable expertise in curriculum building, in management

_____

[5]The details of this arrangement are discussed on pp. 153-54, in connection with project arrangements for release of materials.

techniques, in sources of information, in contacts with the professions involved, and with schools, to stop after a single job, such as the development of sixth grade anthropology or tenth grade geography, seems inefficient. An expert staff may be assembled and developed into an efficient and effective work team. For example, the BSCS art staff, which was gradually dissolved after the versions were published, was probably the largest, most competent biological illustrations staff in the country. Not only were the artists competent, but they had mastered the problems of working with writers and with publishers. Furthermore, all the expensive equipment they required for the various kinds of artwork had been assembled.

There is a very definite know-how in many of the tasks of developmental work. Even the mundane details of running a meeting or a writing conference, putting out a newsletter, preparing exhibits for professional meetings, trivial as they may appear in contrast with the basic curriculum-policy decisions and the preparation of curriculum materials, can be time-consuming and unduly expensive the first time. And if these tasks are not handled expeditiously, they may limit or debar successful implementation of the project or acceptance of materials by potential users.

Just as it is far easier for a manufacturer to diversify his products than it is to establish a new company every time a new model is to be put out, so it is far simpler and more economical to diversify curriculum-building activities as new editions or other materials—whether directly related to the original or not—are desired. However, in the case of a manufacturing company or of a developmental study, sometimes the loss is greater than the gain. A new organization may have a dynamic atmosphere, difficult to create or maintain in an older organization. And the dead hand of the past and past commitments may unduly restrict new activities.

Some of the curriculum projects, as they are first set up, have an *esprit de corps* that many participants have said is unique in their experience. Even the best-run organization cannot maintain this level of enthusiastic commitment indefinitely. Newly established projects may be more inventive. Since they have never done the job at all, they may be less committed to one method or set of procedures than is a project that has worked successfully in the past. For example, as the BSCS starts work on classroom materials at a different grade or ability level than it has done before, it sets up summer writing conferences that in many ways are prototypes of previous, successful BSCS writing conferences. While this may be the very best way of preparing classroom materials, it is possible that there are other, equally good ways. Perhaps the BSCS would not be as likely to explore the alternatives as would a new group that had not had previous experience with developmental curriculum work. It must be remembered, however, that just because a group is new and has not had prior experience, does not guarantee systematic exploration of alternatives or a branching out in dynamic directions. In fact, the reverse might be true. Perhaps an older group can better afford to experiment, to take a chance with a radically new procedure.

Another problem of continuity of projects is personnel. A continuing project may not be able to continue to attract top-flight personnel. The kinds of persons who staffed the early projects initially often would not take on such assignments as career assignments. Many were scientists—research people who were willing to leave their academic activities for a year or two to make a unique contribution and to try out some ideas they had. Many would not be willing to make the departure from scientific pursuits permanent. This is not a matter of leaving or not leaving a college campus. Rather, it is a matter of leaving research and teaching in a discipline, for a career in education.

If top-notch people outside of education are to be associated with projects, this will probably not be a long-term commitment involving full-time or even half- or quarter-time work. If it is, such scholars may not remain at the top of their disciplines long. For the more permanent projects, there has already been a shift in the types of personnel involved. True, many have the eminent scholars working on a consultant basis, or for summers, but there are fewer of the outstanding scholars from the disciplines working with existing projects, and these are more difficult to obtain, even for the projects that have commendable records of success.

What kinds of staff rewards are needed to maintain quality staff over long periods of time without the professional rewards that come from the staff member's usual pursuits? The problem may be somewhat alleviated on a collegiate campus, where staff, if they have regular faculty appointments, can maintain professional contacts, perhaps teach a few classes, and work with graduate students. Nonetheless, recognition from their professional peers is not the same as it would be for research pursuits. Generally, the physicist or historian will not receive professional recognition—and perhaps not receive promotion in rank—for work on a curriculum project. He does receive it for research in physics or history. Will people who are not caught up in such value systems be able to do the job as well?

It has been suggested that the reward system will have to be changed in some way if the level of personnel in developmental projects is to be maintained. One suggested change might be the payment of royalties to authors— a system not used heretofore by the major curriculum projects—as a means of compensating the individual for loss of research time and also time for outside consulting, which generally pays far better than curriculum work. At the least, some change in payment arrangements is clearly needed for those publicly financed projects which currently are allowed to pay only a basic per diem for attendance at project meetings—a payment not covering expenses of attendance—and no honorarium for the time involved. When a project is new, participants may be willing to take an active part, even at a penalty; over the long run, with financial arrangements that penalize the participant rather than reward him, the quality of participants may not be maintained.

It is difficult to say to what extent the success of developmental projects to date has reflected the newness of the developmental technique, the development of new organizations, the idea of experimenting with few precedents to rely on for guidance, and the enthusiasm of the personnel. But if these factors were major contributors, the momentum for change through the developmental process may slow down as projects mature and existing projects take on new functions.

STRUCTURE OF THE ORGANIZATION

There is a variety of organizational patterns for developmental projects, and the nature of the organizational structure influences project alternatives, and can enhance or deter certain kinds of activities. The developmental project may be part of a large ongoing organization. It can be local, regional, or national in vista and operations. It can be sponsored by a university, a professional organization, an independent organization established for that purpose, a commercial publishing venture, a research organization, a school system or group of school systems, a state educational office, a multipurpose, educational, nonprofit or profit organization. Operations can be physically centralized or decentralized. And responsibility can be centralized or decentralized, and hierarchical or nonhierarchical. There are existing projects exemplifying each of these alternatives.

Sponsorship

While the earlier curriculum projects were generally under the aegis of a university, today there is a wider variety of sponsors. BSCS was initiated by the American Institute of Biological Sciences, a professional society. The American Sociological Association established SRSS; and the American Geological Institute established ESCP. UICSM and SMSG are part of universities, and grants to these projects are channeled through their universities. PSSC was initially part of Massachusetts Institute of Technology and later became part of an independent nonprofit research organization—ESI, now EDC—which combines a number of curriculum projects at various school levels in a number of disciplines.

Some cities—for example, New York—have their own developmental projects. Others take part in cooperative ventures; for example, they may be member systems of the Joint Council for Economic Education DEEP project, with the JCEE encouraging and providing some consultation, or part of the Greater Cleveland Council (now the Educational Research Council of America—ERC) established by school systems in the Greater Cleveland area, with developmental curriculum work carried on by council staff rather than by the individual school systems.

A number of textbook publishers have established developmental projects, either under a separate division of the company set up specifically to oversee such projects, or as part of the regular textbook division of the company. The OE Regional Laboratories and OE Research and Development Centers have developmental projects as part of their activities.

While in theory, it would be possible to establish a curriculum project on an entirely autonomous basis, in practice, projects generally have some kind of parent organization. Complete autonomy is generally not feasible either for a new or an existing project. For an existing project, it is difficult; for a new endeavor, the difficulty is still greater.

ESI was able to set up as an independent organization after the initial success of PSSC, its forerunner. However, the BSCS was unsuccessful in its attempt to work out an independent status after the NSF arranged for its removal from the aegis of AIBS, its initial sponsoring agency, and its affiliation on an interim basis with the University of Colorado.[6] Here, even after the BSCS achieved a considerable record of successful curriculum development and responsible operation, it was made clear by funders that the BSCS was free to become independent, but that funders would probably not look with favor on grant proposals in such a situation.

To set up a new, independent organization for developmental curriculum purposes without sponsorship of a parent organization of some kind is even more difficult. Some kind of financial backing is needed during the planning period; while grant funds for planning are available from public and private foundations, these are generally awarded through sponsoring organizations. The same is true of grants for operating the project.

Understandably, public funding agencies must have some guarantee of continuity of operation, some assurance of fiscal and operational responsibility, before awarding funds, and such assurances are more likely when there is an established organization to act as sponsor. Funds generally go only to existing,

---

[6]The background of the NSF action is discussed in Greenberg (1963) and Walsh (1965). This NSF action reflected a loss of confidence in the AIBS fiscal management, with a continuing confidence and support of the BSCS.

going concerns with a history of responsibility, but a concern cannot come into existence and build such a history without funds. While it is not impossible to set up a new, independent organization to operate a developmental project, such efforts would run into extremely difficult financing problems and interim staffing problems before operating grants are received, unless a private foundation were particularly interested in the endeavor.

Degree of Centralization of Operations

One important variable in curriculum-project organization is the location of the central office and the extent to which staff and operations are centralized in that office. Geographical centralization of developmental project staff has some clear advantages. Communication is facilitated. Managerial services can be centralized with a minimum of delay and red tape. The day-to-day interaction of staff can be an enriching factor in policymaking as well as in actual operations. A great deal of time is saved in traveling, in shipping manuscripts and reports back and forth, and in getting prompt, informed decisions. This would seem to provide a reasonable, logical method of operating a curriculum project, and many large and small projects operate in this way. For the most part, UICSM staff has worked in Urbana at the University of Illinois. SMSG staff was located first at Yale and now at Palo Alto at Stanford University (though summer writing conferences have been held elsewhere). HPP staff is in Cambridge at Harvard, although housed in a number of locations there.

However, some projects, both large and small, are not so centralized. The BSCS, which maintains most of its staff at Boulder, on the University of Colorado campus, has maintained a separate organization and staff at the University of Texas for the Committee on Innovation in Laboratory Instruction work, and that committee's writers remained at their home institutions when preparing their materials. And the BSCS has maintained other offices for six-month periods in New York, Seattle, Palo Alto, and Berkeley, and has had full-time and part-time staff members in other locations for short-term appointments. SRSS has a central office staff, but the initial writing on units is done at the home institution of the author(s) selected to prepare a particular set of materials. Still more decentralized is the DEEP program, with developmental work carried on entirely at the local level by the thirty participating school systems.

While such decentralized operations have their drawbacks, there are some advantages. It becomes possible to take advantage of a variety of staff, laboratory, and library facilities that would not be available in a single location. Some people, not available on a full-time basis away from home, are available on a part-time basis at their home locations. Further, in such projects as DEEP and

SRSS, the project takes on less of a localized geographic identity, a factor which can make its activities more acceptable.

In the balance, unless there are some compelling reasons for the dispersion of activities, a central location is undoubtedly more efficient in terms of management services and also in facilitating communication. Since sharing of ideas during the developmental period of curriculum production is a major feature of the most successful developmental projects, this would appear to be a major factor in locating staff.

Why then did such a project as BSCS have full-time personnel located away from the headquarters office? Even higher on the BSCS priority list than facilitating communication among persons working on different major facets of the program was the desire to have the most appropriate people working on the materials. When these people agreed to undertake the assignment, one of their conditions was that the work would be done in Palo Alto, New York, or Seattle. This then influenced the locale of the work. And in these instances, all the writers on a single project or phase of the work were in the same location; had this not been the case, the quality of the product would undoubtedly have been lessened.

For IME, the decision to decentralize was based on financial considerations; a large portion of the writing was done at the home location of the writers as a supplemental activity to regular teaching and other professional assignments. The development of laboratory equipment was also a part-time activity for the people involved, and so had to be accommodated to the locale of the people doing the work. For DEEP, the decision apparently was not a financial one, but rather was based on the JCEE long-standing practice of working through local groups in implementing programs to improve economic education.

When operations are not centralized, it is particularly important that attention be given to maintaining frequent and open communication. This may involve considerable expense, but is far more efficient than failing to do so, since it permits avoidance of costly errors. For example, in the DEEP project, on occasion, office quality-control interventions concerning locally prepared materials were too late to be effective; on several occasions, work had gone too far to permit backtracking for improvement.

On several other projects, the authors of materials prepared away from the headquarters office considered these materials ready for very minor revision and copy editing when they had not been seen by anyone but the authors. In some instances, these products entirely missed the focus of the overall project and failed to implement project goals. Some materials prepared in this manner have been highly traditional in approach, even when intended for projects that were inquiry-oriented.

In one project, on no occasion did persons constructing tests have face-to-face contacts with persons developing materials, and there were no detailed and systematic statements of intent or objectives by the authors to which tests writers could turn. Because of lack of open communication channels, the test writers had to guess what it was the authors were trying to teach.

Thus, decentralization has its hazards. These hazards are not insuperable. But unless they are recognized, and steps taken to minimize their potential effects, the project may suffer quite seriously, both in terms of money wasted and a less than adequate product.

Degree of External Control

The nature of the funding is one determinant of the amount and kind of outside control that can be exerted on a developmental project. The nature of the parent organization is another. While some of the aspects of control by the parent organization are predictable and consistent over time, others are not.

Projects operating under state or local auspices probably have more frequent and detailed day-to-day external control over business management than those operating under the aegis of a professional organization. They may be subject to civil service regulations, central purchasing requirements, state and local preaudit of expenditures, and close budget control, as well as a considerable degree of policy control. These may be the most severe constraints on projects. However, other types of projects—those under university auspices, those sponsored by publishers, those sponsored by professional societies, and those sponsored by nonprofit organizations—are also subject to various types of controls and interventions.

A professional organization, such as the American Sociological Association or the Association of American Geographers, may be expected to exert a very different kind of control on its projects than a university, a publishing house, or a nonprofit organization dominated by noneducators. But there does not seem to be a typical pattern or norm.

In some instances, the professional society has made the major directional decisions for the curriculum project under its aegis—as, for example, the type of materials to be prepared, and the content and relative emphases—while in others, such decisions are left almost entirely to the project staff and policy board, with only the most general reviews by the parent organization. Or the professional society may intervene more with one project director than with an earlier or later director of the project; or one executive director and executive council of a professional society may intervene more frequently than their successors.

In a nonprofit corporation, there may be more intervention in one project than in another under the same aegis. Except in matters of fiscal accountability, a project under the sponsorship of a university probably has less external control than similar projects under professional organization or publishing house sponsorship.

While a professional organization might question the appropriateness of the content treatment in materials produced by its project, a university would be far less likely to do so, and probably only in extreme instances would a university fail to continue cosponsoring a project fund request on the basis of content of materials being produced. One might expect the strongest policy control of projects by the publishers sponsoring such curriculum projects, yet this may not be the case. One publishing house may leave its curriculum projects pretty much alone, while another may give them close and constant surveillance.

The control may operate only in particularly sensitive matters. For example, in the DEEP project, content review by the DEEP staff was advisory only, and generally no other JCEE personnel read the materials. The JCEE had no control over content beyond its powers of persuasion. However, in one instance, where one JCEE board member strongly objected to the use of some excerpts from the *Congressional Record* to illustrate an economic principle, the JCEE was able to obtain a modification even though there was no specific authority to require a change.

The nature and degree of control in any one situation probably reflects the interests of the policymakers in the parent organization, the interests and personalities of those administering both the parent organization and the curriculum project, and a variety of historical accidents, rather than systematic planning. Many of the control and intervention practices that become major factors in the project direction develop without conscious decision, or even the awareness of the participants that long-term patterns are being formed. The director of the parent organization or the chairman of its board may expect to review all materials before they are printed, simply because on one occasion he happened to be visiting the project when a decision on content for a final edition was being made and, as a courtesy, he was invited to sit in on the meeting. Examples of control policies established inadvertently are legion.

At first glance, it might appear that those projects freest from outside interventions would be in the most advantageous positions. This is not necessarily the case. On occasion, the interventions—whether in terms of policy, financial audit, or content review—may be too infrequent or too tardy. Infrequent interventions may result in the development of a deleterious situation beyond the point of repair—as, for example, where the complete inadequacy of materials prepared is not caught before the materials are virtually completed; or, in a questionable fiscal policy, noted only after hundreds of thousands of dollars have been misspent. While the nature and timing of interventions related to various aspects of the operations may be so frequent and detailed as to hamper operations, in some instances, they have been too few and too general to stop damaging trends or practices in time to prevent a disaster or gross waste of funds and manpower.

A different type of external control reflects a kind of social control—a control by forces external to the curriculum project, but delimiting the scope of the project indirectly. All projects face some such external controls. Thus, College Entrance Examination Board tests, school requirements and expectations, expectations of the profession, and parental expectations and prejudices operate as constraints or external control mechanisms on curriculum projects. Constraints also include the expectations that colleges have of high schools, the expectations that senior high schools have of junior high schools, the expectations that junior high schools have of the intermediate grades, and the expectations that intermediate grades have of the junior primary grades.

Some developmental projects have been highly sensitive to such control factors. Others have more or less ignored them. And some have compromised. While at least temporarily accepting the framework of some controls, they have tried to change other of the control factors rather than being changed by them. Thus, some controversial issues may be left out of a curriculum, while a few may be included. Or some textbook selection restrictions by school systems—for example, that all textbook materials must be hard-cover—may be accepted; and others—that the state textbook selection committee may require change in content after adoption—may be rejected.

Curriculum projects may not feel the impact of the indirect control mechanism as early in project work as is the case with the more direct control by sponsors and funders. The indirect controls may not be felt at all until materials become available, at least in preliminary form. The full brunt of this kind of control may not be felt until materials preparation is nearly completed and the project becomes concerned with dissemination. Until the information about what the project is doing becomes known outside the project, there may be little evidence of such controls.

Because of the delayed impact of the indirect type of control, the project may not be fully aware of the potential problems involved; and so, it may not be fully prepared to cope with them. Or the project may not anticipate the impact in time to attempt to modify the control mechanism. Thus, some curriculum projects at the high school level became concerned quite early about College Board examinations, and attempted to alleviate the problem without compromising the curriculum or jeopardizing the student. Others either did not recognize a problem, or expected the situation to work itself out in the long run.

However, some projects have been too sensitive to the possible ramifications of the indirect control mechanisms and have jeopardized their curricula. They have anticipated unfavorable reactions to some kinds of materials and treatments. Some have made no attempt to insure that their assessment of the public reaction is accurate. And some have made no attempt to modify possible public reaction. As a result, some projects have entirely avoided controversial areas in their curricula. Some have compromised in grade level or coverage where such compromise was neither wise nor necessary.

Certainly, a project cannot operate in complete isolation from schools as they exist in present society and from that society itself. Yet, some projects have been too bold and unrealistic in terms of the indirect external control factors; some have been overly cautious and equally unrealistic in viewing these factors. Perhaps the most effective path for a project is one of calculated risk, of careful assessment of the pressures and risks, and a thoughtful decision of which risks to take and when to take them.

Internal Management and Decision Making

Hills (1966) suggests that managerial functions can be broken down into three categories: (1) Making decisions about what and how much to produce; (2) Procuring the human, monetary, and physical facilities necessary for the performance of technical functions; and (3) Supervision of technical operations.

In curriculum projects, often only one of these functions—the procurement of facilities—is systematized, and decision making and supervision may be quite loose. There is not always a clear responsibility for decision making and after the fact, it may not be clear just who made a decision, or even when the decision was made; and a decision or manner of operation may just be explained as "This is the way we do things."

Patterns of management and operation may reflect the policymaking structure in the project, and perhaps most important, the people involved.

Projects vary widely in the designated locus of decision making within the project. Some projects have rather strong policy boards or executive committees, with frequent review of policy and major decisions made by one or the other of these groups. Others may have some advisory committees, but the project director is the final arbiter on major decisions. In some, major decisions are by consensus. And in some, it is difficult to determine where policymaking authority lies.

The size of a project may exercise a major constraint on organizational structure, since large organizations of necessity have more complex organizational structure than small ones require. However, size does not necessarily determine the locus of decision making or the amount of openness in decision making.

The pattern of decision making followed by a project may be strongly influenced by the manner of the project's initiation. For some projects, the director of the project was the initiator; he developed the ideas and sought the original grants. In others, the ideas may have been quite fully developed before a director was sought. For some, the director, while not the initiator, was selected relatively early in the planning stages, and worked along with the initiators in establishing the format, structure, and purpose of the project. Perhaps it is more likely to be those projects where the director was the initiator and creator where the project and the director are virtually synonymous. For example, there is close identification of Edward Begle and SMSG, Max Beberman and UICSM, Jerrald Zacharias and PSSC, and each of these men was the project initiator; there is little identification of the materials of EDC or its predecessor, ESI, with an individual; and CHEM Study and BSCS are linked with several persons, rather than with a single individual. And it may be in the director-initiated projects that there is less supervision by a policy board or parent organization.

The degree of geographical centralization does not necessarily determine the administrative organization of the project or the arrangements for decision making. Some projects in a single location operate on a tight hierarchical structure; others do not. Some projects, spread over several geographic locations, centralize decisions more than others or systematize decision making more than others. For the BSCS, the degree of delegation of authority has varied with the function, rather than with the geographic location. Thus, while those activities in Boulder are serviced by the headquarters office for personnel, purchasing, and fiscal matters, the policy delegation has not necessarily been less than for those activities located away from Boulder. It has been the function and the individuals involved, rather than the geographic location, that have been the determinants of policy delegation in this instance.

For DEEP, complete responsibility for policy regarding materials preparation and dissemination is in the local school system, with materials prepared by persons designated by the school system and on its payroll, and with no line authority emanating from the central DEEP office and staff. Where funding, including staff costs, is financed by the central DEEP office, the payment goes to the school system, not to individuals, and there are very few strings attached. Thus, the project consists of thirty individual developmental efforts, coordinated very loosely by a central staff. Within each of the thirty systems, the organization of the developmental work is a local prerogative. This results in a variety of arrangements for organization and decision making, with some of the DEEP local projects having little systematic decision making, and others having highly structured routines for decision making.

Some developmental projects operate on a relatively rigid, traditional organizational structure, with the hierarchy of authority clearly defined and each employee—professional or auxiliary—reporting to his superior in the line of command. At the other extreme, some are so loosely organized that it is difficult to determine who has authority for any given decision or, after a policy is in effect, who made the decision to adopt that policy, and how and when the decision was made. For some projects, certain kinds of decisions—for example, fiscal management or housekeeping decisions—are routinized through specific channels, while the responsibility for substantive decisions— for decisions concerning materials development and dissemination—is less clearly allocated.

Perhaps the most important decisions made by a project are those concerning basic purpose and those involving basic value judgments. For some projects, the purpose was decided before the project was staffed; for others, the broad purpose was decided by those who became staff; and for others, there is a mixture of both kinds of policy setting. Thus, for BSCS, the broad purpose was decided by the parent organization, the AIBS, before the BSCS was created and the director chosen. DEEP was developed and funded before operating staff was employed and participating school systems selected. For IME, the director and staff developed the project themselves.

For Regional Laboratory or R and D Center curriculum projects, the curriculum building may be a facet of the director's prior interests—as with Individually Prescribed Instruction (IPI)—or it may represent one facet of a new interest, where the idea is developed by laboratory or a request is made to the laboratory to undertake a new activity. Thus, a city school system or an industry may come to the Center for Urban Education (CUE), one of the Regional Laboratories, and request help in building specific developmental materials for an urban school or a training program for the company. The decision of whether to accept this task is made by someone or by some group on the existing staff, and then CUE either assigns this activity to an existing staff member to organize or direct, or adds a unit or staff for the purpose.

In considering organizational arrangements, often the formal structure—the organization chart—is considered independent of the informal structure and of the personalities involved; this does not give a representative picture (Smith, 1966; Hills, 1966; Likert, 1967). The nature of the formal and informal organizational structures and the way in which these operate may be primarily a factor of the personality of the director of the project and his staff.

In some circumstances, even the most cumbersome types of organization may work, given certain incumbents. For example, HPP has a tripartite head. There are three directors, and, according to staff members and the directors themselves, the responsibility is not clearly divided among them. Thus, it is not merely a matter of talking to one director on one type of problem and another on another type, though there are some rather general allocations of responsibility among the directors. Furthermore, the three directors have not had offices in the same building, and at times one or two may be out of the city or even out of the country on rather extended trips. This would appear to present a completely chaotic situation, but evidently this has not been the case. While there have doubtless been some problems in this diffusion of authority, these have certainly not been insurmountable. However, despite HPP's rather satisfactory experience, this is hardly a type of organization to be commended to other projects.

The organization chart and the established systems for making decisions may not entirely indicate the actual decision-making process. As the incumbent of the position of director changes, the norms for decision making, authority, and control may be changed with no deliberate or formal change in the project's organization chart. Thus, the BSCS has had two different directors and six different assistant and associate directors. But, except when a new assistant director post was created and specific responsibility and authority were delegated to the appointee, the formal organizational structure did not change; yet the way decisions were handled did change.

This reflects the personal styles of the incumbents and their relationships with others on the staff. Thus, one incumbent may be more prone to consult with a wide variety of people than another; one may be more prone to seek advice from authority figures either within or outside the project; one might prefer group consultations, where another prefers consultations with an equal number of people individually; one might be somewhat slower in coming to a decision than another. For some incumbents, the decisions made, or courses of action taken, were likely to be emergent, resulting from discussions of an initial proposal, and then amending and adapting it; for another, it might more often represent a choice among previously outlined possibilities.

IME, which on paper is largely a one-man responsibility, in practice operates on the basis of frequent, broad consultation with a wide variety of people, even though project participants and consultants are scattered throughout the country. Decisions are likely to be emergent, and probably involve more wide consultation and discussion than is the case in many of the projects with centrally located staffs.

To persons not familiar with recent literature on organizational management, a hierarchical structure—a structure where authority and status flow from the top down, and where decision making follows the line of authority —is more or less taken for granted. Such a structure looks efficient, orderly, and comprehensible. However, for the kinds of activities involved in developmental work, it is probably inappropriate.

Where a hierarchical structure is maintained, there is a tendency for less communication, both between staff members at the same rank and at different ranks, if communication is defined as a two-way flow of ideas rather than as a giving of ideas by one person or a receiving of ideas by one person. In a hierarchical structure, there is less interchange of ideas, and a single person can cut off an idea that seems to him divergent or unsuitable.

In those situations with less rigid structure, there is generally more communication, and more people may be exposed to an idea. Thus, an idea that could be stopped at first hearing in the former situation might, in a less structured organization, have several hearings, and be accepted or adapted by one or more of the listeners. As Bennis (1966) and others have pointed out, a hierarchical organizational structure is less appropriate to creative, flexible dealing with novel problems and with problems requiring novel solutions.

A number of developmental projects are characterized by such flexible authority structures. In such projects, it is not unusual to have a young high school teacher argue with or even veto an idea of an older, highly respected subject-matter specialist. This represents a healthy concern with the intrinsic worth of ideas, rather than a valuing of ideas based on the prestige of the source. In one project, the director reported that after initially working in a traditional, hierarchical structure, he found that he had to change to a more flexible *modus operandi* in order to get the job done properly.

A different kind of flexibility exists in some situations where it is impossible to get any answers, where the location of responsibility is so vague that staff members cannot get answers, where no one will assume responsibility, or where several individuals assume responsibility for the same situation. This type of organization, which may purport to be democratic, lends itself to unfortunate manipulation by a few staff members, may preclude effective operations, and may waste an enormous amount of staff time. Particularly in the case of project contacts with persons outside the project—for example, with schools cooperating in trying out experimental materials—a diffusion of responsibility or lack of clear contact channels with the project can result in contradictory or impossible commitments being made, or in confusion when the school does not know precisely whom to contact when a problem arises.

It is difficult to say why any project is productive, and loose organizational structure is not a sufficient cause for lack of productivity. But it has certainly been a contributory factor in some projects.

There is no single successful pattern of organization or delegation of authority that characterizes the most effective curriculum projects. However, a great many project participants express considerable satisfaction with those projects which have a clear focus for decision making accompanied by open lines of communication that transcend status barriers. Such projects more often seem to have creative products than those which are organized on a conventional hierarchical basis with information flowing upward and decisions flowing downward.

Perhaps there should be an identification of the kinds of decisions being made; and a clear pinpointing of responsibility for various kinds of final decisions would seem necessary. Unless the decisions made in projects are clearly identified as such, the project may find itself involved in some decision-making processes it deplores, or would deplore if it recognized them. For example, in one project, the last person to work on materials before they went to the printer was a layout artist. It was not recognized for some time that this assignment had major substantive implications far beyond artistic considerations. Other projects have found themselves committed to including schools and school systems in experimental programs and furnishing free student materials, as a result of a casual comment of a staff member or committee member visiting a meeting or a school system.

A clear pinpointing of decisions and of responsibility for decision making would help in avoiding such situations. However, the process for coming to these decisions might best be left open, and formal status considerations should not be paramount, either in arriving at decisions or in allocating the decision-making authority. Thus, the responsibility for deciding what school systems participate in materials tryouts should be clear, and only the individual with this authority should make commitments. However, in arriving at the decision on how schools should be chosen, what criteria to set up for selection, and what commitments will be asked of participating schools, ideas should come from those who will be concerned, or those whose background is relevant, regardless of their project or preproject status. In the same way, one individual should be the final authority on content of material, to permit a coherent and responsible product, but this person need not be the highest in the organizational hierarchy, even where the project director is involved in materials preparation. And pertinent suggestions need not come through a usual chain of command.

It is impossible to operate a developmental project without making value judgments. At many points, there are choices that cannot be made solely on the basis of data available; there is a choice involving values. Some of these value judgments are basic ones, some are not. Such questions as: Should controversial materials be included? What kinds of people should be involved in materials preparation? and What cognitive processes should be stressed in the materials? are very different in nature than questions of: Should school A be included in the experimental sample? What working hours should the staff follow? and Which expense forms should be used?

While in retrospect, many questions can be identified as basic value judgments, they may not be considered as such at the time the decision is being made, and there may be no different procedure for making decisions involving the basic value judgments than for making those that involve less basic value judgments. A strong case can be made for a distinction between the two types of decisions, with provision for broader participation and more time allocated in decisions involving more basic value judgments. In practice, this is not always the case, and sometimes the reverse has been true.

Further, there should be consideration given to the question of what kinds of expertise should be involved in different kinds of decisions. Who should decide what is good sociology or what is good economics? Should it be the same person who is asked: What is good teaching? What is good testing? What is good teacher training? and What are good diffusion techniques?

To whom should the project go for answers? Should it always be the same source or same kind of source? Or are different sources needed for different kinds of decisions? When the question is posed in this manner, perhaps the answer seems obvious—that a different kind of expertise is needed for different kinds of questions. Yet, project practice does not always reflect this answer. Certainly, the project must make the final decision on all such questions, but the sources from which advice and information are sought should be wider, and should reflect the kind of question that is being asked.

PROJECT PERSONNEL AND PERSONNEL POLICIES

Organizations are made up of people; and the kinds of people in an organization, the way they were chosen, and the informal structuring of inter-relations among them inevitably influence the organization, its policies and products, and its ability to attract other people to the staff. Thus, the importance of the situational and structural considerations notwithstanding, once a project is initiated, it may be the people involved who make the greatest difference among projects, and the people who constitute the more critical factor in the success or failure of a project.

The Director

The project that initially seems to have the best ideas is not always the one that works out best. Perhaps the project director may be the key to the entire ecology of the project, to the way the project develops, the paths it takes, the kinds of people who want to work with the project and who are hired to work with it, and the philosophy of the project.

This is not simply a matter of how he works with people, though that is certainly a factor of major importance. It also includes his contacts, his appearance, his professional reputation, and professional background. One director can do things another cannot, simply because of a professional reputation, or professional contacts, or ways of working with people. Thus, a project with an eminent scholar as a director may be able to attract different kinds of funding or different kinds of participants than a project with a less eminent director, regardless of the basic worth of the ideas behind the project.

Many developmental projects clearly reflect the personality, background, and personal styles of the director in some way, and those that do not are quite different from those that do. This does not mean that the director who is authoritarian in operations, who tends toward a strict chain-of-command type of organization, is the most influential in determining the project ecology. The director's personal stamp on the project may be as basic, though less obvious, in a less rigidly organized project; the very fact that the project is less rigidly organized may reflect his personality and modes of operation.

The personality and methods of operation of the director are probably most influential in those projects that are housed in single-purpose organizations, that is, in organizations created for the specific purpose of carrying out the project, or in projects where the director oversees a cluster of related projects. Thus, in the BSCS, which may have three or four developmental projects in high school biology carried on at one time and under one director, the personality of the project director may be quite influential.

In a project carried on in a multipurpose materials development or educational complex, where an individual project may have its own director but where the general organizational patterns of work may be highly structured, the personality of the director may show relatively little influence in the project. In fact, in such situations, the director may have been appointed at least in part because he fits the general organizational expectations concerning operational behavior of supervisory staff. Thus, the role of the director would be a more sensitive one in a project such as SMSG and UICSM than would be the case in any single project under the aegis of one of the larger and more diverse Regional Laboratories or educational development complexes.

One area of influence of the director is in terms of establishing a climate for the project. It is the director who can establish or discourage a climate that provides security to the individual in an ambiguous and uncertain situation— a situation where it is better to try the unknown than to stay with the comfortable known; a climate where mistakes or tentative thrusts do not result in loss of esteem or status, a climate where it is safe to try new ideas or to admit that an experiment did not work.

The director's personal influence may also be reflected in the project organization chart in the type of formal organizational structure used; this structure may be one particularly compatible with his personality or philosophy. But especially in an ongoing organization, the type of formal structure may be far less influenced by the incumbent director than is the case with the informal structure, the day-to-day *modus operandi* within the specified general organizational pattern.

BSCS, ESCP, and CHEM Study all have had several directors. As directors changed, there was not necessarily a change in the formal organizational structure, yet, in at least some of these changes, the informal structure was clearly modified to a greater or lesser degree. And the extent of the change in informal procedures was not a determinant of whether the organization chart was changed.

Given similar formal organizational requirements, one source of the differences in the way projects operate is in the decision-making process, since it is here that the noticeable as well as subtle changes in direction of the project occur. It is here that morale may be built or destroyed. And it is here that the whole flavor of the project may originate.

With similar organizational regulations, one project director may tend to consult more widely than another. One may consult with subject-matter specialists, while another seeks the counsel of educators or psychologists. One may seek the advice of high-status persons, while another seeks advice from persons, regardless of their status or rank, if he considers them sound. One director may seek more advice or share more decisions than another, even though, according to the project's formalized procedures, the decision-making prerogative is his, and the final decision rests with him.

One director may be more prone than another to seek emergent decisions through group discussion, while another may ask individuals or groups for preferences among specified alternatives. Another may make the decision by himself, either rapidly or after much deliberation. And still another may make decisions by default, by postponing decision making, and by avoiding clear-cut decisions.

Such differences in decision-making strategy undoubtedly have a long-run effect on the outcomes of the project, yet the outsider cannot identify this influence from analyzing the products of the group; often he cannot identify it even from reading about the organization of the project and the conduct of its activities. And even the project personnel may not be sufficiently sophisticated in skills of analyzing organizational processes to be able to identify the cause-and-effect relationships between the long-run outcomes and the project's decision-making and communication patterns.

And so, the question of what went wrong or why a given project was particularly productive or effective becomes an elusive one. Project-evaluation efforts may simply indicate relative success or failure of a given venture, without anyone being able to pinpoint those factors that should be replicated elsewhere, or those that should be avoided elsewhere, or to determine why one project was relatively successful and another project, ostensibly using the same procedures, was not.

For example, there is one project with little centralization of activities in the headquarters office, with much of the materials-preparation activity dispersed through the country, with no project policymaking board, and with considerable policy and materials control in the hands of the director. The project was a highly successful one. One might, therefore, conclude that this type of organization is appropriate for developmental activities. Yet, such a conclusion would overlook some highly germane aspects of the process used. In this case, there was more broad consultation before decision making, and more sharing of decisions than in many projects that have staff in a centralized location, that have policy boards, and that carefully outline provisions for sharing decisions.

This tendency by this project director to delay decisions pending wide consultation and to share decisions—a tendency that reflects a personal operational pattern, rather than a structural requirement—may be the key to the ability of his project to attain its goals, despite organizational handicaps of wide geographical dispersion of staff and infrequent face-to-face encounters.

But the outsider, judging the formal organizational mechanisms from the adequacy of the materials produced or the comments of project personnel about their degree of satisfaction with the way the project was run, would be in no position to replicate what was a highly successful process without some knowledge of the day-to-day operational patterns of the project director. In this case, as is the case in HPP with its tripartite directorship, clearly the personalities involved and the relationships among them make what might be an awkward or impractical *modus operandi* reasonably effective.

While a given organizational structure may facilitate some kinds of operations, this is perhaps less influential in terms of the total nature and direction of the project than is the consideration of the nature of the incumbent director. For some projects, this may mean that should the directorship change, the project either stops suddenly or gradually drifts to a halt. Or the project may take a direction entirely different from that pursued successfully under a previous director without a clear-cut decision by the policymakers that such a change should occur. This is not a criticism of the major impact of the director on the project, but rather an observation concerning it.

Certainly, there have been extremely effective projects with strong, single, and one might say, permanent directors. There have been equally successful ones where there have been several directors over a period of time. But there have also been a few that have ceased to function effectively or ceased functioning entirely when the director has changed. It is difficult to look back after the fact to determine the reasons for this failure.

It would be easy to attribute the failure to a strong director who left his group unprepared for decision making or unable to find a substitute strong leader. However, in at least one case, the problem was not the departure of an effective leader, but rather a lack of a clear sense of purpose and direction of the remaining staff, which, doubtless, was at least part of the reason the succeeding director was unable to provide these. There was no great clarity as to the job to be done or the media to be used, and so the project drifted without clear direction until its grants were cut off by a dissatisfied funding agency.

Background and Qualifications of Staff

The director and his mode of operation are only two aspects of the staff of a project. In terms of locating and retaining other members of the professional staff, developmental projects often present problems different from those in staffing of other materials-development or research activities because of uncertainties of how a college professor, research person, or classroom teacher will fit into a role that is new and untried for him.

One of the serious staffing problems reflects the fact that developmental work is relatively new and a very different kind of activity than has been carried on by the individuals being considered for the staff heretofore. It has been difficult to predict who will be able to meet the demands of the various kinds of assignments involved, assignments that may be quite different from those generally performed by persons with the requisite qualifications in teaching, writing, and research in the discipline.

Some highly talented writers, who not only have the subject-matter background, but have already written successfully for the target audience, may not be effective members of a developmental writing effort. They may not work well as collaborators in a large and diverse group, or they may find it difficult to cope with the give and take of the feedback systems. Some skilled classroom teachers cannot fill a leadership role in teacher orientation, or in materials preparation, or even in visting schools for observation or to give assistance. And some are unable to work comfortably on a peer basis with college and research personnel from the discipline.

Some projects are staffed largely by college level personnel, reflecting a tacit assumption that the profession, as represented by the college professor, knows best what in the discipline should be presented, and how it should be presented. Some have heavy representation of school people, and some fluctuate in a mixture of college and school people. Some tend to use college personnel for one type of activity, such as writing, and school people for such other activities as teacher orientation or school visiting. Some projects use generalists, some use specialists. Some call on existing staff from other projects carried on under the aegis of the same sponsoring agency; for example, a Regional Laboratory may transfer staff from one ongoing or completed project to another. And some recruit new staff for each new project.

Many projects bring in people who are not familiar with school systems, with education, with the age group of children for whom materials are being prepared, with state school systems, and with other aspects of the target population, with developmental projects, with interproject relationships, and with relationships with sponsoring agencies and funding sources. Use of such people can bring an invaluable dimension to developmental work. At the same time, it is time-consuming. The new individual either must have a great many things explained to him or find them out himself, or there will be shortsighted decisions that are inappropriate and do not take into account the relevant factors in a situation.

UICSM expects its authors to be able to teach at the grade level for which materials are being prepared, since the authors themselves become pilot experimental teachers. It expects exploratory work before the start of systematic materials preparation. This exploratory activity may involve a year or two of trying out ideas, observing, and occasional teaching. This kind of materials preparation, free of deadlines and highly exploratory, involves different kinds of staff and different kinds of staff assignments than is the case in a project with deadlines and with firm commitments to schools that a year or semester's materials will be provided for a complete course.

Another facet of staffing is whether the staff members are project-oriented or research-oriented, whether their primary interest is in the project or in accomplishing some specific research in which they are interested. Smith (1966) and Hills (1966), in their studies of the Center for Advanced Study of Educational Administration, the R and D Center at the University of Oregon, point out that for some personnel, the project represents an opportunity to carry out research or development that is a most basic personal concern.[7] For such individuals, the project, in effect, exists to facilitate the pursuit of their own interests. Others are more "company men"; they are project-oriented and the project goal becomes their prime goal in the organization. This, according to Smith and Hills, represents not just a different view of the major task to be performed, but also is reflected in different ways of working, different value systems, and different types and channels of communication.

While the orientation of some projects is rather directly opposed to the research orientation, many college faculty members, both in the disciplines and in education, may take the research-oriented view, with serious consequences to the project. The question perhaps can be summarized in terms of what part of developmental work is development—which is completely product-oriented —and what part is research. There are many arguments about the role of research in development activities and in developmental projects. Regardless of the merits of the various arguments, the fact is that if projects draw on certain types of individuals for staffing, there will be a research interest and commitment, whether or not the project desires this emphasis. Such interests can provide a source of enrichment for the project or can bring friction, misunderstanding, and ineffectiveness.

The kind of background the staff has and its assignment to various activities may reflect a deliberate attempt by the project to communicate an image of one kind or another—for example, an image that the project represents various facets of the discipline, that it is multidisciplinary, or that it is a cooperative effort of educators and researchers in the discipline. It may represent the appointment of the best-qualified person for the job, regardless of image. Or it may reflect a combination of both kinds of considerations.

Regardless of intent, staff selection and development will affect the project's image. For example, in one project, a top position was assigned to an

---

[7]While CASEA is not a developmental project in the sense the term is used here, the kinds of staff and the nature of the organization parallel those in many of the organizations sponsoring developmental projects, and many of the points made in these two studies appear germane. These studies are highly recommended to project directors to give an insight into some unusual aspects of the sociology of developmental efforts.

obviously unqualified school principal (who was unfamiliar with the subject area and grade levels involved in the project work, as well as with curriculum development) because of the sponsoring agency's feeling that his presence in a position of wide visibility would enhance the acceptability of the materials to the target school system. Similarly, a project wanting to project an image of representing education throughout the United States should hire staff that is more widely representative geographically than is the case if this is not a project concern.

A project that desires an image of genuine use of school personnel in all its phases should be sure that much of the project staff with which the public comes in contact are from this group, and that such staff members have been genuinely involved in all phases of the work, not just used as symbols. If the project materials are prepared largely by college professors, no amount of publicity will convince the public that school people were consulted and had an integral role in materials preparation.

Despite what the project may say about project staff or the use of school personnel in all aspects of the program, if the only people the public sees are from the college level and from the discipline, the image projected to schools may be less favorable than would be the case if such representatives were more broadly selected. In the former situation, not only may the ensuing product be suspect, but there may be a level of empathy and credibility that is lacking, since in some situations, a practitioner can communicate where another person, regardless of his sincerity or accuracy, cannot.

For example, when, based on his own experience, a high school teacher tells other high school teachers that something is teachable or that students will enjoy doing things far more sophisticated than they have done before, or when he describes his own difficulties in using the material and how he handled these, the audience—even a nonteaching audience—may be more prone to accept his statements than is the case with similar statements from another source. Further, when a schoolteacher asks for help about a classroom problem —and he may be more likely to ask such help from a project representative who is a teacher—the project representative may be in a better position to give realistic advice.

No one pattern of staffing guarantees success, but the mixture of competent and appropriate college and school people throughout the work of the project, rather than only at certain points, more often seems to produce a satisfactory project both in terms of practicality, appropriateness for classroom use, and acceptability to the target population of schools. Those projects that have brought school people in at a late date or have used them only in an incidental role have often found the materials produced impractical or unacceptable, and the project may face the accusation that the use of school people is tokenism or window dressing.

Size of Staff

The volume of the output of a developmental project is no indication of the size of the permanent or part-time staff of the project. For some projects, the permanent staff consists of a part-time director and a part-time secretary, with no more than six or eight others added for short term work from time to time. For others, there may be sixty or seventy people on the staff at one time, with the number increasing to one hundred or more during peak periods of writing, as during a summer writing conference. Some of the very small projects have been able to prepare complete classroom materials for a full-year course, steer these through two experimental editions, try these out in the schools, and then prepare a final edition in the same time it has taken a larger project to do what appears to be much the same kind of job.

At first glance, this does not make sense. It looks as though the larger project is wasteful and inefficient. This is not necessarily the case. The size of staff may reflect the nature and complexity of the developmental work to be done, the variety of skills needed to do the work, the ability to predict activities to be carried out, the project time schedule, the productivity of the individuals employed, and the kinds of activities in addition to materials preparation that will be carried on.

While sheer numbers of people do not improve the product, some materials do take more people or more skills than others. Some materials require several areas of specialty within one discipline or several disciplines; and some require a variety of skills, as in the preparation of films, artwork, learning programs, and laboratory exercises and the development of laboratory equipment. So, the nature and diversity of the tasks to be done are factors in staff size. The extent to which the project farms out work through contracts with other organizations is another. For example, some projects contract out illustrations, film production, and evaluation; others do these in-house.

Another factor is the ability to predict the skills to be needed and the suitability of potential staff for performing these. If a writing conference is to last six or eight weeks during the summer, and the resulting experimental materials must go to the printer at the end of the eight weeks, it is important to insure the availability of all the skills that may be needed, even though not all the anticipated needs materialize. There simply is not time to recruit competent people during the writing conferences, and it is difficult to contact people during the summer when most writing conferences are held.

For example, the only previous developmental activity in biology that was even roughly comparable to the BSCS 1960 summer writing conference effort was an earlier NSF-sponsored writing conference to prepare laboratory exercises; but this activity was only remotely similar to the BSCS work, and the people planning the BSCS conference had not been observers at the earlier conference. They did turn to those who were familiar with this earlier conference for recommendations on staff, and a number of BSCS writers were invited on the basis of such recommendations. However, not all of these were equally effective in the BSCS situation, a fact which may result from the differences in the task to be done, or from inappropriate recommendations that had been given to the BSCS, either because of an error of judgment or because of a failure to appreciate the nature of the BSCS task.

Still another facet of size of project staff is the level of services to be provided. Some observers believe that projects operating on public funds are wasting money if they operate on more than a minimal, Spartan basis. Others feel that to provide a wide variety of services is not only essential for effectively producing and trying out materials, but also for their acceptability and usability in the schools. They point out that simply building better materials will not improve eduction; if the job of the developmental project is to improve eduction, then the chance of success can be enhanced by providing certain types of activities that other projects may not feel are essential.

For example, how should routine inquiries be handled? To answer correspondence is not a small matter; it can constitute a major office activity. During at least one year of the developmental period of BSCS materials, the BSCS was receiving some 500 routine inquiries each month—over 6,000 per year—about its materials and programs, and for several years, one secretary's assignment was to type individual copies of one of three or four form letters, with an occasional extra sentence added to take care of special contingencies. Projects must decide: Should correspondence from schools and teachers be answered? If so, should these inquiries be answered promptly? Should mimeographed or printed form letters be used, or should all replies be individual? In handling correspondence with a printed checklist—with a check mark indicating the appropriate response—the reply may cost $.25, whereas an individually-typed letter using a standard form would cost $1 or $1.50. The form reply may answer the question quite adequately; it may also lose a large number of influential potential supporters of the project. It would be helpful if the recipients of form letters understood the problems involved in individual replies, and the large saving of funds through use of form letters—funds that might be used for materials development—but often, they do not. And the project cannot know in advance which individuals will be offended by a form letter and which ones will not. And it has no way of knowing how far-reaching the effect of one or two offended individuals will be.

Other decisions that are reflected in staff size involve such questions as: Does the project want to visit schools where materials are being tried out, or will it depend on written reports from teachers and on test data? When visitors come to project headquarters, will they be handed printed materials, see a secretary, or have a member of the professional staff spend half a day or a full day with him? For some projects, handling of visitors to the project can require the equivalent of the full time of a professional staff member.

When educational groups request speakers, will the project send a speaker, which may involve a three-day trip—one day for a speech and two days of travel? Will it send brochures? Or will it simply send regrets? Will it pay the expenses of the speaker or charge the inviting organization? Will the project seek opportunities to make presentations at national, regional, state and local educational meetings? Will it take exhibit booths to such meetings in order to reach more of the potential audience? Will project staff members accept invitations to address teacher-training institutes? Will they seek such invitations?

Another aspect of staff size involves the question of continuing professional activities of staff. For example: Is the project primarily a developmental one, or are there extensive research activities involved? Research can be time-consuming, yet have no impact on volume of materials produced. Other relevant questions include: Are staff members encouraged to contribute to the scholarly literature in education and in the discipline? Do they limit themselves to writing general descriptions of project activities? Or do they do no outside publishing? Are professional staff members encouraged to maintain professional contacts and make contributions to professional societies in the same manner that universities encourage and support such activities as officeholding in professional societies, editing scholarly journals, arranging professional meetings, etc.? Are they encouraged to maintain their professional competence through attending meetings and seminars in their scholarly field, even when these are not directly related to the work of the project?

Projects vary from one extreme to the other on these matters. Some feel that it enhances the project to have staff members active professionally, even when such activity is not directly contributing to the project focus. Others suggest that staff members wishing to attend professional meetings do this on their vacation time and at their own expense.

The wide variation in size of existing project staffs in large part reflects the project's reaction to such questions as these. The project's answers to these questions may reflect its self-image and image of the job it wishes to perform.

Those projects that have set as their total goal the production of materials may not spend as much time in contacts with the target audience as those that are concerned with actually changing the day-to-day practice in the schools.

The project taking the broader view will need a staff two, three, or perhaps six times as large as that taking a narrower view. To some projects, the larger view is clearly impractical in terms of funding. To others, such activities seem a waste of money. However, some projects have been able to finance many of these activities, and argue for the financing of all such activities from the standpoint of building and maintaining professional excellence of staff and effectively producing desired change in school practices.

Permanency of Staff

Some projects operate with a very small permanent staff, bringing in consultants for short-term appointments, or contracting out work as the need for specialized services arises. Others have larger permanent staffs in the central office. Some have relatively stable staff in terms of total staff size, as well as in the individuals involved, with staff members assigned to a variety of project activities or to other projects as the work load varies. This practice may be most frequent in such multipurpose organizations as Regional Laboratories, which tend to have a number of simultaneous, diverse projects and activities.

For such multipurpose groups, there is undoubtedly more flexibility of assignments. However, this is not always a clear advantage. Because of funding uncertainties, some multipurpose groups may tend to select staff more because of the flexibility of the individual—because he is a jack-of-all-trades—rather than because of his high level of expertise in one area—that is, because he is a master of one. Thus, in some projects, the premium on staff flexibility rather than on expertise may not result in the best-qualified person doing a particular task.

In the multipurpose organization, a particular person may be given responsibility for an assignment simply because he was on the organization's staff before the project was developed and the project has a moral or a legal commitment to him. Such a person may not always have the expertise necessary for the responsibility, while there may be persons outside the organization who are available and who do have this expertise.

Several projects, including BSCS and HPP, have deliberately established a policy of staff rotation for professional positions; most of their professional staff are on a one-year basis, with an occasional renewal of contract. Such one-year appointments coincide with the school year and the appointees are generally public school or college people on a leave of absence from their regular positions.

This has the advantage of bringing to the project a variety of specialized skills. It permits the short-time employment of the best available person for specific tasks. It protects the project from long-term commitments to individuals who may not be the most appropriate staff members as the nature of the work to be done is shifting. It enables the project to obtain people who may not be available for longer-term appointments. And it keeps feeding back into school and college situations persons who have some expertise in the materials being developed. Furthermore, it builds a large corps of resource people who can later be called on by the project for short-term assignments in the project office or at their home locations, who can knowledgeably fill posts on the project's policymaking committees, and who will be useful in later teacher preparation for the materials being developed.

These are great strengths. However, the policy also has weaknesses. Regardless of the calibre of the new appointee, he is not as effective during his first months on the project staff while he is learning the ropes, as is the equally qualified individual who has been on the staff a year or more. For even the most able new staff member, the first few months are spent largely in orientation; this means that not only is he an inefficient employee for these months, but the time of other staff members is taken in training him. Where staff appointments overlap—for example, when appointments are for fourteen months, from June of one year through August of the following year—and the departing employee and the new one can work together for two months, the transition is eased somewhat; nonetheless, this procedure is expensive and time-consuming.

The lack of continuity resulting from a policy of rotating staff can also be detrimental in terms of public relations, when outsiders find a different person involved each time they contact the project. Further, the institutional knowledge of the project can be highly inaccurate. Thus, when a decision is made, there may be no one who remembers what the full background is, or what previous similar decisions have been made, and what the consequences have been. Or it may be that only the business management staff—generally on more permanent appointments—becomes the repository of the project history and background. Such staff members may have a different perspective or interpretation of the past events than the professional staff member would have.

During the second five years of the life of the BSCS, except for the fiscal officer, there was no one on the full-time professional staff at Boulder who had been with the project for more than one of its first five years. While several of the current staff members had various assignments with the BSCS during that period, such work was not on a day-to-day basis, and they cannot be as familiar with the background of decisions and processes as would be the case had there been more continuity. Thus, while the policy of staff rotation permits tapping more resources and broadens community contacts with the project, it clearly limits the ability of an ongoing project to capitalize on its past experience.

Some Special Staffing Problems

In addition to the problems of obtaining staff appropriate to a relatively new kind of activity, projects face other difficulties because of the kinds of staff usually involved, and because many of the projects are affiliated with colleges and universities. These problems involve relationships among members of the professional staff, and between the staff and the sponsoring institution; and while many of the difficulties may appear trivial, they can seriously jeopardize morale, and limit the ability of the project to recruit personnel.

One such problem is the relationship between staff members with doctorate degrees and those without. Another is the relationship between college and university people on the one hand and school people on the other. Do the higher status and title necessarily go to the person with the doctorate degree? Does the higher status go to the person from the college or university? If the college person automatically has the higher rank, the project is accused of permitting domination by academicians; if he does not, some college people may face a difficult readjustment in their expectations, a readjustment not all can accept easily. And regardless of the intent of the project to ignore previous rank or position in making appointments, some school people on the staff, as well as many outsiders, will have difficulty accepting the situation.

Another related problem is how the salary of the college and school people compares. To obtain competent staff, the project must be able to compete on the open market. With a few noteworthy exceptions, the college people come from a higher paying market than the public school people. Furthermore, to the college person, participation in the project may not be professionally enhancing; on the contrary, leaving his usual research activities for a year or two may constitute a deterrent to his professional advancement. Thus, he may expect sufficient renumeration to make up for this sacrifice. For the school person, association with a project is generally considered to be professionally enhancing, and so an extra financial incentive may be less important.

The ideas of equal pay for equal work, and pay commensurate with level of responsibility are both completely reasonable in the abstract. In a curriculum project, given the mixture of school and college personnel, both may be impractical. Yet, the converse is not entirely justifiable. In projects, often college and public school people are doing comparable work, or the public school person may supervise the work of the college person. To pay the subordinate double the salary of his superior is open to question. Yet, this may be the only basis on which the subordinate can be hired. Similarly, to have three parallel positions filled by equally competent people, but with a wide range of salaries for the same work, may seem unreasonable. But this may be the only practical solution to a particular kind of staffing problem.

For example, over a period of three years, the BSCS employed five or six different individuals to obtain feedback from schools and to analyze this feedback for the version writers. This group included people from universities and school districts with widely varying pay scales, so that one person filling this assignment might have come from a position paying more than double that of another. The BSCS felt that the individuals selected for this assignment were the optimal people for these positions. It welcomed the diversity of backgrounds as an asset in viewing the schools. All of these feedback people were well qualified. All had the same responsibility.

To have paid all the same salary would mean that the salary set would, of necessity, have to be based on that of the person coming from the highest paid job, a policy that would have been open to serious question by the NSF in the budget review. Yet, to pay different salaries for essentially the same job violates the idea of fairness in terms of equal pay for equal work. The only simple answer would be to staff such parallel positions with people from similar professional backgrounds—either school or college, but not both—and from institutions with similar pay ranks. Such a practice would completely preclude the desired diversity of backgrounds the BSCS was seeking. It would also mean that staff selection would be based on arbitrary criteria unrelated to the job to be done.

This is a situation that permits no simple or perfect solution. The approach used by the BSCS to cope with the various problems of pay and rank was admittedly a compromise, but it did reduce some of the potential sources of friction and difficulty on the points of job title and relative pay. Assignment of responsibility was independent of salary, and both were independent of job title. Aside from the director and the assistant and associate directors, all professional staff members were titled consultants, regardless of their job assignments and levels of responsibility. This was occasionally misleading since these consultants were full-time employees, and so, perhaps some term other than consultant should have been used.[8] Also, the title consultant did not

---

[8]On one occasion, the funding agency questioned the magnitude of payments to consultants, since it was under the impression that the word was used for persons who consulted occasionally with the BSCS, rather than served as full-time employees, and what were taken as payments for very occasional work were, in fact, annual salaries on full-time jobs.

indicate to outsiders the kind of work the consultant was doing. However, the practice of using one title for all professional personnel did minimize problems of comparative ranks. It also eliminated the problems of promotions—that is, change in rank and title—as a reward for merit; salary increments and later invitations to serve on BSCS committees after employment terminated were alternative rewards for merit.

Salaries for all professional personnel, including the director and assistant and associate directors, were based on the salary paid the individual in the position held previous to his BSCS employment, the position from which he took a leave of absence for the duration of his BSCS employment. This salary was adjusted by a standard percentage increment to compensate the individual for loss of credit in his usual retirement plan, the greater expense of maintaining a home in a new community for a relatively short period of time, and the fact that most job changes in qualified personnel are accompanied by some increase in pay.[9] This meant that the director and assistant and associate directors need not be the highest-paid employees, and that each salary was set independently.

A number of other incidental, yet quite troublesome problems—some trivial and some rather basic—arise unless project personnel are regular staff members in a permanent organization; that is, unless they hold regular tenure appointments in a university or similar organization. While the consequences of these problems may appear limited, the effect can be devastating, not only on morale, but on the ability of the project to recruit and retain qualified staff. Not all projects face all these problems, but such difficulties do recur with annoying frequency.

Some projects have no university connection. Here, there may be a reluctance of some college people to accept an appointment, unless there is an opportunity for an adjunct professorial appointment of some kind at a nearby collegiate institution. Sometimes the individual may arrange such appointments himself; sometimes the project facilitates the arrangements; and sometimes no such arrangement is practical. In the latter case, there may be considerable reluctance of college professors to work with the project on a continuing basis.

For those projects located on a university campus, the project may be only a visitor, renting space from the university, as was the case of the BSCS for the first three or four years of its existence. Or the project may be sponsored by the university, either using university staff, or bringing in new staff. Particularly in the case of the project that is located at but not part of the university,

---

[9]The salary in their regular positions also provided the basis for setting compensation for the participants in writing conferences.

potential questions range from whether the staff members are eligible to join the faculty club, whether they receive the lower faculty rate for football tickets, and whether wives of staff members may join the faculty women's club, to the more serious problems of whether staff children are eligible for the tuition waivers granted faculty children, and whether the staff members may be covered under various fringe benefits, including health insurance, disability insurance, and a retirement plan.

For the short-term employee, the retirement plan may not pose a serious problem, and often he can maintain his pension coverage in the school system or university from which he has taken a leave of absence; some projects even provide funds for this. For other employees, it can be a serious factor. For example, in one project, employees worked for as long as five years, with no retirement plan coverage at all.

For projects that are part of a university, a major issue is whether appointments to the project are joint appointments with a teaching department. Joint appointments are much sought by staff members with collegiate backgrounds, since this is enhancing to their professional stature. Many also enjoy teaching and maintaining contacts with colleagues and graduate students. However, the department concerned may not need a staff member in that area. Or the requisites for employment, and the relative importance of one or another candidate attribute may be quite different for the project and the department.

If the person the project most wants to hire is not a particularly attractive candidate to the subject-matter department, will the department be saddled with this individual after the project is completed? What course is taken when the person the project is extremely anxious to hire does not have the standard qualifications for academic appointment at the sponsoring university? Can there be joint appointments for some positions and not for others? If so, how will this affect the prestige and morale of those not on joint appointments?

While from the candidate's point of view, the joint appointment may seem quite attractive and the project may seek a policy of joint appointments in order to attract the people it wants, the subject-matter department may be quite reluctant to consider the idea, or may reserve the right to veto any appointment unless the candidate has its complete approval. Where a joint appointment is made, new problems arise. Who determines the person's salary? Are project salaries comparable to departmental salaries? Who is responsible for the person's promotions and raises? Will the employee suffer because of the division of his loyalties and efforts between two employers? Are the same criteria germane for advancement in both the department and the project? If not, will this interfere with the performance of duties in one or in the other?

Where a joint appointment is not made, the staff member may not receive credit toward tenure or promotion. Thus, he may be a temporary employee for a number of years, doing important and exemplary work, but accruing no credits toward tenure at that institution. He also is not able to enhance his professional status in terms of seeking another position by citing a professorial rank held. This puts him at a clear competitive disadvantage with his professional peers who have been engaged in professorial posts and the research activities concomitant to such positions.

Projects located on or near college campuses often are able to use students as part-time or full-time employees or as unpaid researchers while they are working on theses or dissertations related to the project. This can be an excellent source of relatively inexpensive, qualified and skilled personnel at the same time that it provides valuable training for the neophyte. Many projects identify the training of graduate students as an important objective; others have provided effective training, even though such training is a peripheral consideration, and the training is an incidental by-product rather than a deliberate stratagem. However, while use of graduate students can strengthen the project and provide valuable training, there are some ramifications that should be kept in mind.

Which is more important, curriculum development or training of students? Should students be assigned in terms of where they can produce most, or in terms of where they will learn most? The most appropriate activities for training purposes may not be those most appropriate for moving the project ahead as rapidly as possible in the project's major task—curriculum development. Where there is a conflict, which consideration takes precedence?

If students are to do research connected with the project, does the project select the student, or is he selected by the student's major advisor? Who decides what research he will do—the student, the major advisor, or the project? If the student has the traditional freedom and responsibility for selection of his research problem and the methodology to be used, will the research be of use to the project? If he does not, will the research be appropriate for a graduate degree? That is, is problem identification a necessary part of the expected process of graduate research? Does the student's chairman see eye-to-eye with the project in terms of the manner of data collection and treatment, or does the student have to serve two masters? If he does, will this preclude satisfying either, or prove so time-consuming as to limit the utility of the data as far as the project is concerned.

If the student does research compatible with the project needs, will the data be available in time for the project to use it? Doctoral research generally takes longer than the student and his chairman anticipate. Also, class commitments and examination schedules may interfere with data collection activities; data for project evaluation often must be collected late in the school year, at a time when the graduate student may be involved with his own examinations.

In one project, a bright, apparently conscientious graduate student who was collecting and analyzing data for the evaluation and also using this for his thesis, had done an excellent job collecting data on schedule, but the analysis, which was a very time-consuming process, was not completed until one and-one-half years after the project was terminated. Not only was it impossible to feed the findings into the ongoing project activities, they even missed the final evaluation report of the project. Unfortunately, this example is not entirely atypical.[10]

The training of future research personnel and educators has been a major contribution of a number of projects which use graduate students as employees and also encourage them to pursue doctoral research in connection with the project. This contribution far outweighs the possible problems in their use on project work, and such contributions should be encouraged. However, projects planning to involve students should be aware of the potential difficulties, and try to anticipate them insofar as possible.

Discouraging as these staffing problems may seem, many projects have recruited and maintained highly competent staffs, often incurring serious professional sacrifices on the part of some of the persons involved. The calibre of such staffs reflects a personal commitment to curriculum improvement and a personal excitement with an idea. In the short run, this was possible particularly when the developmental project idea was new and revolutionary, and a number of projects had a spirit of personal involvement rare in employment situations. However, in the long run, as developmental projects become an accepted method of curriculum change, the novelty will cease to be an attraction, and more satisfactory arrangements will be needed, if appropriate staffing is to be achieved on a long-term basis.

---

[10]Similar problems of meeting deadlines may be faced when outside researchers are given permission to work on research related to the project. This can provide valuable supplementary expertise in project evaluation, thereby increasing the resources available to the project. However, when an individual is not on the regular project payroll, there is little pressure the project can bring to bear on the tardy individual. Particularly during the formative period, where data or analyses arriving late may be useless, this can pose a serious problem if the project is depending on the data in its work.

III

AIMS AND PURPOSES OF THE
DEVELOPMENTAL CURRICULA

Variations among projects in terms of purposes are legion. While all projects are concerned with effecting some kind of change, the extent and nature of the desired change vary from one project to another. Some projects want to work within the present educational structure and media, others want to break new ground, to use completely new approaches. Some projects want to change the subjects taught in the schools; some want to change what is taught within a given subject already taught; some want to change the way the curriculum is taught; and some want to learn more about learning. But all want to effect some change in the student. This desired change may be immediate or long-run.

Before looking at project aims, it may be well to look at the ways of classifying or describing aims. There are many valid ways of distinguishing among educational aims, or classifying such aims. Thus, aims can be immediate or long-range aims; they can be general or specific; they can be oriented to subject matter or not. And within the subject-matter orientation, they may be concerned with one discipline, with a cluster of related disciplines, or with a broad, multidisciplinary approach. The aims may be difficult to achieve or relatively simple. They may deal with intellectual skills (the cognitive domain), with attitudes and values (the affective domain), or the manipulative and motor skills (the psychomotor domain).

Projects often include method or techniques for effecting change as part of their aims, and it is difficult to separate these entirely from the aims themselves. Even though the eventual aims may deal with change in the learner, there are often intermediate aims, relevant to change in teachers, systems, media, and techniques; and, while in theory, one should be able to separate changes in learning or in end product from techniques in achieving this product, in practice, such separation may be difficult.

THE RESEARCH—DEVELOPMENT—APPLICATION CONTINUUM

Projects vary in the point on the continuum between research and application with which they are concerned. Glaser (1969) discusses five functions necessary for the successful relationship among research, development, and application:

1. *Exploratory research* is the theoretical, basic research characterized by questioning attitudes and relative independence of the application or further development of existing procedures or knowledge.

2. *Fundamental development* involves the investigation of the many variables relevant to the principles discovered in exploratory investigation.

3. *Specific development* is the stage at which the fundamental developments are put into a program, tested on a small scale, taken into the classroom, tested further, and revised.

4. *Design and proving* involves the redesign of the program for general use through detailed modifications, which may take into consideration development of new equipment and techniques, and reflect teacher work habits, school conditions, and structure of the classroom. Here, the problem is to demonstrate product effectiveness under field conditions, to test out the efficiency and economic value of variations in the conditions of use.

5. *Training and follow-through* concerns the further implications of the program—passing on knowledge by providing a training program for key people in the schools, and keeping open channels for feedback about new problems of developments with the product or procedure.

Glaser points out that these five components are necessary parts of the structure required for transforming knowledge from the science of learning into practical educational efforts.

Some projects phrase their concern purely in development terms, and enter the continuum at the specific development stage, stage number three. Others start earlier on the continuum, and phrase their concern with learning more about learning and teaching. Some projects are concerned with only areas three and four, with specific development and with design and proving, and for some of these, the design and proving stage is given only cursory consideration. Although Glaser points to the final stage, training and follow-through, as essential if effective application is to be achieved, this is not always included in project aims.

Projects generally do not couch their intents in terms of these five steps. They do not state specifically that they are concerned with one, two, or three of these steps. Yet, project intents may be categorized in terms of these steps, and use of this system in examining project aims and outcomes may throw some light on why some projects have not fully implemented their aims, since they may have neglected some of the steps or given some short shrift.

THE COGNITIVE, AFFECTIVE, AND PSYCHOMOTOR DOMAINS[1]

Educational aims in terms of learning outcomes can be divided into three categories or domains—the cognitive, the affective, and the psychomotor. Most projects have cognitive aims as a primary focus.

The Cognitive Domain

The cognitive domain involves six categories of functions which may be placed in a hierarchy in terms of complexity of mental operation (*see* Illustration 3). The lowest level is *knowledge,* including recall—the recall may be of fact, or it may be of ways of dealing with specifics: the knowledge includes knowledge of methodology, of principles, or of theories. The intellectual skills included in the rest of the cognitive domain involve doing something with what is recalled. Skills include: *comprehension* (similar to direct application); *application* (indirect application); *analysis* of new problems or situations (if the analysis is not of new situations, the activity is either comprehension or application, or may even be recall); *synthesis* (the putting together of elements to form a whole that is new to the learner); and *evaluation.* In this hierarchy, each higher level includes all preceding levels. Thus, a task classified as analysis would include knowledge, comprehension and application. A task classified as application would include knowledge and comprehension.

The classification of a task to a given level of the cognitive domain depends on the curriculum in which it occurs, and the context in which the curriculum is to be used. What is an original task involving analysis for one student or in one curriculum, may be a repetitive task, requiring only direct application of previous learning for another student, or another curriculum. The classification level of the task depends on what has gone before in the specific curriculum or in the past experience of the learner, either in other courses or in out-of-school contexts.

Within the cognitive domain, most projects have a subject-matter orientation, though there are a few that have an entirely process orientation, free of subject matter.[2] Thus, it is rare to find a project interested in problem solving

---

[1] The classification of educational aims into three domains is taken from Bloom (1956). A summary of the classification system within each of these domains based on Bloom (1956), Krathwohl (1964), and Simpson (1969) is included as Appendix B. It is suggested that readers not familiar with the work of Bloom and Krathwohl read Appendix B carefully before proceeding with the remainder of this chapter.

[2] The Eastern Regional Institute for Education defines process education as applying to both cognitive and affective domains. "In the realm of cognition, the long list of desirable processes includes observing, classifying, inferring, inquiring, reasoning, and remembering. Processes in the affective realm are associated with the exploration of values and the attainment of positive attitudes and motives for learning." (Eastern Regional Institute for Education, undated.) When used in the cognitive domain, a process orientation may have a specific subject-matter content or it may be content free.

ILLUSTRATION 3

Levels in the Cognitive, Affective, and
Psychomotor Domains

Cognitive Domain	Affective Domain	Psychomotor Domain
1. Knowledge	1. Receiving	1. Perception
2. Comprehension	2. Responding	2. Set
3. Application	3. Valuing	3. Guided response
4. Analysis	4. Organization	4. Mechanism
5. Synthesis	5. Characterization by	5. Complex overt response
6. Evaluation	a value or value	6. Adaptation
	complex	7. Origination

NOTE: For each domain, the levels constitute a hierarchy in which each advanced level must include all previous levels.

SOURCE: Based on Bloom (1956), Krathwohl (1964), and Simpson (1969).

or in building deductive thinking in the abstract; and where these do occur, they are generally concerned with the elementary school level. It is not at all rare to find a project concerned with problem solving or deductive thinking in a subject area—such as economics, sociology, history, or science—or a project concerned with developing process, but using a subject area or cluster of subject areas as a vehicle. Thus, a project may focus on the processes of science, using physical science and/or biological science as the medium—as is the case with the AAAS project—or teaching the processes of the social sciences using history, sociology and/or anthropology as the medium.

There can be varying emphases on subject matter and skills or processes. For the most part, the question of process/subject orientation is a matter of degree, rather than the inclusion of one to the exclusion of the other. Some projects have process as a major thrust. Thus, Suchman's Inquiry Project and AAAS Science as Inquiry Project are highly concerned with development of processes; BSCS, IME, and IMB are a few of the many projects combining subject goals with process goals. In the AAAS project, the major concern is with the process, but the process involved is the process of science, and the various disciplines in science are used as the vehicles for teaching the process.

Most projects express some concern with process, though this concern may be implemented in different ways. Thus, some curricula involve students in process. Some merely describe the process as one of which the students should be aware. AAAS and BSCS materials involve the student in actual process—that is, they ask the student to learn by doing. Some other projects provide students with descriptions of how others carry out the process.

Some projects appear concerned with process—inquiry, problem solving, flexibility—as an end in itself. However, such process concerns may also be considered means for achieving other ends. Thus, Bruner (1966) stresses the desirability of flexibility, but does not mention commitment to specific ends; apparently to him, flexibility *per se* is good. Brameld (1965) is concerned with the process, but this concern is clearly with the process as an intermediate goal, as a means for achieving a long-range goal, which, for Brameld, is social reconstruction.

Some of the projects are concerned with bringing into the schools a subject not taught at all heretofore, or not previously taught as a separate subject. Thus, there are projects concerned with the development of elementary school astronomy curricula, or with high school sociology, geography, and economics. Other projects are concerned with modernizing the curriculum in a subject area presently taught at a given grade level, so that the coverage of the course more accurately reflects the present state of the discipline. This has been a concern of SMSG, BSCS, PSSC, CHEM Study, and CBA.

These same studies and others are also concerned with changing the emphases within the subject area. This may be in terms of content, where the emphasis shifts from consideration of detailed, isolated facts, to presentation of clusters of facts which are organized around concepts—that is, with giving a more valid reflection of the discipline.

Or the project may be concerned with mastery of different skills related to the discipline. For example, it may emphasize mastery of more complex cognitive skills, rather than knowledge and direct application of knowledge. Or the project emphasis may be on activity—on doing, rather than talking and reading about the activity—to achieve a different kind of learning, or a more effective kind of learning. Thus, a number of developmental projects have included an emphasis on laboratory and field work in their aims. This has been a concern not only of science projects, but also of projects in the various social sciences and technology.

In each of these cases, the idea of the project is to produce a different kind of learning. But in all of these cases—whether the content is different or not, whether the focus is on process or on a discipline, whether the approach involves a single discipline or several disciplines, whether the subject matter has been taught as a discrete area or at that grade level—the major thrust is generally in the cognitive domain—in the building of intellectual skills.

The Affective Domain

The affective domain has to do with the development of attitudes and the building of values. It includes five levels, and again, these levels form a hierarchy, with each higher level building on the preceding levels. The five levels of the affective domain are: *receiving* (awareness, willingness to receive, and controlled or selected attention); *responding* (acquiescence in responding, willingness to respond, satisfaction in response); *valuing* (acceptance of a value, preference for a value, commitment to a value); *organization* (conceptualization of a value, organization of a value system or hierarchy of values); *characterization by a value or value complex* (generalized set, characterization by the value—that is, consistent operation on the basis of the personal value hierarchy). With few exceptions, the affective objectives identified by projects take a secondary role to the cognitive objectives. Many projects are interested in building favorable attitudes toward a discipline. Some are interested in increasing enrollments in that discipline; for example, HPP is concerned with declining enrollments in physics, a trend not halted by the older PSSC activity. Some are concerned with the image and attitudes students hold of practitioners of the discipline—with a student's impression of scientists or economists, or of chemistry, or economics. Yet, while the building of favorable attitudes and values is common as a secondary level aim, the usual primary focus of projects deals with the cognitive domain, and generally this is specific to a subject area or cluster of subject areas.

The Psychomotor Domain

The psychomotor domain is less often involved in the project aims, particularly in the written aims, and when included at all, such references are often short-run objectives that serve as vehicles or steps for achieving longer-run aims.[3] While many of the tasks involved in achieving the cognitive goals involve motor skills (e.g., the writing of answers, the operation of equipment, the manipulation of objects), the specific motor skills are not often mentioned, but are implicit or assumed steps in the achievement of cognitive goals. When the psychomotor aims are specified, they generally involve cognitive goals as well.

While most goal statements of projects are in cognitive terms, the affective and psychomotor are, in fact, goals of projects. Recognition of this and of the kinds of skills desired, and of the levels of expectation within each of these would give a clearer sense of direction to projects.

Interrelationship of the Cognitive and Affective Domains

Not widely recognized by projects is the fact that *achievement of all cognitive objectives requires parallel, concomitant achievement of affective objectives; achievement in the cognitive domain must include achievement in at least the first two levels of the affective domain, and also probably includes some involvement of the third level of the affective domain—the building of values.* Desired cognitive achievement is not possible without involving the receiving category of the affective domain—that is, unless students receive some stimulus. In this sense, receiving does not mean mere exposure to the stimulus, but it involves the student's awareness of the stimulus, a willingness to receive it, and perhaps controlled or selected attention to the stimulus. Putting a book or teacher in front of a child will not result in the desired cognitive gains unless the child is aware of the teacher or book, and takes in what is being presented.

In other words, teaching does not necessarily result in learning. Teaching need not even involve awareness of the teaching—witness the student who

---

[3]The psychomotor domain has not been as clearly described as the cognitive and affective domains, and the parameters of this domain are not as clear-cut. While Bloom (1956) and Krathwohl (1964) describe this domain as including "manipulative or motor skills," Simpson (1969) apparently is broader in her definition, and includes sensory perception—including taste, smell, and hearing—as a first step in the motor act. (See pp. 239 .)

daydreams, or is simply unaware of his surroundings during the school day, or some parts of the school day.

The curriculum project cannot determine whether the desired cognitive learning has taken place, unless the child responds in some way (the second level of the affective domain, responding). Unless the child is willing to answer or perform in some way—whether the performance is on a test, in a nontesting situation, or even a nonschool situation—one cannot determine whether he has learned. Thus, at least the first two levels of the affective domain are involved in achievement of all cognitive aims.

Further, in many cases, cognitive aims are concerned not with whether the child *can* do something, but whether he *will* do it. *Can do* and *will do* are not synonymous, and, as Krathwohl (1964) points out, the distinction may reflect the third category of the affective domain, valuing, at least to the point of acceptance of a value and perhaps preference for it. For the student, the value involved is not necessarily a liking for the subject or a preference for it. It may be a valuing of not being penalized for failure to study, either by the teacher, the rest of the class, or the society—including parents, potential employers, colleges. Or it may be valuing a specific reward for mastery of the cognitive goal, a reward in terms of grades, commendation, friendships, acceptability within group norms, absence of conflict.

In addition, achievement of some aims at the organization level of the affective domain may be prerequisite to the desired *will do* level of performance of cognitive aims. The student may face a conflict between values, and the desired performance may require the reference to a hierarchy of values which sets a higher value on the performance desired by the curriculum than the value set on another activity. For example, unless the valuing of systematic, careful work is higher in the student's personal value hierarchy than spending in a different way the time that can be saved by doing sloppy work, the performance of systematic, careful work will be a *can do* rather than a *will do* outcome.

In other situations, unless the student has developed a hierarchy of values as a reference point—that is, unless he has reached the organization level of the affective domain—the performance of the desired cognitive skills may be impossible. Aims relevant to the cognitive skills of synthesis and evaluation often involve reference to personal value hierarchies. For example, unless the individual is able to identify his own values that are involved in making a decision, and sees how these values are interrelated or how they conflict, he will not be able to weigh alternatives involving conflicting values rationally. Such weighing of alternatives may be the aim of the project.

Thus, a project may have as a cognitive goal that students will be able to make rational decisions *vis-à-vis* social problems with scientific implications. Such decision making involves personal value judgments and relative personal priorities among values. It may involve a choice between valuing the quality of the environment or valuing of technological progress; valuing of individual freedom or of group convenience; valuing of physical resources for their economic potential, for their recreational potential, for their scientific potential, or for their aesthetic potential. Often, projects hope to improve the decision making by students so that in the future, they will be able to make rational decisions on such questions as appropriate level of armaments, appropriate levels of taxation, and development of supersonic transports and jetports. Such decisions cannot be made on the basis of facts alone. They involve value judgments. And appropriate value judgments cannot be made rationally without an organized system of values, without a stratifying of the more important and less important values.

Decisions on whether to continue development of new weapons—for chemical and germ warfare, for example—whether to defoliate the countryside in a war, with the resulting long-run, ecological and social ramifications, whether to undertake a health program in an underdeveloped nation, thereby increasing the dependent population to the point where the starvation rate becomes critical, the question of national priorities, of whether we have guns or schools and houses—all these are questions that involve not only the highest levels of the cognitive domain (analysis, synthesis and evaluation), but they equally involve personal value hierarchies.

The correct answer depends not simply on accurate analysis of facts. It also requires a systematic analysis of the values involved, and the relative importance, in a personal value hierarchy, of a number of conflicting values. There is no *right* value hierarchy we can give students. It is something that has to be worked out by a student, if he is to achieve the cognitive skills desired.

Clearly, the achievement of desired cognitive goals involves achievement of affective goals. But, *even when the desired cognitive learning is not effected, the affective domain is involved, and values are being built in the teaching/ learning situation of a curriculum.* As Tyler (1950) points out:

The most frequent method (of developing attitudes) is through assimilation from the environment. . . . A second and perhaps the next most common method of acquiring attitudes arises from the emotional effects of certain experiences. In general, if one has had satisfying experiences in a particular connection, he develops an attitude favorable to some content or aspect of that experience, while if he has had an unsatisfying experience, his attitude may become antagonistic. The third most frequent method of developing attitudes is through traumatic experiences, that is, experiences which have

had a deep emotional effect. . . . Finally, a fourth method of developing
attitudes is through direct intellectual processes. . . . Unfortunately, attitudes
formed through definite intellectual processes are not so frequent as those
obtained in other ways.

Attitudes are not directly taught through such procedures as telling students
how they should feel, what they should like, and what they should respect.
Attitudes are assimilated; they are developed.

Deliberate attempts to tell people what their attitudes and values should
be may result in the acceptance of the opposite rather than the apposite value
or attitude. Didactic statements that a subject is important—intended to implement an objective relevant to building a value about the importance of the
discipline—may build the obverse value, or it may contribute to a host of other
negative values about school, teachers, education, and books. (Tyler, 1950; H.
Grobman, forthcoming.)

Thus, it seems quite likely that the achievement of cognitive and psychomotor aims involves prior or concomitant achievement of some affective
outcomes, whether or not these are identified by the project. Regardless of the
long-term, primary goals of the curriculum project, perhaps such affective
outcomes should be the most important areas for project concern, since without achieving some positive, affective outcomes, at least through the level of
valuing, achievement of any other goals in the cognitive and psychomotor
domains may be precluded.

This hypothesis, if valid, has rather serious implications for curriculum-
project work. If supported, it would indicate that the affective domain should
receive far greater attention from curriculum projects.

LONG-RUN, INTERMEDIATE, AND IMMEDIATE AIMS

Project aims can be regarded in terms of a time dimension—that is,
whether they are for immediate achievement or long-run achievement,
whether they are the goal for the day, week, or unit, or an eventual outcome
of the curriculum at the end of a year or a level of schooling, or whether the
outcome is to be achieved during adulthood. While it is conceivable that a
project could have a single aim—e.g. the improvement of reading—most projects have clusters of related long-run aims. Some projects translate these into
intermediate and immediate aims; others make this translation implicit in their
work, without verbalizing the short-run aim.[4]

---

[4]Krathwohl (1965) speaks of global aims (e.g., citizenship), intermediate aims (at grade and
course level), and detailed aims (such as specific mastery tasks).

Illustration 4

WHAT IS COMMUNICATED DOES NOT NECESSARILY REFLECT THE INTENT OF THE COMMUNICATOR OR THE CURRICULUM.

CHARLES M. SCHULZ

Long-term aims are often rather global and diffuse, perhaps of necessity. They often deal with such areas as developing civic competence, understanding economic concepts, mastery of scientific modes of inquiry, contributing to the liberal education of the student, and understanding science. Such aims tend to deal with a distant future, and are directed to the development of competence and/or attitudes to be used in situations that cannot now be predicted, often situations for which there are no existing prototypes. Thus, a science project might have as a long-run aim that when the student reaches adulthood, he will be aware of the scientific implications of new developments, and will make decisions concerning these in a rational, systematic manner.

Decisions concerning today's radioactive fallout problems, or present national priorities could not have been precisely anticipated thirty years ago, and the kinds of data needed to make systematic, reasoned decisions could not have been identified thirty years ago. Similarly, today we cannot precisely identify the kinds of problems with scientific implications that today's students will face as adults. Yet, today's developmental projects are concerned with the future actions of their students in identifying and coping with the new problems of the future.

In looking at the long-run aims of a project, there are often serious semantic problems involved in clarifying what the project means by the terms it uses. This difficulty may result in problems of translation from the future, general aims to the intermediate and immediate aims. The general, imprecise nature of long-term aims, and the failure to translate these systematically into short-run aims can have serious consequences, because it may result in lack of clarity inside as well as outside the project concerning what is to be done; and without a clear sense of direction, there are no criteria or bench marks for determining whether the project's task has been accomplished.

It is impossible to determine the extent to which a project is doing what it set out to do, unless there is some understanding of what it set out to do. With a mandate of improving mathematics education, what constitutes improvement? Is it the change in nature of what is covered? Or is it the more effective learning of what has been covered in the past? Is it an increased ability to score well on traditional tasks? Or is it the ability to do new tasks well?

The project that aims for understanding economic concepts, or developing basic scientific literacy, leaves a wide area of leeway. *Understanding* is an indefinite term with different meanings for different people. For some, understanding economic concepts requires only verbalizing a memorized concept; what may be required is the recall of a general idea, which puts the task at the lowest level of the cognitive domain. To Bruner (1960), knowing cannot be separated from doing, and a student does not know something unless he can use it in a variety of contexts. Bruner (1966) insists that knowing is a process rather than a product. Thus, understanding can mean knowing, the lowest category of the cognitive domain, or it can require the more complex intellectual skills, including analysis, synthesis, and evaluation, the highest categories of the domain.

When projects specify their goals in behavioral terms—when they state precisely what behavior is expected of the student—the meaning of the aim becomes clear. A project that asks the student to identify given words, to identify equipment, to specify causes, to solve problems dealing with sets, or to build hypotheses, makes its purposes clear. There is less room for ambiguity in such situations, and for this reason, a number of persons concerned with developmental work are strong advocates of the practice of specifying objectives in behavioral terms—that is, in terms of the immediate and observable behaviors desired. In such instances, project purposes are unmistakable. There is a clear, agreed-upon sense of direction. And the achievement of the purpose is measurable.

The earliest developmental projects stated aims rather generally; they talked of improving the curriculum, building understanding, and stressing inquiry. Some projects never defined objectives more clearly. In others, more detailed objectives were emergent; they developed as the project personnel attempted to work out programs and materials, as writers were more able to verbalize what they meant by understanding and inquiry. Thus, for the BSCS, the vague statement of learning the way scientists work came to include such more specific statements as having students identify problems, build hypotheses, and test them in a laboratory setting, coming to answers and building generalizations from them. The BSCS never prepared a complete list of specific objectives, yet there was fairly general agreement about many of these, and there were lists prepared (and amended as needed) of more general objectives.[5]

Other projects have been more conscious of objectives, and some have made a very deliberate effort to specify objectives not only precisely, but in terms of immediate, observable behavior. The AAAS project was one of the first to place this clear emphasis on immediate outcomes and on observable behavior.[6]

---

[5] Such lists or statements appeared from time to time in the *BSCS NEWSLETTER* (Boulder, Colorado: Biological Sciences Curriculum Study, 1959-present).

[6] A popular source on how to state objectives behaviorally is Mager (1962). For samples of the kinds of objectives verbalized by the AAAS project, see Kurtz (1967); and for complete lists, see *Science—a Process Approach* (AAAS, 1969; AAAS, 1970). See also Popham *et al.* (1969) on instructional objectives.

The way in which objectives are stated—whether the statement is general or highly specific, and whether objectives are stated in terms of immediately observable behavior—influences a number of aspects of the project. It influences the ways in which materials are prepared in terms of the immediacy of the focus on goals, and it influences the manner in which achievement of goals can be checked.

Undoubtedly, the statement of goals in behavioral terms facilitates the materials-preparation task, because it gives those responsible for materials preparation clear goals. It makes evaluation in terms of goal achievement more feasible, since the goal statement includes the bench mark against which performance may be evaluated. Why then is there a reluctance or outright refusal of many projects to state goals behaviorally, and a hostility to the idea by many persons in the education-research community (Broudy, 1969; Raths, 1968; Atkin, 1968; Tyler, 1966)?

Some of the objections are based on a preexisting bias. To some of the people working on developmental projects, the preparation of statements of objectives carries an aura of an education-establishment approach, and for some people from the disciplines, this approach typifies what is wrong with education and with educators. They foresee endless semantic hassles and arguments over wording, which preclude getting on with the job at hand. Whether justified or not, many of the discipline people are highly prejudiced in advance over such an approach.

Others feel that any but the broadest objectives in experimental programs must be emergent; that to set specific objectives—whether behavioral or not —in advance, unduly delimits the project. UICSM, for example, believes in an emergent development of materials and the setting of day-to-day objectives, with next week's or next month's short-run objectives growing out of today's experience in the classroom. Such individuals identify the problem of clearly charting in detail the direction of the curriculum when it is experimental, when it is difficult to anticipate what is possible, and before one can tell which directions will lead to a desired long-run goal.

Others demur because behavioral objectives are generally specified in immediately observable terms, and there is a difficulty in insuring that what is immediately observable is related to the long-run desired outcome. Also, since affective outcomes are difficult to observe, affective objectives may be entirely ignored. Some critics of the behavioral objectives approach feel that this approach reflects a belief that life consists of specific and predictable activities. They point out that being a parent, for example, is not like bricklaying—it does not consist of specific, predictable activities.

Some critics of the behavioral objectives approach feel that this approach encourages proponents to deal with minutiae and overlook the real purposes. They consider the behavioral objective proponents exemplars of Peter's *side issue specialist* (Peter and Hull, 1969) whose watchword is: "Look after the mole hills and the mountains will look after themselves."

This raises serious problems of validity of the short-term, specific objectives, a matter which has not been adequately investigated. Often, projects that specify immediate aims jump from the broad, generic, long-run aim to the immediate, precise aim automatically. They may jump from an aim of developing understanding to an aim such as the mastery of a glossary, or a series of concepts, with the assumption that the latter are the natural and logical precursors of the former—that learning words, memorizing principles, or solving some routine problems will result in preparing students for the broader, future problem situations to be faced.

Such projects tend to assume that the traditional, or nontraditional, daily task that they propose for the student does, in fact, contribute to a global aim in the distant future. While it might be difficult in most instances to prove a direct contribution of any given day-to-day task to a long-range end goal, there is rarely even a systematic analysis of the assumptions underlying the implication of a connection, followed by a rigorous examination of these assumptions.[7]

While the discrepancy between long-run aims and short-run aims and activities may be more obvious in projects specifying behavioral objectives, the same discrepancy may occur where short-run objectives are implied rather than specified. Such projects, too, are prone to make tacit, though unwarranted, assumptions linking immediate and intermediate objectives with long-run objectives—for example, the tacit assumption that learning how to operate a microscope today will enhance the degree of scientific literacy of the individual twenty years hence; or that the ability to identify five causes of the Civil War or World War I today will increase the individual's ability to analyze rationally, and cope with public issues in the future.

While it is not possible to prove conclusively that this is or is not the case, it is possible to identify and analyze the assumptions underlying such hypothesized relationships. For the most part, careful, systematic analyses of the relationship among immediate, intermediate, and long-run goals have not been made, either by those specifying objectives in terms of immediately observable

---

[7] Edward A. Suchman (1967), Chapter 4, includes a cogent discussion of the problem of validity of aims and the relationships and assumptions involved between the immediate and long-run aims.

behavior, or by those verbalizing only long-range or nonbehavioral objectives.

Sometimes, the relationship between short-run and long-run objectives has been considered. But when this is the case, the existence of a direct relationship is generally considered to be a strong presumption, even though many of the short-run objectives, both specified and implied by the materials, are neither logical nor plausible precursors to the long-run goals. Drawing graphs, answering fact questions, completing drill, and analyzing situations in Ancient Rome are assumed to increase competence in adult activities in future decades, despite the fact that past experience has indicated that such long-term outcomes do not generally follow. And so, some of the new curricula may be merely teaching more efficiently what we have taught in the past, which perhaps should not be taught at all.

In the last decade, the pendulum has swung from the statement of goals in the most general terms to the statement in highly precise terms. And now it may be swinging back to a midpoint, to a compromise position, where there is a recognition that global objectives are clearly inadequate to set an appropriate framework for curriculum development or evaluation; and precise statements, in terms of immediately observable objectives, may be overly restrictive.

Certainly, the statements related to knowledge and understanding could be somewhat delimited by the reference to Bloom's (1956) cognitive levels, so that it would be clear whether knowledge and understanding mean recall, or involve the entire cognitive spectrum. Or projects might provide general statements of objectives, with examples of what would constitute satisfactory performance; such examples would be illustrative only (Tyler, 1966). Thus, a project might state that by understanding is meant ability to use selected, identified concepts in that discipline, at Bloom's level of analysis, synthesis, or evaluation.

Or the project might provide a few examples of the kinds of tasks that would be considered as achievement of understanding. For example, it might state that when a student comes across a nonschool situation, new to him— such as a report of an oil slick on the ocean—a situation that has basic biological implications, without prompting he will be aware of the biological implications. However, such examples should only be illustrative of the kind of activity expected of the student, rather than indicative of the precise activity he will be expected to perform.

Even preparing such examples as these is a time-consuming task. For projects newly organized to work in an area, the delimitation of the ball park cannot be done overnight. Further, for many projects, the objectives are quite properly emergent. This does not reflect lack of planning; rather, it is a matter of becoming familiar with the area, with what can and perhaps cannot be done. It simply may not be possible to assess the full potential of the materials until the work is well under way.

Particularly in instances where a project wants to involve people from diverse specialities, people who have not had previous curriculum-development experience, it may not be able to start out with clearly defined, precise statements of objectives. The group does not yet know exactly what it wants to do. Participants would not accept objectives developed by others. They have to work into the building of objectives.

While some people work best if they have a detailed, long-term blueprint in front of them, others, who are at least equally creative and productive, have only a general idea of where they are going, and could never write a book if they had to completely outline it in advance. This is a matter of personal style; and forcing people out of their style results either in their dropping out of the activity, or their resentment and less than optimal performance. If the people involved in the project are accustomed to curriculum development following the precise specification of objectives—and many people working on developmental projects involving programmed instruction have this background—and if they like this way of working, the statement of precise objectives poses less of a problem.

While the author tends to reject the notion that to be valid, objectives must be stated precisely and in immediately observable terms prior to the preparation of materials, the complete failure to state objectives is not accepted as satisfactory either. A number of projects have run into serious trouble because they never decided what it was they wanted to do, beyond improving education in the discipline or building understanding. They assumed that whatever activity or materials they developed must be doing this, because these materials were in the subject area, and were built by intelligent people. There was often an assumption that for the students using the materials, doing would automatically follow knowing, that having knowledge was synonymous with being able to use that knowledge.

While specifying detailed objectives is not an acceptable alternative to vague generalizations as a guide, developmental projects need to be somewhat specific, to tie down in more understandable terms what it is the project hopes to do, even if the statement is not immediately observable, or observable at all. Undoubtedly, more precision of statement is needed, even if this precision is not as detailed as some advocate, and even if it does not result in immediately observable behaviors.

Further, statements of objectives should be subject to reevaluation and modification. No statement of either short-term or long-term objectives should be considered permanent and immutable. As the project develops, as it has an opportunity to work on materials, receive feedback, and evaluate its experiences, a reexamination of its objectives is clearly indicated. And a project's changes in objectives should not necessarily be looked at askance. Perhaps those projects which do not modify their objectives over time are more open to criticism than those which do.

ASSUMPTIONS UNDERLYING THE CURRICULUM

Projects vary in the extent to which they include in their objectives skills which are not specific to the discipline. This is separate from the question of whether the project focuses on a single discipline or is multidisciplinary. Even a single-discipline project—a project in economics, history, English, or one of the sciences—may be concerned with the development of some of the broad skills that are part of the schools' general educational responsibility. For example, school systems usually include in their general objectives developing well-adjusted students, developing student skills in self-expression, improving manual dexterity, developing favorable attitudes towards self-directed education, developing certain attitudes toward the role of the individual in modern society, and certain values *vis-a-vis* society and the individuals in society.

Such aims are not specific to a single subject area or grade level, and cannot be effectively taught in one course or at one grade. They are considered the responsibility of all courses at all grade levels. But, as is so often the case, what is everyone's business becomes no one's business. Only rarely do projects consider whether they are making a contribution to such general goals as these, and even when they are making such a contribution—for example, to the improvement of communication skills—they may not be aware of this contribution and may not include it in their bench marks for progress.

Perhaps some of the projects concerned with the disadvantaged or the lower-ability student are more conscious of such general aims as increasing student feelings of personal adequacy, building the student's confidence in his ability to do schoolwork, or decreasing his sense of alienation to school and society. But even here, such broad concerns are not always identified. The fact that the broad concerns are not identified generally means that attention is not directed toward them and, as a result, the project may be hampering the development of these general goals rather than encouraging their realization.

Similarly, a failure by a project to identify the theories of learning and philosophy of education espoused, may result in a dilution of the project's efforts. With some noteworthy exceptions, few developmental projects identify a psychology of learning which they accept. Still fewer identify a guiding educational philosophy or the value judgments basic to their curriculum. Yet, all curricula reflect some philosophy of education—the purpose of education, the role of education in society, the definition of a good society—and a theory of learning. Such philosophies, theories, and value judgments may be implicit rather than stated, but they are present in all curricula, are basic to the curriculum, and are an essential part of the assumptions underpinning the curriculum.[8]

All curricula reflect some notions on such questions related to learning as:

How do students learn most effectively? Do all students learn best in the same way?

Do students learn because they are rewarded and/or punished? That is, what is the role of motivation in learning, and how is motivation fostered?

Can one train the mind or train the faculties of the mind, with the result that general competence in all intellectual areas will be enhanced?

Will knowledge of the past—particularly of the classics of the past—prepare students to deal with problems of the future?

Will training in one area be transferred automatically to other areas? Can such transfer be expected to occur only with specific preparation for transfer? Or can transfer not be expected under any conditions?[9]

What is the role of insight in learning? What kinds of insight are important, and how are these developed?

What levels or types of cognitive skills enhance retention of learning? What levels of cognitive learning increase ability to use present learning in later, high cognitive level tasks?

Is learning most effective when it proceeds from the known to the unknown, or from the unknown to the known?

Should learning go from the abstract to the concrete, or from the concrete to the abstract?

Should learning be sequential, and pyramided on previous learning?

Can complex cognitive abilities be mastered during the child's first school years? Or can they be mastered only when taught initially during the child's first school years?

To what extent are children born unequal in terms of intellectual potential? Is there a great variation in the innate, intellectual ability of students?[10] Barring prenatal or postnatal injury, can all children be brought up to an effective functioning level?

Several of these possibilities reflect theories of learning that have been discarded as inappropriate decades ago. Learning theorists have amassed evi-

---

[8] The following analysis is based in part on criteria and principles for selection of curriculum content developed by Hines (1950).

[9] See Klausmeier (1969) on research on transfer of learning.

[10] Boyer and Walsh (1968) indicate how different assumptions in this area where no conclusive data are available—result in widely differing approaches to education. Schwebel (1968) indicates a belief in a far greater innate intellectual potential than is generally recognized.

dence that a mental discipline approach, attempts to train the faculties of the mind and theories of automatic transfer of training,are not valid explanations of how children learn. Yet, these theories are often implicit in the kinds of materials and activities involved in developmental materials, and in the short-term and long-term aims of developmental projects.

On several of the notions concerning retention and later ability to use materials or skills, there is clear evidence that one approach or teaching technique is not as successful as another; regarding others, the available evidence indicates that there is no clear advantage to one kind of approach, and no single, best approach. Such evidence is not necessarily reflected in the assumptions underlying developmental curricula to date.[11]

Few projects have systematically investigated available knowledge about learning—as exemplified in the summaries by Gagné (1964), Gagné and Gephart (1968), Klausmeier (1969), and Glaser (1969)—and have attempted to incorporate such evidence in their approach to teaching. Few projects have considered the nature and the variety of facets of human intelligence.[12] Few have made systematic decisions about which facets of intelligence concern them, and which do not, in the light of kinds of cognitive achievement effected.

Curricula also reflect such value judgments as whether skills should be taught at the earliest possible age. For example, if the theory of sets or if Spanish can be successfully taught at third grade, should they, in fact, be taught at this grade? Are the gains of such teaching worth the possible penalties in terms of loss of time for other skills (such as computation), loss of time for other subjects (the addition of Spanish must reduce time for something else), or detriment to other subjects (for example, possible increased difficulty in mastery of English or reading)?

At what cognitive level and in what degree of depth is it worth teaching a subject? That is, if some parts of algebra can be taught in the primary grades, is it worth doing so, if they can be taught only at the memory or direct application level, without a basic understanding of what is being done and why, and to what use this skill can be put?

Is the gain of reducing the grade level at which a subject is taught worth the loss in sophistication or depth of understanding possible with greater maturity? When a subject is moved to a lower grade level, is any loss in understanding compensated for by the gain in time? An obvious example may

---

[11]Undoubtedly, some members of the developmental project staffs are unfamiliar with learning research. However, others are probably familiar with it, but are not aware that it is germane to do their developmental tasks as they are working on these tasks; perhaps this is because their initial contacts with psychology were not at an appropriate cognitive level to enhance its use at a later date in an unfamiliar situation.

[12] Guilford (1967) identifies 120 different dimensions of intelligence.

be human reproduction, which can be taught at any grade level from kindergarten on. At what point can this best be taught as a basic, biological function to students who are sufficiently mature to put this learning into suitable context? If the tenth grade student is able to handle a sophisticated presentation of human reproduction as a biological function, as part of his regular biology course, should the same course be moved down to eighth or ninth grade, to students of less maturity, simply because the students can master the content? Or should the information be included in the regular seventh or eighth grade, or perhaps in the fifth or sixth grade course? The knowledge certainly could be mastered there. In fact, there are advocates for moving this biological presentation into the early school or preschool years. What is the relative gain and loss involved?

Is it worth teaching a subject at an early age if this does not mean a greater long-run gain in mastery? For example, is it worth teaching reading at age three or four just because this is possible, if the average eight-year-old reads at the same grade level, regardless of the age at which he was initially taught to read? Is it more important for a student to handle a broad range of material, or to master less material without feeling frustration and being overwhelmed?

Perhaps the most important kinds of assumptions underlying the curriculum are those related to the philosophy of education, including ideas about the purpose of education and society, and the role of the individual in society. All curricula reflect ideas about such questions as:

Is education an investment which should pay off to the economy, or is its main purpose to increase self-realization?

Should education be concerned with the past, present, or future? In the latter case, is the future to be any future that develops, or is it the future we deliberately and systematically create?

Who should decide on the curriculum and on its content and activities? Should the child have a role in deciding what and how he is to learn?

Should the teacher select activities? Or should the curriculum builder decide these? Or should the child have a part in selecting them?

Are the student's needs when he becomes an adult the controlling concern of education? Or are his present needs as he, or someone else sees them, a controlling concern?

Is subject matter important because it has survived through time? Because it is significant to an organized field of knowledge? Because it is of particular interest to the child? Because it is of use to him at the moment? Because it is of use to adults in today's world? Because it will probably be of use to him in the future? Because someone thinks it will be good for him? Or because it is relevant to the crisis of our times—to the survival of democracy and to reconstructing society?

Is it the job of the school to perpetuate present society, or to encourage a restructuring of society? And if the latter, in what direction should the restructuring go?

Are free enterprise and capitalism as we now know them essential to democracy?

Are flexibility and/or creativity traits to be encouraged or discouraged?

What is a good society?

What constitutes progress? Technological advances? Increased gross national product? Changed social conditions?

Is change desirable? Should change be welcomed, or viewed reluctantly? What are the criteria for desirable change? Are moral and ethical implications of a change important in encouraging that change? Should schools teach students to make value judgments and choose among alternatives? Should schools be concerned with the implications of technology?

Is competition good? Is cooperation more important than competition? Is interdependence more important than independence?

What is a good citizen? Is a good citizen a conformist or a noncomformist? Is citizenship a political phenomenon or a social phenomenon—that is, is it concerned with the individual's political role, or with such social roles as being quiet and following school regulations?

What is a good or typical person? A middle class conformist? A rugged individualist? A warrior? A peaceable resister? An American? An employed person? A parent?

What is the individual's proper role in society? A passive participant? A rebel? An agent for encouraging rationally directed change?

Some persons consider the reconstruction of society a major purpose of the schools (Brameld, 1965). Some suggest that the extent to which a curriculum contributes to this end, in any subject area, is a valid criterion for selecting or judging a curriculum (Hines, 1950; Grobman and Hines, 1957). Bobbitt (1924) suggests that "effective education is a progressive remaking of our environment." Bode (1927) states that " . . . any subject that is worthy of a place in the curriculum must contribute to the attitude which places upon men the responsibility for the continuous re-creation of the environment and of standards for conduct with reference to that respect for men which we identify with democracy." The "social dynamite" of our slums and culturally disadvantaged is an inescapable responsibility of schools; is it the concern of curricula?

Morrison (1967) indicates the tremendous repercussions on social arrangements that are resulting from technology, repercussions that have largely been ignored by schools and society. Solandt (1969) is among the many scientists who have recently been concerned by the growing number of decisions about the future use of technology that "in total, may be much more important to mankind than even 'the bomb.' " Starr (1969) emphasizes the conflict between social benefit and technological risk, and the price society would have to pay for safety. Ripley (1969) illustrates the failure of society to recognize the conflict between human safety and technological change, even when the lives of hundreds of individuals are imperiled needlessly. Bennis and Slater (1968) indicate that a major task for education must be "teaching how to live with ambiguity, to identify with the adaptive process, to make a virtue out of contingency, and to be self-directing." Are these questions to which developmental curricula are addressing themselves?

It is fairly obvious that the social studies reflect involvement with many of these questions. It is less clear that such subjects as mathematics or chemistry do so. Nonetheless, they do. Perhaps an extreme example is the trade book, *The Science of Chemistry* (Freeman and Patton, 1968). Intended for an adolescent audience, it includes under the heading of "More good things from chemistry," an illustration of a steel-helmeted policeman, who resembles a storm trooper, squirting mace at some teenage students. The obvious implications are that progress includes development of mace, that rebellion is not a part of good citizenship, and that being a student is a dangerous occupation in this society. In mathematics, the recent textbooks developed in Egypt, phrasing problems in terms of numbers of Israeli planes and snipers shot down, and of numbers of Egyptian planes and commandos returning unharmed, provide unmistakable evidence of the possibilities of communicating philosophical and social implications in this apparently impersonal discipline.

"Pressures on Children" (1968) provides inescapable evidence that schools and every subject area within the schools have placed destructive pressures on students, and the highly undesirable concomitants of such pressures are identified. Studies of the increasing suicide rate among adolescents and the rate of ulcers and other physical ailments resulting from environmental pressure, among even first and second graders, further reinforce this point. The National Advisory Commission on Civil Disorders (1968) concluded that "White racism is essentially responsible for the explosive mixture which has been accumulating in our cities since the end of World War II." While the degree to which the schools have contributed to this white racism may be debatable, the schools' responsibility for combating it, and their ineffective role in doing so, are not.

While being interviewed about school by an educator, one student commented, "Well, curriculum is curriculum. We have it for twelve years. We haven't mentioned it to you because we wanted to tell you first about the things that really matter." (Mallery, 1962) The extent to which the developmental project is concerned with the state of society, with the pressures on students, with what is really important to students, should be clarified.

hat theories of learning, philosophy of education, and value
not been identified by developmental projects as guidelines,
that they are not part of the assumptions underlying the
curriculum. Where these assumptions are not identified, it is harder to evaluate
them, to check them for consistency, to be sure they are mutually compatible
and supportive, and to insure that they represent a valid reflection of what the
project wants to do.

AN OVERVIEW

All projects have some kind of specification of purpose—of what they are
trying to do. These lists of purpose may be more or less complete; but all
developmental projects have as a goal the effecting of change. The dimensions
of the change to be effected differ markedly from one project to another. Some
projects want to change content or sequence in materials that are available.
Some want to change ways of teaching. Some want to prove the feasibility of
different content or method. And some want to effect actual lasting change in
the schools, on both content and method. Regardless of the scope of their
intent, all projects want to change students in some way.

As projects justify their existence, they express an overt or implied concern with long-run change, and while they express immediate and intermediate
goals, there is a long-run goal that is the basic justification. Thus, a project may
have as an immediate goal the improvement of word-recognition skills, and an
intermediate goal of handling unfamiliar words, with the long-run goal concerned with speed, accuracy, and ease of reading. Or the immediate goal may
be the mastery of a working vocabulary in economics; the intermediate goal,
the mastery of principles in economics; and the long-run goal, the improvement of problem solving in an economic context by an informed citizenry.
Many of the developmental projects are concerned with developing students
who, in later life, will be of an inquiring mind, will use sophisticated, critical,
thinking abilities in approaching problems, and will be self-educating and
rationally self-directing, particularly in the context of the subject area.

Some projects have a specific, mission-oriented focus, such as teaching
disadvantaged first graders to read. Others have a general focus, such as
improving mathematics education, teaching inquiry, developing creativity, or
"messing around" in science. The job of the former projects is more specific
and more clear cut; for the latter, it is more diffuse.

Proponents of specific goals, with some justification, point out that you
cannot decide on direction, or measure attainment of goals if you do not know
where you want to go; NASA probably would not have gotten to the moon
in 1969, if it had not been decided, specifically, that the moon was the goal,

and that it should be reached in 1969. Others, supporting a less-directed approach, believe that the specific goals must be emergent, developed with experience. The former type of objective is easier to tie down, to break down into subobjectives. In the latter case, the distance between the general aim and the specific, immediate objectives is harder to bridge successfully.

Some of the ways of looking at project goals are dependent on the context of the curriculum; others are not. Thus, the classification of aims on the basis of difficulty in learning involved, or importance to the learner, must be in the context of a given curriculum, since what is important in one context may not be important in another, and what is difficult in one context may not be difficult in another. What is difficult for a sixth grader may not be difficult for a ninth grader. What is important in an American history course may not be important, though still relevant, in a sociology course.

Classification based on degree of specificity, or in terms of cognitive, affective, and psychomotor domains, is independent of context. An aim that is highly specific is highly specific regardless of context. Similarly, a skill that involves problem solving always involves intellectual and attitudinal skills, regardless of the curriculum or audience.

There are also some classifications that are partly independent of context, and partly dependent on it. For example, the implementation of some aims always involves motor skills as well as cognitive and affective involvement, regardless of the curriculum in which they are found. But even here, the context in which the aim appears will affect the classification of the aim within the general categories of cognitive, affective, and psychomotor. For a student who has had no practice in analysis of mathematical problems involving sets, an aim including this might be at the analysis level in the cognitive hierarchy; where, for a student who has already studied a parallel problem earlier, it might be at the knowledge, interpretation, or application level.

Projects have both verbalized and implicit goals. And there may be disparities between what the project says it is trying to accomplish, and what it appears to be accomplishing, or between what the project says its goals are, and the goals implicit in the materials.

Further, project goals are hierarchical, whether or not this hierarchy is recognized. Some aims become more important than others; yet, the hierarchy of a project's aims is not always systematically established. Or the project may not be aware that it is, in fact, operating on the basis of a hierarchy of goals, perhaps a hierarchy that would not have been adopted, had it been subjected to close scrutiny. For example, a high-level cognitive or affective goal may result in the development of a short-run, immediate cognitive or psychomotor goal; thus, developing scientific literacy may be translated into a goal of mastering the vocabulary of science, or manipulating several scientific instruments. Sometimes, a project loses sight of the fact that the latter, short-run goals are only vehicles for achieving the former, long-run goals. In such cases, the immediate goals become ends in themselves, and this may preclude achieving the long-run goals.

Preparation of curriculum requires choices relating to relative importance of goals. Should one sacrifice coverage for process—for example, coverage of American history for development of the process of how historians work? In theory, the sacrifice of coverage may be espoused, but do the tests covering the curriculum reflect this? Are encouragement of an inquiry process and development of creativity more important or less important than understanding the basic concepts of physical science? If one must be sacrificed, which one? If students are encouraged to pursue independent lines of thought as they begin to inquire and come up with original, creative ideas, what happens to coverage? In a project attempting to improve English education, goals may include increasing the student's interest in English and American literature, and also, mastery of grammar and spelling. However, achievement of the grammar and spelling goals may preclude achievement of the interest-stimulating goals by building a disaffection for English. Which goals should take precedence?

The matter of goals for projects is a far more complex one than is generally appreciated by most projects. Many projects pass over the matter quickly. Others focus on immediately observable, behavioral goals and consider the matter adequately handled. While the possibility and desirability of advance, detailed specification of goals are questionable, there appears to be a need for a greater continuing concern with goals, with awareness of direction, with redirection as needed, and with relative priorities and consistency among goals.

A story—perhaps apocryphal—about developmental projects concerns considerable film footage shot for one purpose and found not useful. The project then built a new effort around the existing footage, and after the fact, rationalized the new curriculum package in terms of a whole series of aims and theories of learning. Whether or not this story is true, certainly some of the project materials now available do not reflect either the initial intent of the developers, or a planned deviation from the initial intent. Rather, they represent an accidental outcome rationalized after the fact, because of a lack of awareness of where the developers wanted to go, and of the underlying assumptions that were creeping into the materials.

IV

WORK ON THE DEVELOPMENTAL CURRICULUM

DEFINITION OF CURRICULUM

Projects vary in their concept of what is the curriculum. Some see the curriculum as a book for the students. Some see the curriculum as clusters of student materials with a multimedia approach, including a variety of kinds of materials for all children in all classes. Some see a variety of materials from which the teacher can select for his class. And some see the curriculum as a series of materials from which a program is selected individually for each child.[1] Or, curriculum can be broadly viewed as including everything needed to achieve the curriculum goals—all classroom contacts, and all materials, for student and teacher, and possibly training for the teacher.

Actually, the developmental approach need not include the preparation of materials, but may focus on the teacher—training him to operate differently in the classroom—as does one British project in elementary science. Or it can train the teacher in the discipline with the expectation that he will be able to develop his own materials, or use existing materials differently than was possible earlier, an approach used by some of the JCEE-DEEP school systems.

Generally, new developmental projects have not initially recognized the complexity of change. They have not been aware that when one segment or element in a situation is changed, others must also be changed; that a change in student books may require a change in teacher training, in time allotment for the subject, in facilities, in equipment, in extra teacher-preparation time, in different criteria for testing and for grading, and in the curricula that precede, occur concomitantly, and follow the new curriculum. Thus, projects do not necessarily make a single advance decision on exactly what will be their activities in curriculum materials, or even whether they will prepare materials at all.

---

[1]This can be accomplished in a variety of ways, with or without computer-assisted instruction (CAI). The teacher can select materials for the child, as in IPI, based on the child's past performance and interests. The materials can be selected automatically, based on past performance, either through branched programming, where the child is directed to one pathway, or another, based on his speed and performance record. Or the teacher can be instructed to follow a system of presentation based on past performance, with no judgment on the part of the teacher in this assignment.

A project may simply plan to do something to improve a situation in a given discipline, study the situation, and perhaps decide to prepare some kind of student materials. After preparing these materials, it may find that something more is needed, since teachers are not ready to use the materials. The project may then decide to conduct teacher-training sessions. Or it may prepare teacher materials. Or it may supplement or modify student materials with other kinds of materials to facilitate teaching and learning. Or the project may want teachers to develop their own materials and so it may start with teacher training in the subject area. It may then realize that, even after special training, the individual teacher, who is teaching full time in the classroom, has neither the background nor the time to develop classroom materials. This realization may lead the project into materials development, when it had not initially intended to do this.

The BSCS provides an example of a changing view of curriculum and the project's task. The BSCS started with the idea of preparing a series of discrete units. It then turned to preparing combined laboratory-text materials, with accompanying teacher materials and teacher preparation sessions. It then added tests for students, films for teachers (the *techniques films* in biology), films for the students (the *Single Topic Film Series*), materials for those responsible for training teachers, and even materials for administrators who would be introducing materials into their school systems. Some of the JCEE-DEEP school systems started by preparing teachers and subsequently decided to initiate development of classroom materials, as they found that teacher preparation was not enough.

Such emergent series of decisions may not represent a logical way of developing a program, but it may be a necessary reflection of the very nature of the developmental process. By definition, the developmental process is an experimental process, where feedback and experience determine the next steps —and some steps may seem to be backtracking. Hindsight is always easier than foresight, and if one is breaking new ground, not everything works as anticipated, and not all advance steps can be predetermined at the start of the job.

This does not mean that projects could not think through the job to be done more effectively than has sometimes been the case. Some projects have made quite shortsighted mistakes, which could have been avoided, had there been a careful analysis of the situation, the possibilities, and the ramifications before the project initiated its programs. Some projects have not been sufficiently thoughtful, or have not drawn on the experience of other projects.

However, this is not a general rule. There has been careful thought by many projects, even though the direction of such projects may have changed later. This ability to change when such change is indicated is one of the greatest strengths of the developmental movement; and as freedom to shift and to modify is curtailed, the effectiveness of the developmental process is curtailed.

THE ROLE OF THE TEACHER IN IMPLEMENTING
THE CURRICULUM

Projects differ widely on their views of how materials should be taught, how much flexibility should be built into the curriculum, how many choices teachers and students should have, and whether all students should use the same materials. The decisions on these matters can make for basic differences among developmental curricula.

Some developmental curricula provide educational packages, including virtually all of the materials that will be needed for course implementation. This may include text, films, slides, tapes, supplemental readings, teacher materials, equipment and tests. Others provide only some of the major materials, and leave the building of the entire course with the teacher. The latter situation may be intended to provide greater flexibility. But it may also place a great burden on the teacher in terms of locating the other materials needed for implementation. The teacher himself must search out the materials needed and build them into a unified framework. This may prove more time-consuming than is practical, given the teaching loads of most public school teachers today.

Further, there is no assurance that the other materials the teacher locates or selects will be compatible with the intent of the developmental curriculum. For example, where all needed student materials are not provided, the teacher may supplement with materials that are not supportive of the basic course materials, or that may even detract from the overall aims of the developmental curriculum. Where tests are not provided as part of the new curriculum, and standardized tests or teacher-made tests are used to check student achievement, the emphasis in the developmental curriculum may be inquiry, while the emphasis in the tests may be recall of isolated facts. For these reasons, many of the developmental projects have created multifaceted educational packages for implementation of their curricula.

The ways in which such curriculum packages can be used vary widely. At one extreme, the curriculum provides a model, rather than a definite operational pattern and materials to be used time and again. Or the material can permit use in a variety of ways—for an expository or an inquiry approach. At the other extreme, the approach and materials may be completely prescribed. Here, there may be one set of materials to be used by all teachers. This involves provision of a complete package, including everything teachers and students need. It includes no options and no alternative routes. It may delimit the teacher role to distribution and collection of materials, with the remainder of the activities rather inflexibly set.

Some curricula involving programmed materials are presented in this way. Such materials are often designated as teacherproof. This is an indication that the teacher cannot influence the learning situation. The term also often carries the implication that the teacher cannot damage the learning potential of the materials. (Simply because the materials are in the form of a teaching program does not mean that they are inflexible. IPI programmed materials, for example, build in flexibility of approach for both teachers and students, and they delineate a new and critical role for the teacher. However, some others do not.)

Some materials which include a complete package, encompassing all the materials needed by the teacher and the student, build numerous options into the package. These may include alternative pathways to the same learning end, supplementary materials, review materials for students who are not progressing well, and activities that may be uniquely suited to some kinds of students or some kinds of schools or classes. In other words, instead of mandating what it considers to be an optimal program, such projects suggest the broad parameters of a program, and provide different alternatives or pathways at various points during the implementation. This presentation of alternatives within the package may reflect a belief that both students and teachers are not always the same; that learning progresses best when the materials are suited to a given situation; and that the existence of choices for students and teachers is desirable, and provides a more favorable attitude toward the materials.

The inflexible program may not represent a deliberate rejection of these ideas. Rather, such a program may reflect the difficulties encountered in using other approaches to effect change in a short period of time. Thus, an inflexible approach is sometimes used when the teachers lack subject-matter preparation needed to teach a new subject, or a subject with a new emphasis. It may be used when the teachers lack the training in the specialized teaching techniques appropriate for the developmental materials. Or it may be used when the project simply does not trust teachers, when the project feels that the teachers cannot do justice to the materials.

The lack of teacher familiarity with new, specialized subject matter, or with new teaching techniques, constitutes a very real threat to appropriate implementation of materials. Despite the best of intentions, a teacher cannot teach well when he is not familiar with the subject matter. A teacher who has been directive in his teaching often will not know how to shift to an inquiry approach. A teacher who has presented most of his material by lecture and direct questioning will have difficulty encouraging students to seek out their own information, and to develop their own generalizations.

While the desire of a teacher to change from his customary teaching techniques to other techniques may be a necessary condition for such change, it is not a sufficient condition to permit such change to take place. The teacher must also know how to change. Thus, the teacher, when occupying his traditional role in the teaching/learning situation, constitutes a critical factor in effecting change.

One way of handling the problem is to bypass the teacher, thereby removing him as a critical variable. Such an approach was used in one situation where the teachers generally lacked the sophistication in subject matter to permit them to teach the course. At the same time that long-range efforts were being made to improve the teachers' subject-matter background, the students were provided with a course consisting of a series of filmed lectures. For some thirty or forty minutes a day, the students heard a lecture by a specialist, presented on film. By and large, the role of the classroom teacher was to turn the closed-circuit television set on and off.

The justification for this medium of presentation was the concern of the project and school system that the subject area be presented to students in the interim years while the teachers were receiving more specialized preparation. The fact that the filmed presentation was restricted to the knowledge level of the cognitive domain, and that the presentation might be boring to the students, or not fully understood by them, was apparently of less concern to the project and the school system than was the fact that the subject was being taught.

Another kind of approach is to program the role of the teacher so that his performance is compatible with the general approach of the developmental curriculum. This method is used by the BSCS in its *Invitations to Inquiry* and *Single Topic Film Series.* In both of these series of materials, the teacher and students are guided through a programmed discussion. The invitations and the film series both provide basic information to be presented to the students, in one instance, by the teacher, in the other, by the film and the teacher. At certain points in the presentation, there is teacher intervention with specified questions, which are provided for his use. The teacher is also provided with prototypes of the kinds of answers he may receive, and with suggested ways of handling these answers so that he does not cut off discussion or discourage inquiry. IME and IMB also use this programmed discussion approach.

For BSCS as well as IME and IMB, the intent is to enhance the teacher's ability to conduct a discussion. The guidance that is given by the programmed approach is intended as a temporary crutch, to enhance the teacher's ability to lead group discussion, rather than as a permanent delimitation of the teacher's role. And in BSCS, use of the programmed material is entirely optional. Thus, in the long run, the intent is to free the teacher, rather than to delimit his freedom.

This type of programming of the teacher, even when it is intended to be supportive and short-term, is not universally accepted as desirable. For example, in the social studies materials being developed for twelfth grade in the *World History through Inquiry* Project (Massialas and Zevin, 1969), the authors provide suggestive questions for the teacher, but nothing in the way of possible sample answers. This is the case even in areas where the teachers may have no more initial preparation than the students; for example, in historiography and in archeological interpretation.

The authors initially explain to the teacher the nature of inquiry in the social studies. And for each unit, they provide some appropriate questions to be asked. But they do not provide the teacher with information on what kinds of answers are likely to be volunteered by students, which answers should be encouraged, which are incorrect, and what further questions might be asked to elicit a different kind of response or a different focus. And they do not advise the teacher how the students are to arrive at reasonable answers. This is by deliberate intent. The authors want to give the teachers freedom. They want to encourage discussion. They do not want to provide a set of right answers.

Noteworthy as this intent may be, for some teachers, the materials may seem extremely difficult to teach. And some teachers may not be able to realize the full potential of the materials, since they may not know what general ideas should be brought out. While the project's special training session for teachers may be useful to the teachers in this regard, it may not be sufficient to permit optimal utilization of the materials.

A third approach to the problem of the teachers' lack of familiarity with materials and methods is for projects to focus first on teacher preparation, to prepare the potential users before they start to teach the developmental materials. This has been done by a number of projects. But it usually provides only a partial answer. This approach very clearly delimits the potential market for the materials, and so may preclude widespread use once the curriculum becomes generally available.

Perhaps the most desirable approach is a combination of several techniques. For some materials, programming of some sort may be necessary. Special teacher orientation seems indicated for many of the new programs. And special teacher materials may be useful to assist the teacher in terms of subject matter he will need, techniques in teaching, questions he may be asked, and difficulties he may face.

This view is an important contrast to the approach taken by some enthusiasts that programming is an efficient method of studying school materials, and that the schools of the future will depend in large part on programmed materials, with the student and his program largely independent of the teacher/student relationship as we know it today. While for some advocates of programming, this is a question of how learning proceeds most efficiently, for their critics, the question involves the basic purpose of the schools and what is to be taught. There is evidence that programming is an effective way of presenting knowledge. There is less evidence that it is effective for implementing other educational objectives.

DEGREE OF ACCEPTANCE OF EXISTING STRUCTURE AND MEDIA

Some projects want to develop new approaches within present frameworks; some want to break new ground, and they reject many or almost all previous frameworks. Some start within the present framework and find they must develop new approaches going beyond existing frameworks. In part, the decision of whether to stay within an existing framework is influenced by a time factor. It is generally easier to effect rapid change within the existing framework than in a new or radically modified framework. However, some goals cannot be achieved fully, or even in major part, within an existing framework.

Generally speaking, PSSC and CHEM Study stayed within existing framework and media; they used laboratory manuals and text to present physics and chemistry at the eleventh grade level, where these subjects had previously been taught. The BSCS deliberately decided to stay within the existing grade level and ability level framework. It accepted the tenth grade level placement of biology and the existing audience for biology, including most average and above-average tenth graders. It accepted use of written materials, with both laboratory and text presentation (though changing the relation of these by increasing the emphasis on laboratory, and making it complementary rather than supplementary to text). It accepted the teacher's existing role as directing activities, though shifting the emphasis from the teacher as a monitor and strong leader to a leader of inquiry. And it accepted much of the existing laboratory situation and time allotments.

Yet, after working within this framework, it found itself forced to break new ground in a number of ways, an example is its *Single Topic Film Series*. This program is a series of brief (4 minute) silent, 8mm. film loops, intended to bring into the classroom materials that could not be presented through text or laboratory, while retaining an inquiry-oriented approach. This was not to be an information-giving series, but rather a series in which the students used an inquiry approach to develop new concepts.

This effort was started in 1962, but the first films were not released until 1966 or 1967, and the series took some seven years to complete, compared with the three years required to prepare the basic course materials—the laboratory manual, texts, and teacher guides—for three one-year courses. While problems of financing hampered the project, the more important factor in the time required for the film series was the problem of developing a new kind of format that would be appropriate to the task. Once the first two films were completed, the remaining films followed without too much difficulty. But developing the appropriate format was a difficult, time-consuming, trial-and-error task.

In contrast to the CHEM Study and BSCS approaches, from the start, IPI focused largely on new formats, new subject matter, new methods of presentation, new environmental requirements, new time allotments, and new teacher and supervisory roles. This gave it a freedom from many of the constraints operating on other projects. It permitted a greater flexibility of approach. However, it also made the job of effecting change more difficult. The more radical the change in grade level placement, in manner of presentation, and in facilities and arrangements needed, the more difficult it is to bring about actual change in schools, to produce a product that is acceptable and will be accepted.

Work in completely new areas, requiring new arrangements and new formats, is bound to be slower than work which accepts more of the existing structure of schools and materials, and probably, it is more expensive in personnel and other resources. The potential difficulties involved in breaking new ground are not always recognized when a project is undertaken. Certainly, the BSCS had no idea of the complexity of the task involved in successful implementation of the *Single Topic Film Series,* and the initial time schedule, which anticipated the completion of several films in a year, was revised time and again.

When faced with this unexpected difficulty on entirely new ventures, some projects modify their initial plans, even to the point of compromising the outcome in terms of verbalized aims; some modify less drastically; and some abandon the venture. Doubtless, ventures that are dead-end should be abandoned. But perhaps some have been abandoned or compromised too soon, because of the unrealistic, initial expectations of the developers and the funders. Again, this involves the experimental nature basic to developmental work, and the unavoidable fact that the more different the idea is from current practice, the more difficult it is to predict success, ways of achieving success, and the time and resources needed to achieve success.

TARGET AUDIENCE

The target audience of materials has several facets. The most obvious is the student for whom the materials are intended. But the target audience also includes kinds of schools and teachers.

Some projects are concerned with a single grade level, some with a sequence of grade levels, and some with several grade levels, not necessarily in a sequence. For example, the BSCS has been concerned with biology for the tenth and twelfth grade, and is presently concerned with eighth grade biology, but it has not become involved in the work of the intervening years; in contrast, the AAAS project has been concerned with a sequence of years. Some DEEP school systems have worked with three or four discrete grade levels within the school system, while others have been concerned with a coordinated and sequential kindergarten through twelfth grade (K-12) approach.

Some projects have been concerned with all students at a grade level, regardless of ability level; others have focused on a given ability grouping at the grade level. Thus, materials for a given grade may be directed to the average student, the average and above-average student, the above-average student only, or the lower-ability student only. Materials may be directed to a given socioeconomic or geographic sector of the population, e.g., the disadvantaged student,[2] the urban student, or the students of a given geographic area. Thus, there may be an English, reading, or sociology course for the city dweller or for the inner city, a socioeconomics course for students in Atlanta and the surrounding county, or an ecology course for students of the school systems having access to a specific arboretum west of Philadelphia. Or, there may be a combination of ability level and socioeconomic-geographic direction to the materials. Thus, the materials may be directed for the slow reader of inner city New York.

The target audience may also be described in terms of prerequisites, future direction, or interests of students. For example, PSNS is Physical Science for Nonscience students in college. High school science courses may be for the college-bound student or for the noncollege-bound student. They may assume some background preparation in mathematics or other science, or no previous background. They may be for students not planning further science courses, thus constituting terminal courses; or they may be for students who will probably take further courses. They may be aimed at students in a given curriculum, such as industrial arts, or with specific professional inclinations,

---

[2] A wide variety of terms is used in literature to refer to the culturally disadvantaged, including *slow learner, culturally deprived, inner city child,* etc. At different times, different terms become popular, but generally speaking they are synonymous.

such as medical technology or engineering careers.[3] Such expectations limit the target audience.

The project may limit its target audience in terms of certain kinds of schools, or it may intend its product to be appropriate for most schools in the United States today. The materials may be only for schools that have certain subject sequencing, or certain kinds of scheduling, facilities or teaching and space arrangements, or the implementation may be enhanced by certain facilities or arrangements.[4] Some curricula in science, social science, or language may require laboratories and/or field work. Some require longer class periods, or more frequent periods than are scheduled in some schools; for example, a thirty-five minute class period may be inappropriate for some curricula. Some need special library facilities, computers, or specialized language, audiovisual, or playback facilities. Some are more appropriate for situations with team teaching, double periods, or facilities for individualized study.

Some materials imply a well-trained teacher in the subject area, while others are directed to any teacher. And some require no teacher, or use the teacher merely as a distributor of materials, while the curriculum carries itself or is teacherproof.[5] Most take a middle role, with some background on the part of the teacher assumed and requisite to the implementation of the materials, but the amount of teacher background required may vary considerably. For example, in the social studies, materials may be produced for teachers, most of whom have had no previous, specific training in the specialized area of the discipline under consideration, such as demography, sociology, or anthropology. Some assume training concurrent with the introduction of the materials. And some have as a prerequisite considerable teacher sophistication in the subject area.

Materials prepared for the elementary grades generally require less teacher background than do high school materials. Thus, elementary science materials may imply only the inservice training course offered with the introduction of materials, or only a teacher manual, where a high school science course—BSCS, CBA, CHEM Study, or PSSC—while enhanced by a special orientation, requires that the teacher have far more background in the specific science, such as a college major or field of specialization. Junior high school

---

[3]Particularly in the large cities, students may elect or be assigned to specific, specialized curricula, often reflecting academic success or socioeconomic background, or they may be in specialized high schools—such as science, arts, or technical—and special courses have often been designed for this very selected audience.

[4]For example, BSCS Bulletin No. 3, *BSCS Biology—Implementation in the Schools* (A. Grobman *et al.,* 1964) indicated the facets of school situations most conducive to effective use of BSCS versions, in terms of teaching arrangements, facilities and administrative arrangements.

[5]Probably no materials are entirely teacherproof, even if the role of the teacher is limited to distributing the materials and collecting completed work. However, some materials minimize the role of the teacher to a major extent, so that the target population is not highly delimited by the type of teacher or his background.

materials may take a middle course; IME and IMB, for example, have had brief training sessions (two days), extensive teacher handbooks, and require little specialized background in one of the sciences, since junior high school science teachers today tend to teach all areas of science rather than specializing in only one.

The designation of the target audience in terms of pupils, teachers, and schools in many instances represents a compromise. Some studies want to do everything at once, want to hit all possible audiences with the same curriculum, since they feel their subject and goals are imperative and of value to all. This commitment to the value of the goals may blind the project to the realities of schools, teachers, and students; and when this omission is indicated, the project may produce quite unrealistic materials.

Others modify the target audience or the materials as experience indicates. For example, one project that did not analyze the target audience of teachers in advance started with materials that required considerable teacher sophistication; when initial expectations were not met, it turned to the preparation of teacherproof materials, materials in which the teacher had a minimum role and minimum choices. Thus, the target audience remained a broad one, and the materials were changed when the initial materials were found unsuitable for this audience.

Other studies start with an appraisal of the potential audience and deliberately limit themselves to this. For example, the BSCS was criticized initially on its versions because they were oriented to the average student, who might not be taking other science courses in high school and, even if he were going to college, might not be enrolling in science courses there. The initial aim did not include college preparation, preparation for advanced high school science courses, or specific courses for the gifted student at a time when there was a high level of concern for the gifted in science. The materials also were not directed to the low-ability student. (A separate program was prepared for such students at a later date.) While some evaluation studies did indicate the suitability of the materials for college preparation and for the gifted, this was a by-product rather than a primary direction for these particular materials.

The BSCS courses were designed for use by biology teachers, not by anyone who happened to be teaching a course in biology; that is, it was anticipated that teachers using the materials would have had college preparation and certification to teach biology. It was not assumed that all teachers would have extensive special preparation to teach BSCS biology, even though such preparation was recommended. It was not assumed that all teachers would be current on all new developments in biology. It was also not assumed that they would all have had experience with the inquiry method of teaching. It was assumed that there would be some access to laboratories, and that laboratories would have at least a basic minimum of facilities, including electric outlets, gas, running water, microscopes, and glassware. These were some of the constraints the BSCS set for itself.

In contrast, the IMB materials do not assume that the teacher has had a broad background in biology; also it is recognized that many teachers will have only brief special orientation, rather than the summer or year-long courses available to prepare teachers in many of the other new science curricula. The IMB materials are intended for a broad spectrum of students, including slow students. And successful implementation is not dependent on accessibility of elaborate laboratory facilities. The course assumes little in the way of prerequisite student skills or knowledge.

PSNS is similar to IMB in its lack of dependence on prerequisite student skills and interest, and its suitability in circumstances where laboratory facilities are minimal. For these projects, the constraints in terms of target audience are deliberate, and directly reflect the aims of the project.

The nature of the target audience must affect the nature of the curricula developed if the curricula are to be used successfully. Yet, not all developmental projects clearly specify the target audience in advance. Even after the curriculum is developed, many cannot describe what an appropriate audience is.

Some projects develop materials and then try them out to see where they work, sometimes at considerable discomfort to the student groups involved in the tryouts. For example, in one developmental project, there was a tacit assumption that the experimental materials would be appropriate for anyone at the grade level where it was being offered, and this included all students at that grade level, since the course was part of the required social studies sequence. It turned out that the high reading level of the materials resulted in a situation in which only students above the grade level in reading could cope with the materials, and where the kind of presentation in terms of examples used was neither interesting nor meaningful to a large proportion of the students in the tryout program.[6]

---

[6]Unfortunately, when experimental materials are being tried out in the first feasibility tests, many projects use rather large groups for the first tryouts, and many fail to make advance provision for halting or changing the experiment when initial feedback indicates that the materials either are not producing the expected result, or are actually detrimental to the classroom learning situation. In some cases, the experiment is difficult to stop, or no one even considers stopping it because no alternative arrangements are available, no other books or materials can be substituted, and the teacher has to have some materials to use with the class for the rest of the year.

Further, after the research experiment is designed, some feel that it should be carried out as designed, and the grant funds may imply an obligation to do this. *Thus, the research design or the grant requirements may be considered more important than the children involved.*

In the instance cited above, the experiment was carried out far longer than was desirable. And students who were already alienated from school and from society at the start of the course were exposed for months to additional experiences likely to cause further alienation, despite recognition fairly early in the experiment that the materials were patently unsuitable.

Some projects never do determine the precise parameters of the audience that can use the materials, since the samples on which the materials are tried out are never precisely described, either in advance or after the tryout. Thus, the target audience is a vague one, defined only in the most general terms.

Developmental projects may accept the existing situation as the circumstances for their curriculum, and build materials accordingly, materials that fit into the preexisting situation without modification of that situation. Or they may aim at an optimal situation and require it for their use. Or they may take a middle ground, where certain minimums are present—some teacher preparation, some laboratory facilities, some limits on class size, and the materials are usable in this situation. But such projects may also encourage the enhancement of this situation, if optimal advantages are to be garnered from use of the materials.

Thus, a course may require a sophisticated laboratory or it may require only a minimum laboratory, but stimulate improvement of the laboratory facilities, of teacher background, or of time allotted to the course. A course can be designed for the time allotment customarily given in the schools—often one period daily for high schools—at the same time that it encourages adding one or more double periods a week. It may require little more than running water and a sink for laboratory equipment at the same time that it encourages improvement of the laboratory.

The availability of federal funds for school equipment has made it possible for projects to require more in the way of equipment, particularly in science and foreign languages, than would have been practical a decade ago. For example, when BSCS materials were used in Baltimore city schools in 1960-61, all BSCS teachers obtained refrigerators by the end of the experimental year; none of them had refrigerators at the start of the year. Clearly, this equipment was needed; it had not been seen by the supervisors or principals as essential earlier; and funds could be made available. In the 1950's, funds for such purposes were far more limited.[7]

The target population is highly local (a city, county, local region) for some materials, and broader (state, region, or nation) for others. For some projects, the potential audience is international. Thus, anthropology materials building on the Atlanta and Macon County history and resources may be intended for local consumption, and would be inappropriate elsewhere; an economics unit

---

[7]One facet of the evaluation of the science programs might be the extent to which science laboratories have become more prevalent in schools adopting the program, or the increase in time allotted to the teaching of the subject. Here, one face of the coin is the improvement of the circumstances for teaching a science; the other is how the money would have been spent otherwise, and at what cost the additional time was achieved—that is, what would have been taught if the extra time had not been allotted to science?

built on local economic activities of the Minneapolis area would be inappropriate elsewhere, and is not intended for use elsewhere. However, many of the
projects have taken the entire United States as the target audience, and some
have even gone beyond this.

Thus, the BSCS intends its materials for students in the United States—
from Alaska and Hawaii to Florida and Maine—despite the disparities in flora
and fauna and ecosystems within the United States and its possessions. But it
considers its materials appropriate only within the American culture,[8] and
does not give permission for direct translation of its materials into other
languages. While the BSCS gives permission for adaptations to overseas countries and offers assistance to such countries with technical advice, it does not
authorize direct translations. The rationale is that biology is closely tied to
local educational systems, environments, and cultures, and that to be effective,
a biology course must build on the experience of the student and on the
subtleties of his surroundings. And so, students in Taiwan, Brazil, or Israel
should be using the local ecological situation for the study of basic biological
theories and concepts, not the flora and fauna of the United States.

According to the BSCS, animal specimens discussed should be those that
are indigenous to the country, not those in an imported book. In requiring
adaptation rather than permitting translation, the BSCS is trying to avoid the
situation reported by a visitor to Hong Kong, where students in a biology class
were following the laboratory directions in a British book for the dissection
of an earthworm, as preparation for the British University examinations; but
the students were dissecting local earthworms. The students' laboratory reports describing their dissections conformed with the information in the
laboratory manual, even though the earthworms they were dissecting did not.

The BSCS adaptation policy also reflects a recognition that national
mores vary. In India, discussion of evolution or of genetic differences among
races presents little problem; dissection of animals does.

However, the BSCS has not entirely resolved the problem of the ecological
diversity within the United States. Thus, the Philippine adaptation of BSCS
biology may be more appropriate ecologically to some of the U.S. possessions
in the Pacific and to Hawaii than are the U.S. editions currently used there
and in U.S. overseas armed services schools and private schools for Americans
throughout the world.[9] Here, students are studying the book, not studying

---

[8]It does include Canada as part of the American culture, and both the regular English
language edition and a French translation are used in Canada.
[9]The OE and NSF copyright regulations specifically indicate that the U.S. government may
use materials as they see fit. Thus, no project using public funds for materials preparation may
limit the use of its materials in schools operated by the U.S. government—for example, schools
operated by the armed services and schools in the Virgin Islands and the Pacific territories.

nature. And here, too, the BSCS has not been able to solve the problem of appropriate materials for all situations.

In contrast, some other developmental projects consider their materials suitable for broad use, and authorize translations. Thus, SMSG and PSSC materials are available in a number of languages at present, in direct translations from English.

The question of whether to permit direct translation is not just one of content, but also of philosophy. Some content is more directly tied in with a culture or geographic area. However, there is also a feeling by some that American materials, even when relatively appropriate, are not as functional as is the case when there is a deep local involvement in the adaptation of materials. Thus, when the Philippine people, on their own initiative, undertook an adaptation of BSCS materials—an adaptation in English—and prepared one that was truly Philippine, the commitment was greater, the pride in local achievement was quite deep, and the effort had an important ripple effect. The initial adaptation and teacher-training effort led directly to the development of the Science Education Center at the University of the Philippines, to work on all science curricula for Philippine schools.

This kind of broader effect would be far less likely from a superficial local involvement in adoption of foreign materials, or even in translation of foreign materials and the importation of teacher-training techniques to accompany the translated edition. This is another of the instances in developmental work where the more expensive and time-consuming technique may bring a different type of concomitant outcome in terms of long-run adoption and use.

The project decision on target audience, and the extent to which the project's curriculum will fit into an existing situation or will require major school change, not only may restrict the magnitude of the potential audience for project materials, but it may also place a constraint on the possible effectiveness of the materials produced. For example, geography is now not taught as a full-year course in most secondary schools. To prepare a one-semester or one-year course would delimit the potential audience. To prepare series of units which could be combined into one-semester or year courses permits use in far more situations. It automatically increases the target audience without requiring major changes in school schedules. From the practical viewpoint of increasing the amount of geography taught, this clearly makes sense. More schools will use some geography materials if such materials can be fitted into the existing curriculum, rather than requiring a major revision in time schedules, with the allocation of a semester or full year to geography.

However, to prepare independent units rather than a sequential course means that one unit cannot build on another. If there are any skills essential to all geography, each unit must teach these, assuming no prerequisite knowledge. Thus, there will inevitably be repetition. Further, no unit can build on the previous learning of other units. This not only limits the degree of sophistication of the presentation, so that later units cannot be more sophisticated than earlier ones, but it also sacrifices the repetition of a skill or an idea, or reference to a skill or an idea in several different contexts, a practice which is conducive to later recall and ability to use the learning in out-of-course situations.

Clearly, the situation is one that calls for a compromise. Either one must forego a large part of the potential market and the potential influence on the curriculum, or one must sacrifice some sophistication and effectiveness in presentation. High School Geography Project (HSGP) chose to develop discrete units. SRSS has also undertaken the preparation of discrete units (two-week episodes) as its first task in materials preparation, a deliberate decision, reflecting the fact that sociology is generally not taught as a separate semester or year course in secondary schools.

In contrast, the BSCS tried to use discrete units for its second level BSCS biology, the second course biology, often taught at the twelfth grade. Initially, an attempt was made to use four BSCS laboratory blocks—six-week, laboratory-oriented units, each centering around a major area in biology, and intended originally as supplementary materials for the tenth grade biology course—as a year-long course. This was not satisfactory, since there was inadequate continuity. Next, an effort was made to build connecting materials, linking the laboratory blocks. This, too, was unsatisfactory because of unnecessary repetition, lack of increasing sophistication from one block to another, and failure to integrate earlier learnings into later activities. As a result, a complete restructuring of the materials was undertaken, maintaining the emphasis on laboratory but building sequentially. The new second course did not replace the blocks; rather it served a different purpose.

Some decisions delimiting the target audience should be made early in the developmental work so the writers can have a general direction. The more precise parameters can emerge as materials are tested experimentally. There is no ideal set of parameters. None is optimal. The setting of parameters depends on the wishes of the project, on the role it sets out to fill, and on the needs of educational systems. There are some parameters that are unreasonable. There are some subjects that are inappropriate for a given grade level or sequence.

Once the appropriateness of the parameters in terms of grade or maturity level is accepted, it is not necessarily better to aim at all children, or at a given locale, or a given ability level. However, the project should be aware of what it intends to do in terms of its potential audience, analyze this audience, and try to work in these terms, rather than prepare materials and then see if an appropriate audience can be located. Too many children can be harmed and too much effort expended in this scattershot approach. When additional audiences are added to the initial target population, this should be done following a careful analysis of the population and the probability of success. Initial use of the materials with these additional groups should be cautious and on a small scale.

PREPARATION OF MATERIALS

In materials preparation, some of the major decisions are those relevant to: duration of writing effort; location of writing effort; staff—how many and what kinds of people; allocation of responsibility—who makes the ultimate decisions, who reports to whom, how assignments are made and who reviews what; work methods—whether writers work alone, in pairs, or in teams; and mechanisms for quality control.

For some projects, materials preparation is an ongoing task, either with or without firm, rather short-term deadlines. For others, it is a short, one- or two-month effort. Many projects have relatively firm deadlines for all materials, and some have firm deadlines for just course materials. Thus, while it may be necessary to have the materials representing a semester or year-long course ready for school use by mid-August of the year in which they are to be tried in schools, for single supplemental units or for films to supplement a course, there may be no real reason for a firm deadline.

Where there are no firm deadlines, materials preparation may be an open-ended task. Whenever materials are completed in draft form, they are tested, but they do not have to be completed for a given target date. While the open-ended approach has the advantages of a more leisurely pace which permits thorough checking of details, completion of all desired tasks, and polishing the materials as they are being prepared, some projects working in this way seem to go on forever, taking far more time than the end product warrants. Thus, perhaps some time limit may be helpful in imposing a kind of self-discipline on the project.

For projects preparing materials as an ongoing activity, writing may be done by regular staff, by special consultants, or by persons hired specifically for this purpose on temporary appointments. It may be done as a part-time or full-time assignment. However, many projects have used a new technique —the writing conference—in an intensive, relatively short-term writing effort. In the writing conference, a group of people—generally more than would be coauthors of a single text—are brought together for an intensive session in which materials are prepared.

Writing Conferences[10]

Many projects have used a writing conference as a technique for materials preparation. This involves bringing together a variety of people at one site for a specified period of time—often part or all of a summer—to work as a team on materials preparation. While the summer writing conference technique was not a developmental project invention, the technique had not been widely used earlier.

Writing conferences are an expensive way of preparing materials, and it is possible to produce developmental materials that have a single author or two or three coauthors; and such authors need not be at the location of the project or at the same location as the other authors. It is obviously far cheaper to have an individual author prepare materials, either at home or in the project office. If more than one author is desired, then coauthors living in the same location can work together, or those not living near each other can correspond.

Thousands of textbooks have been prepared by single or joint authorship without writing conferences. Why spend large sums of money to bring relatively large numbers of authors together in one place? Geographic distance does clearly influence the process, the opportunity for quality control, and the product. Thus, before making plans for production of materials, a developmental project should consider whether a cooperative effort is desirable, the extent and timing of quality control that is desirable, and whether this is feasible, if the authors are in scattered locations or if they are not in the same location as the headquarters staff.

The advocates of writing conferences point to several unique advantages of this·method. Writing conferences permit a greater variety of skills to be brought to bear on the task. The interaction among people of different backgrounds and specialties brings a richer, better product than can be produced by one or two individuals collaborating in the traditional manner of authorship. Perhaps most important, the continuous feedback pattern possible among writing conference participants makes for a better product. If these are the unique advantages of a writing conference, it seems logical that a major consideration in decisions concerning suchconferencesshould be the extent to which the decision will enhance or preclude the possibility that the potential benefits of the writing conference will be realized.

Simply that the writers are in one place does not mean that there will be continuous feedback, or that the advantages of bringing together people with

---

[10]Though the following section is directed to writing conferences, many of the remarks—such as those on personnel and procedure—are germane to other techniques for materials preparation.

varied backgrounds will be realized. For example, at one writing conference, writers were assigned to work in pairs, in different parts of a large room adjacent to the director's office. During more than a month of writing time, there was no discussion of the work among members of various pairs or between writers and the director. The norm was that coffee-break and lunchtime discussions were not work-related, and nothing was done to discourage or change this norm. Thus, physical proximity may be a necessary but not sufficient requisite for adequate communication. Physical proximity can also encourage and sustain a high level of enthusiasm in the writers. But mere proximity does not guarantee high morale or frequent communication.

Duration. The duration of the writing conferences varies. Often, the writing conferences are held during the summer, when academic personnel from schools and colleges are available; and the sessions may last all summer, one month, or just two weeks. Some groups have used a one-semester or two-semester period during the school year, when they have felt that the summer was not long enough, or did not give enough time to meet the printing deadlines on which school tryout of materials the following year was contingent.[11]

While the time required for preparing shorter materials naturally is less than needed for a year-long course, two weeks may be too short a period, even for some very limited purposes. It may take a full week for the writers to become oriented to their task, to get to know their coauthors, and to establish and become accustomed to a *modus operandi.* However, where people have been working together on prior assignments, and considerable work is done in advance of the writing conference, a two-week period may be appropriate.

When experimental editions and the commercial edition of the BSCS second course materials (for a year-long course to follow ninth or tenth grade biology) were prepared, the writing conferences lasted from six to eight weeks during the summer. But, writing of the first 1968 revision of the commercial edition was completed in a two-week session. In the latter case, all participants had worked on these materials earlier; all were familiar with the developmental process and with writing sessions, since all had previously participated in such sessions; all had been involved in extensive planning prior to the intensive

---

[11]If the experimental materials are to be tested in schools in successive years, a winter session to rewrite preliminary materials before they are retested the following year means that the rewriting is concurrent with the school tryout, and so, feedback from this tryout is not available during much of the time that the rewriting is being done. If the writing is scheduled for spring semester, only the first semester feedback would be available for the second semester writing effort. Thus, if preliminary materials for a year-long course are tried out in schools from September, 1969 to June, 1970, a writing conference prior to June would not permit use of all the year's feedback. To postpone writing to the 1970–71 school year would mean a one-year hiatus in classroom tryouts. Thus, many projects schedule rewriting for an interim period during the summer and publish materials late in August for September trials in the schools.

two-week writing period; and the revisions planned were relatively minor. Similarly, writing conferences for preparing a series of tests, for some supplemental materials, or for preparing films might also be of relatively short duration. However, for the preparation of highly experimental materials, for more extensive materials, or for more extensive revisions, a longer period would seem warranted.

Yet, some writing sessions may be too long. For some of the longer conferences, the product does not appear to justify the extra time spent. The intensity of effort possible for one or two months cannot be maintained for six months. Furthermore, if year-long course materials can be prepared in two months—and sufficient developmental materials of high quality now exist to substantiate the fact that this is possible—why is a longer period warranted?

For some projects overseas, where the difficulty of the task has been increased by budget constraints, and where few background resource materials exist, a longer period may be imperative. The writing conference of the Science Education Center of the University of the Philippines, to adapt the BSCS biology materials for use in the Philippines is a case in point. There were problems not faced when the initial BSCS materials were being developed in the United States. The existing photograph and art collections on which writers could draw were more limited. For materials borrowed from the United States, there was a necessary time lag for the mails. There was less research literature available concerning the indigenous flora and fauna to illustrate the biological principles being discussed. There were difficult problems of adaptation of laboratory equipment, so that equipment required for the course would be compatible with limited budgets of schools; and there were problems of development of laboratory exercises involving less extensive equipment. Thus, the need for a longer writing session was obvious.

However, for some projects in the United States with the six-month or year-long writing sessions, the work seems to expand to fit the time available. This does not mean that writers who work for these longer periods waste time or do not work hard. They do. The question is whether they pass the point of diminishing returns in their revising, polishing, supplementing, and modifying. Often, changes have been made in highly successful materials, when the new version can hardly be justified as an improvement on the old. The new edition changes may be like the changes in automobile models, where the new model must look different from the old one, even if the difference is nonfunctional.

Location. Summer writing conferences are often located on college campuses. There is adequate office space on many campuses during the summer, since college dormitories may be turned into temporary offices. Adequate living space for participants may be found either in the dormitory or by subletting houses of college faculty members who are away for the summer. And the location provides access to a substantial library.

The summer writing conference is not always on the campus where the project has its office, or on the campus nearest the project office. ESSP worked summers in Cape Cod. Boulder, Colorado has been a favorite site, not only for SMSG, which was the first developmental project to use the University of Colorado campus for its writing conference, but for the BSCS, the ESCP, and others. This is not a matter of the uniqueness of campus facilities and services offered by the university, though these have been excellent and are certainly a consideration. The plain fact is that people who are invited to participate in such work during the summer are more likely to accept the invitation when a pleasant, cool environment is offered, than when the work is located in a hot, humid, and uninteresting area. Although participants may enjoy coming to New York or San Francisco even during the summer, writing conferences are generally more expensive to operate in an urban situation.

Personnel. There are many questions concerning selection of personnel. How many people are needed to do the job? Are others needed, not as writers, but for other reasons? For example, it may be well to involve in the writing conference a nucleus of persons who will be holding key positions in the field testing the following year, so they will have a better understanding of the program. Or it may be well to involve some teachers who have already used preliminary materials, who can provide further feedback. How will selection of writers affect acceptability of the product? For example, should schoolteachers or people from the discipline be used? Is it important in terms of the project image to have a wide geographic or institutional representation? What kinds of specialists—academic as well as other—are needed? Is each such specialty needed for the entire period? Can one individual be found who has several of these specialties? What qualifications should participants have? Who should make the selection?

It is difficult to predict in advance how individuals will operate in the writing conference situation when they have not participated in one before. Some people do not work well in teams. Some cannot write at the appropriate grade level, or even in such a manner that their writing can be modified to fit the grade level. Some cannot take the criticism of their work by the other members of the team. However, most people, if they are generally competent in the subject area or in some other needed specialty, can play a useful role, even if this is not in the expected writing assignment. For example, unsuccessful writers may be highly successful in selecting photographs, in working with artists, in developing laboratory exercises, in preliminary tryouts of materials or laboratories, in proofreading, or editing. However, this may leave the writing conference short of people who can write for students.

Thus, until a project has considerable experience with writing conferences, it may be wise to overstaff somewhat, to provide a needed margin of safety. It is far more efficient to have a possible abundance of writers than to risk spoiling a product because of personnel shortages. The writing conference period is often too short to permit obtaining additional expertise during the conference itself, and it is difficult to locate school and college people on short notice during the summer, so that once a staffing shortage is recognized during the writing conference, it may not be possible to remedy.

No specific number of writing conference participants can be recommended as adequate, minimal or optimal. ESSP and IME had writing conferences as small as five or six participants. The BSCS had over sixty writers for its first summer writing conference to prepare three different sets of year-long course materials (or some twenty writers per version), half of them schoolteachers.

The criteria for selection of writers vary from project to project. Some use subject-matter experts only, particularly if the materials are to be used in high school. Others use various mixtures of subject-matter experts and educators. Sometimes, these educators are in college or school supervisory positions; sometimes they are classroom teachers who may or may not be from the grade level and subject area involved.

Some projects use only educators, or only educators currently employed in a school system. Some select teachers with relatively little or no specialized subject-matter training, and provide a course or workshop to give the needed subject-area mastery, and then ask these teachers to prepare materials. (This is more common at the elementary school level, but is not restricted to this level.) Some bring in special kinds of writers with little or no specialized subject-matter background—these might be programmers or film script writers, for example—and provide them with a set of specifications, such as a set of behavioral objectives, and turn the task over to them. And some use such people to supplement rather than replace other kinds of writers.

No single formula for participant selection guarantees success of the materials-preparation effort. However, materials development by persons lacking some sophistication in the subject area has obvious limitations, whether these persons are schoolteachers, professional writers, or others. This does not mean that such people cannot contribute, but rather than the major role should be played by others.

Project experience to date appears to support the hypothesis that to prepare highly creative materials that incorporate not just new subject matter and learning tools, but that are interesting and relevant, and provide genuinely new approaches, requires authors who have overlearned their subject—that is, whose knowledge goes beyond a single college text or course, who are so thoroughly familiar with their discipline and its underlying theories that they can design entirely new approaches to old problems, can illustrate ideas in highly imaginative and meaningful ways, and provide interesting materials compatible with the project aims.

The risk of failure seems far higher for projects using relatively untrained teachers than for those depending in large part on persons with a variety of backgrounds, but highly qualified in the subject area. This does not mean that all scholars will be able to prepare suitable classroom materials or that classroom teachers cannot. There are many classroom teachers and other educators whose subject mastery meets this test, and who have had an essential role in the production of new materials. Furthermore, those projects that have not used classroom teachers in their writing efforts have generally been less successful than those using varying proportions of educators and subject-matter specialists.

One earmark of the early curriculum studies was the involvement of subject-matter specialists and classroom teachers in materials preparation. For the most part, subject-matter specialists had not been active in preparation of school materials in the preceding period. According to many observers, this cooperation was a prerequisite to the success of the projects. Some will counter this statement with the observation that such writing sessions were not genuinely cooperative efforts. Unfortunately, there were undoubtedly some cases where the classroom teachers were not full participants, but were invited as window dressing. However, in other instances, this was patently not the case, as is indicated by the fact that for some successful projects, classroom teachers directed writing teams that included people from the disciplines.

There are some who feel that scholars, without elementary or secondary school experience, cannot contribute effectively to the production of materials for these levels. This has not been the case. While some cannot, others have had noteworthy successes.

There are some who do not favor giving teachers an equal role in the writing effort. They feel that the teacher either has no real contribution to make in materials development (the tacit assumption being that discipline people, perhaps assisted by college of education people, are more competent in this role than are classroom teachers), or that the teacher role comes to the fore during the classroom tryout, but not during the writing of materials. Their point is that the average teacher participant in a writing conference is not able to make a contribution equal to persons from the discipline.

This conclusion is not warranted by the experience of various projects to date. True, in a number of projects, not all of the teachers have been highly productive in the writing sessions. They may not have been given the opportunity. Or such teachers may have been poorly selected. In some instances, the teacher participants have lacked subject-matter background and writing experience. For some projects, the determining factors in selection of teacher participants precluded choice of the best potential participants. For example, in one project, selection was by various school systems, with some making nominations as a reward for past performance, unrelated to the project work. In another situation, the incumbent of a given status role was automatically the nominee, with little consideration of the appropriateness of the incumbent's qualifications for the writing conference assignment.

The problems of locating and involving classroom teachers in materials preparation are somewhat different at the elementary and secondary levels. At the elementary level, it may be more difficult to find a teacher with an adequate background in mathematics, science, or economics; at the high school level, there are more persons with a strong background in a single subject area. However, even at the secondary level, in some of the specialized areas not required for teaching certification—anthropology, historiography, sociology— the problem of locating suitable writing conference participants may be difficult. However, qualified people do exist, and it is worth the extra effort to find them. And the classroom teachers should be a part of the materials-preparation effort, not just the tryout effort, if there is to be early enough feedback on approach and treatment to produce the most appropriate materials.

Auxiliary staff. In addition to the writing conference participants, there must be considerable auxiliary staff, if the time of the writers is to be used efficiently. There should be a surplus of secretaries on the staff, or a group of typists, some of whom are on call at short notice, since, unless materials can be typed and reviewed promptly, valuable time is lost. Particularly where there is a large number of participants, facilities and personnel are needed for duplicating drafts of manuscripts so that all participants can be informed, and feedback from colleagues can be fast enough to be optimally useful. Some groups need a resident art staff. Others have had resident editors and specialists in various learning devices—laboratory-equipment development, films, learning programs, etc. Some have had instant students, a core of students available daily or at short notice to try out segments of the materials.

Some projects operate on a rather spartan basis. They economize on secretarial help, and their writers waste time waiting for public transportation to and from airports, picking up their own mail from central locations, going to a central location to use the telephone, and ordering and picking up their own supplies. This appears to be economical. However, taking into consideration the cost of the writers' time, the limited time available for materials preparation, the demanding nature of the job, and the need to maintain the goodwill of the writers, most of whom do not have the incentive of potential royalties from their product, this is hardly an efficient use of resources.

Advance planning.   Some writing teams wait until the writing session starts to plan what they are going to do and how they will do it. Given the short duration of summer writing conferences, unless there is some advance structure, a large job can hardly be completed in the course of a single summer. One alternative—a method used by ESSP—is to spend one summer planning and the next in execution. A contrasting alternative used by some groups assigns detailed advance planning to one individual or small group, which decides the nature of the materials, their format and structure, and the work assignments, thereby giving the session participants a head start, but also giving them little voice in these matters.

For some writing conferences, only general directions are decided in advance by the project or its director or policy group. Some key people in the writing conference are then brought in before the session; they draft and circulate tentative plans to the participants, so that all participants can give some thought to the plans in advance of the writing session, and the session can open with a group discussion of the tentative plans. This procedure has been used with considerable success by a number of projects, and it permits anyone in complete discord with the method of treatment to determine in advance whether he wants to participate. Further, it permits a more accurate projection of staffing needs for the writing conference.

Several individuals who have worked with groups using this type of structuring have later withdrawn from other projects which have been more arbitrary in their advance planning and in making work assignments. These people give as their reason for withdrawing the feeling that the arbitrary manner of proceeding defeats the very basic purpose and unique advantage of the writing conference—that is, that it is a cooperative venture. They feel that without joint decision making and a chance to participate in discussions of plans, content, format, and approach, the writers could just as easily have carried out their writing assignments at home.

Who makes decisions.   Whether or not the preparation of materials is a team effort, someone has to make final decisions. Someone must accept the ultimate responsibility for the product, someone must make the ultimate decision on what is covered, how it is covered, what type of treatment it will receive, etc. In regular textbook publication, the publisher, in one sense, makes this decision. While the author may seek advice from others, and decide what is submitted for publication, the publisher decides whether he will publish it either as is or will incorporate changes suggested to the author.

With curriculum projects, the question of control of content and treatment is more complex. The project director may or may not be a member of the materials-preparation group. Even if he is one of the writers, he may not be the individual directing the writing task. In other words, although he is the director of the project, he may be filling a writer's role for this one activity, rather than being the leader of the activity.

For some projects, the line of control and decision making *vis-à-vis* materials preparation is rather nebulous. When asked about this, project personnel may reply that things are decided by consensus, and there is no point in further clarifying the power structure until the need arises. In others, a clear power structure is set out in advance. Still other projects take a position between these two extremes, with authority being clarified by common assent —or by fiat— as the project builds experience.

While the formality and rigidity of detailed advance structuring may seem unnecessary and possibly irritating, some clear guidelines concerning responsibility and authority may avoid later friction when materials are vetoed without advance notice that such veto power existed.

In one project, where writers assumed they were preparing the final product, the project director completely revised the writers' final draft. The hostility roused among the authors by what they considered arbitrary action became a major deterrent to successful field testing of the materials the following year. The director had not advised the writers of his veto authority; he had assumed that the materials would require only copy editing, and thought that no statement about veto power was needed. He did not review materials during the preparation period. So, when the final review came, it was not a matter of redirecting the writers or making suggestions, but rather of discarding much of what had been written, and rewriting the materials himself.

Some groups work by consensus of the writers, with problems discussed generally. However, consensus is not necessarily good, and does not necessarily bring the best decision. Not all group members are necessarily equally qualified to make all kinds of decisions. Consensus can entail considerable waste of writing time on discussion of minutiae. And it does not offer guidance on which questions are to be discussed, and who is to make decisions when all the writers are not around.

In some projects, the most influential person in shaping the final product is the one who sees the materials last, before they go to the printer. This is not necessarily the person who has been assigned ultimate responsibility, but may represent a matter of procedural convenience. Thus, the person who makes the final changes, the relocation of pictures, the last editing, etc., may inadvertently have a key role in making decisions that would not otherwise fall to him.

Not only does assignment of responsibility for the product vary among projects, but it also varies within the project, for different sets of materials, for different kinds of decisions, and at different times. The BSCS provides an example of such variation. The number of writing conferences to be held, the number of experimental tryouts of a given set of materials, the timing of release, and the selection of publishers were in the hands of the Steering Committee (the policy board), the Executive Committee, and the sponsoring organization. Content and general format were the prerogatives of the members of a given writing team, with the supervisor of that writing team as the final arbiter, under policy guides set down by the Steering Committee.

Some BSCS project supervisors consulted with more people than others. Some worked particularly closely with one or two writers. Some consulted frequently with the entire writing team. When the writing teams were large, consultation was undoubtedly less frequent than with the smaller writing teams for the commercial editions.

Certainly, if any product had been completely inadequate, the BSCS Executive Committee or Steering Committee could have prevented its release, a situation that never arose. In practice, most writing conference products were not critically read in their totality prior to publication by anyone not on the writing team. This was not a deliberate omission or an announced policy, but reflected the tremendous time pressure under which the activity was carried out, the work load of the rest of the staff, and the great confidence of the Executive Committee and director in the supervisors and in the writing conference process.

Feedback. Closely coupled with the question of authority for decision making is the matter of timing of materials' review for quality control purposes, as well as to obtain maximum benefit from the opportunity for frequent interaction among writers on the product as it is developed. For some projects, the feedback process is frequent and routinized. For example, in one large project, everything typed by the writing conference secretaries went directly onto a duplicating stencil, so that copies were automatically provided for all other writers. Also, weekly meetings of writing teams were held to discuss what had been produced during the week. Even where the review mechanism is not this routinized, many projects have a norm of day-to-day interchange of ideas; this process is enhanced in those instances where staff members eat together, even if only at lunch.

At the other extreme are two projects where there was no review of the work of any writer, either by other writers or by the product director, until the writing was completed. In both instances, the director regular staff did a complete rewriting job. This procedure involved an unnecessary waste of time, since the writers kept working on materials that were later considered unsatisfactory, when an earlier intervention might have put them on a different track. The writers were alienated by this rejection, probably more so than if they had been forewarned or criticized and directed toward a different track earlier. The materials deadline was not met because so much rewriting was required. And the materials were, in effect, a one-man job, with all the limitations of a one-man job, even when the one man was highly competent. In neither case was there a genuine team effort.

While physical proximity of writers and project staff does not guarantee frequent quality control interventions, the potential for such interaction is far better than in those situations where the writers are spread over a wide geographic area. The BSCS, for its laboratory blocks, used individual authors or coauthors who did their writing at their home institutions and sent in materials, upon completion, to the center for the block program. Although writers did attend meetings and were visited by project staff members, in the opinion of a number of people who have read and used various blocks, these materials show more variation in terms of the degree to which they reflect BSCS general aims than do BSCS materials which were produced at writing conferences. Furthermore, it was doubtless far more difficult to effect major changes in the initial direction of the materials than was the case with other materials prepared at an assembled writing conference.

The same observation is relevant for the JCEE economics materials. Here, the quality range is even greater. Although here, too, there were some assembled annual meetings, some staff visits with writers, and some review of manuscripts by JCEE and other economists, in many instances, the quality control intervention was too late to permit production of quality materials which would validly reflect project aims.

Some projects encourage full communication in their writing efforts. Others either consciously or inadvertently discourage them. UICSM director, Max Beberman, comments that "full" communication tends to limit creativity and wastes time. However, there are usually at least two writers on a UICSM activity and they work closely. The various UICSM activities are semi-independent projects rather than a single project. The people involved are competent. When they want help or reactions, they are free to ask. And the rest of the time, they are left pretty much alone. Although this policy seems effective for UICSM, it has not had particularly good results elsewhere.

Germane to the matter of communication channels is the question of whether the project wants a group product or a series of individual products, and whether it accepts the idea of group decision making, or prefers a hierarchical basis for organization. The same factors are relevant here that are relevant to organization of the overall project activities, although for the writing effort, the greater time pressure may be more conducive to individual rather than cooperative decision making.

One can find examples of many points on the continuum from one-man decision making to group decision making in the curriculum projects to date. This would provide a useful area for study in terms of relationships and outcomes. The question might well be raised as to whether the writers are more productive—in quantity as well as quality—and as willing to participate in further development work after a one-man show as in a group situation.

Other Arrangements for Materials Preparation

Not all projects use a writing conference. Some have full-time staff members develop materials as part of the ongoing operation of the organization. Others bring in one or two resource people on short-term appointments to work on materials in the same manner that staff members might be assigned to them. While the resources of the organization may be open to such staff members and outside appointees, the situation may parallel the traditional method of book writing by a single author, with the exception that it is an experimental rather than a final product being prepared. The extent to which this is true depends on the working and communication patterns established in the project. And again, this may vary from one project activity to another, with some materials preparation being more cooperative ventures, and others more in the nature of individual authorship.

Within a project, even for parallel activities, there may be considerable variation. For example, in the preparation of its two-week units, SRSS assigned various units to individual sociologists throughout the country. For the experimental editions, each worked in his own way. Some of the writers worked almost entirely alone until they were ready to try out materials. Some cooperated with classroom teachers throughout the development of materials. And some cooperated with classroom teachers at a fairly late stage of materials development.

CUE also uses different techniques for different projects. For some, materials preparation is entirely in-house, by regular staff or staff added on short-term appointments for the particular developmental assignment. For some materials, there is a combination of in-house and outside consultant work. And for some, most of the materials preparation is done by outside consultants. UICSM has had some work done in intensive sessions, and other work done by one or more individuals located at the University of Illinois, in a more leisurely writing effort.

The writing conference does not guarantee a quality product, and many quality products have been produced without writing conferences. However, the writing conference does offer some advantages over other arrangements for materials preparation, in that it provides an immutable deadline, it facilitates the participation of people with a variety of skills, it facilitates feedback among the writers, and it permits more effective quality control.

TRYOUT AND USE OF EXPERIMENTAL MATERIALS

One feature of developmental projects is the tryout of materials during the experimental period. Projects vary in the manner in which they try out experimental editions of materials in the classroom. They vary in the number of such tryouts, in who participates in the tryouts, and in the size of the tryout population.

A number of projects have had two series of field tryouts of experimental materials with students. A typical schedule might provide for preparation of materials during a summer writing conference. A classroom tryout of materials is carried out during the school year starting immediately after the writing. A revision is scheduled for the following summer. And then there is a retrial of the revised experimental edition. This is then followed by a second rewriting prior to general release.

A typical project calendar might include:

1968	Spring	Preparation for summer writing conference
	July-August	Summer writing conference for preliminary first experimental edition
	September	Start year-long trial use of preliminary experimental materials in selected schools
1969	Spring	Preparation for second summer writing conference
	July-August	Second summer writing conference to prepare revised experimental edition of materials
	September	Start year-long trial use of revised experimental materials in selected schools
1970	Spring	Preparation for third summer writing conference
	July-August	Third summer writing conference to prepare final edition of materials

Some projects use more tryouts of all or parts of their experimental materials. Some use fewer tryouts. The decisions concerning the number of tryouts, and the numbers and kinds of students included in trial use of experimental editions of materials inevitably reflect financial considerations. For example, some projects have had to cancel tryouts because of funding problems in 1968 and 1969, when cutbacks of public funding occurred. Other projects have been forced to reduce the size of tryout groups because of budget restrictions from time to time.

In connection with the materials tryout and revision process, some projects appear to have an obsession with perfection. Their classroom materials are tried out, revised, and tried out time and again. For some, the process seems endless. And at the end of several years, the product may be small compared with the potential and the investment of time and money. This situation may occur more often when materials preparation is carried on throughout the year, rather than at a summer writing conference, with its tight schedules and rather rigorous atmosphere.

It is impossible to set an optimal number of tryouts for all kinds of materials. The number of tryouts and revisions should certainly reflect the nature of the product. Thus, projects producing more highly experimental materials probably would need more tryouts than those that are producing less experimental materials. UICSM, as a matter of philosophy, has more tryouts than most studies because the project wishes to be highly innovative. Projects that have a very clear set of advance specifications, and a clear advance structure for the work, may need fewer tryouts than projects that have little advance structure. Thus, SSCP, with a completely loose structure for its materials, required more tryouts than the AAAS project, which had considerable advance structuring and sequencing.

The degree to which the materials are experimental influences not only the number of tryouts but also the nature of the tryouts. For materials that are highly experimental, the advantages of small-scale pilot testing are clear. The more experimental the materials, the more they deviate from customary practice, the less assurance their authors can have that the materials are usable by teachers and students. For this reason, some projects distinguish between the pilot or preliminary tryout for feasibility, and a later tryout, after there is some evidence that the materials are feasible.

Thus, UICSM customarily has pilot tryouts of small portions of materials with one of two classes in the University of Illinois laboratory school during the materials-preparation time. In this instance, the authors of the materials teach the tryout classes. This small-scale pilot tryout may be repeated one or more times before larger blocks of materials are tried with larger audiences of students and teachers.

SSCP used instant students, small groups of students available locally on short notice, to try out materials as the author of those materials wanted feedback. During one of its summer writing conferences, the BSCS organized a special class of students to try out any text, laboratory, or discussion materials on which an author or version supervisor wanted reaction. At other times, the BSCS had staff and facilities assigned for tryout of laboratory exercises as they were being written. Some SRSS authors worked in close contact with a few classrooms, with students using the materials as they were developed, and occasionally, the author assisted in the teaching, or taught some parts of the materials.

Most projects undertake the first tryout with students upon completion of the entire materials, rather than trying materials out in bits and pieces. This procedure is easier than providing for tryouts during the writing period, particularly in the case of curricula prepared during summer writing conferences, when the pressure of deadlines and the difficulty of obtaining appropriate trial groups may preclude substantial amount of pilot testing. However, where highly experimental materials are being used during the pilot testing of an entire course, there is the very real danger of the materials proving unsuitable, and the dilemma of what to teach if the experimental materials are not teachable. Thus, if experimental schools agree to use the developmental materials for a semester or a year, what will they use if the course is unteachable?

While it is easy to assume that any sensible person is able to gauge what is teachable, this is not necessarily the case. In education, many assumptions have been made in the past about what students can and cannot learn. And teachers are not necessarily accurate judges of what their students can learn, since what may seem difficult to an adult may not seem unduly difficult to a student. To the adult, often the unexpected or the new appears unduly difficult. To the student, to whom the entire subject is new, and who has no traditional expectations, the innovative approach may be no more difficult than the traditional approach.

Thus, prediction of what is possible in terms of curriculum approaches may be difficult. In view of this, it would appear wise, in the case of course materials that are highly experimental, to arrange small feasibility tests of parts of the materials before embarking on large-scale testing. Yet, many projects have done their first tryouts on fairly large groups of students. For example, the first BSCS tryout of its version materials included 13,000 students; the second experimental tryout involved 52,000 students. The first tryout of parts of the BSCS special materials (about one semester's work) included 900 students. This contrasts with the first feasibility tryout of the BSCS second course which included 60 students.

Such large-scale, first tryout of experimental materials by projects may reflect the fact that the materials are not so different from previous presentations as to constitute a threat concerning teachability. It may reflect great confidence in the materials. It may reflect an urgency in terms of time and fiscal limitations. Or it may reflect a failure to consider the possibility of difficulty in teaching the materials.

For projects using summer writing conferences for materials preparation, with experimental tryout in the fall, arrangements must be made the preceding spring for enlisting the cooperation of teachers to use the materials. Thus, for such projects, the parameters of the experimental tryout, and the identification of teachers and schools to be used, generally must be completed before the materials preparation is begun. In the case of projects preparing year-long courses, this is the only alternative to delaying tryouts for an entire year.

In theory, this procedure seems highly risky. In practice, it has worked in a relatively satisfactory manner. Those projects that have tried out materials inappropriate for the tryout audience have not always been those that designated the tryout population prior to materials preparation.

Another consideration in the tryout of materials is what the project wants to learn from the tryout. And this may vary at different stages in materials preparation. The question of general feasibility, for example, might be an earlier consideration than a question of precise conditions for optimal use, and would require a different tryout population.

The intended target audience is also an influential consideration. If the intended audience for project materials is a small, highly refined one—e.g., students of average and above-average ability in the Greater Cleveland area —the tryout group is properly limited to samples from this population. If the target audience is more varied, the tryout sample, at some point before the final stages in materials production, should include representatives of the various kinds of subgroups in the target audience. Thus, a project may intend its materials for a national audience—including urban, suburban, and rural schools—for schools that are well equipped and those that are poorly equipped, for teachers who are well prepared in the subject area and those who are less well prepared, and for a wide range of ability levels of students. For such a project, tryouts would have to include a wide variety of schools in the sample to be at all adequate.

For national or regional projects, it might appear most logical to select a random sample of schools through the target area for tryout of materials.

If this could be done, it would insure a representation of the kinds of teaching situations for which the materials are intended. In practice, the use of random samples of schools for testing materials may be neither feasible nor desirable.

A number of projects have found that clustering trial teachers is practical and effective. It permits meetings of experimental teachers, and facilitates training of them. And it facilitates visiting of experimental schools for feedback. SRSS, which initially tried random sampling of schools for its large-scale tryout, changed to the use of clusters of schools as a more satisfactory and realistic technique.

When schools are chosen randomly, even though the school may agree to participate, the individual teacher who participates in trying out materials may be less than enthusiastic, and may even be antagonistic in some cases. A project certainly cannot find out whether its materials are effective if the teacher does not think them effective and does not particularly want them to succeed. While at some point in its evaluation a project may want to learn what happens to its materials under highly adverse circumstances, this is hardly the most important question during the evaluation in the formative period. And if the tryout schools are widely separated and cannot be visited regularly, the project may not even know whether teacher unwillingness to use the materials was a factor in their failure.

A further consideration in selecting trial schools is the willingness of the school to experiment. Particularly at the senior high school level, with the concern for college prerequisites and college entrance examinations, there may be some reluctance on the part of the schools to accept the highly innovative and to implement it fully. While UICSM certainly does not get a typical reaction to its preliminary materials in the highly selective University of Illinois Laboratory School where the pilot testing is done, it is free to experiment. The parents and the school administration give the experimenters a free hand. Further, there is always the regular course work that can be done if the experiment does not work, or the author wants to stop and revise before continuing his experiment. Such freedom to experiment may be more important than typicality of the student group at this pilot stage of materials testing.

In addition to the use of experimental materials for tryout purposes in selected schools, developmental projects are faced with the question of whether they want to permit their materials to be used more widely during the formative period. Should anyone outside the project and the experimental schools see and/or use the project classroom materials, when these are still in experimental form?

Developmental projects are not in the book-distribution business; yet, they can become quite involved in book sales and distribution if they release experimental editions of materials to persons not in the official tryout program. This can become a nuisance. Further, the projects may be reluctant to have unproven materials widely used. This is a matter of protecting students as well as the project reputation and image.

Some projects feel strongly about restricting not only classroom use of the materials during the formative period, but even the release of examination copies to interested people. Such projects will not release even single copies of experimental materials to anyone not immediately involved in project activities. This policy may be in effect only for the first preliminary experimental edition, or it may be enforced for successive experimental editions.

Other projects place fewer restrictions on their experimental materials. They release examination copies of preliminary materials. And they may also sell classroom sets of preliminary or revised experimental editions of materials to schools which provide assurance that the teachers using the materials will have special orientation in their use.

A number of factors are involved in such policy decisions. There is the question of whether it is proper to restrict circulation entirely, even for examination purposes, of materials prepared with public funds. Also, granted the reader of preliminary materials may find errors or unsuccessful activities, he may also provide useful feedback to the project. Further, making project materials available early in the developmental period may be an effective means of preparing the target audience for them. This practice may give schools a chance to become familiar with the kinds of work going on, and to decide whether they want to become a part of it in the future.

Projects that permit classroom use of experimental materials outside the project tryout program generally restrict such use to teachers who have the same special preparation that is given the teachers in the official tryout groups. This policy may reflect a feeling that such preparation is a requisite to successful implementation of the course, even though the special training can only be recommended and not required, once final materials are generally released. Or it may be that the teacher materials which accompany the experimental editions are incomplete, and so the special orientation is of particular importance.

V

DIFFUSION

MANNER OF RELEASE OF MATERIALS AFTER THE FORMATIVE PERIOD

Some projects consider their task completed when they have produced materials that, in their judgment, meet the initial or emergent aims of the project. Others feel that project work should continue with additional activities. But in either case, there is a question of what happens to the materials that have been developed at the end of the formative, developmental period. Are they to be issued by the project itself, through regular commercial channels, or through some other source? If published, should this be through a single publisher or several, and how are such publishers to be selected? Are materials to be placed in the public domain, where they may be used in part or in full by anyone? To date, projects have followed different routes, and often, a single project will use different arrangements for different materials.

The alternatives open to a project vary somewhat, reflecting provisions by different funding sources. NSF projects may copyright materials for limited periods of time. There are severe limitations on copyrighting by OE. For the projects financed by a publisher, the completed materials are, of course, copyrighted by that publisher. Where no copyright is permitted, there can be no selection of a single publisher, as materials are in the public domain and may be reproduced by anyone. In contrast, the Ford and Carnegie Foundations, when supporting developmental curriculum activity, do not limit or prescribe manner of dissemination of completed materials. The policy of both foundations is quite similar:

> In general, we do not put any restrictions on the publication or distribution of books or curricular materials which result from our grants. We see no reason why the authors and publishers should not have a normal financial incentive in producing the materials even though the research and development may be supported by a foundation. Many universities have their own policies in such matters and we go along with them. In some cases . . . we understand that royalties and other income go to support the continuing work . . . which is a system we like but would not require as a condition of a grant.[1]

---

[1] Personal communication from Florence Anderson, Secretary, Carnegie Corporation of New York, October 9, 1969.

A basic consideration in the foundations' policies is to stimulate wide dissemination.

For NSF-financed projects, a variety of arrangements has been made for release of materials. PSSC text materials were issued through a commercial publishing house, and a single supplier was authorized to produce the specialized equipment designed by PSSC.

SMSG issued its materials in paperback editions through Yale University Press; it announced that publication by Yale Press would stop when appropriate corresponding commercial volumes, incorporating SMSG materials and approach, became available. Thus, although its materials were copyrighted, SMSG encouraged publishers to modify and reproduce its materials in regular commercial editions. It was also possible to take parts of the SMSG materials and adapt them, and supplement them with other traditional or new materials.

For a variety of reasons, little of the SMSG materials were published by others in the years immediately following their completion, in a format reflecting SMSG ideas sufficiently to result in the withdrawal of the Yale Press edition. Further, the use of the paperbound SMSG materials was relatively limited, compared to the widespread adoption of materials from other national curriculum projects, such as PSSC and BSCS, appearing at about that time.

Eventually, parts of the SMSG materials did appear in other volumes prepared by individual authors and released through usual commercial channels. A number of books were advertised as based on SMSG or including the "new math," without reflecting the total SMSG approach. Further, some were a combination of the old and new to the point of losing the advantages of both. Thus, though many observers felt that SMSG was an effective effort and produced worthwhile books, these books did not receive as widespread adoption as would probably have been the case had they been issued through the conventional commercial channels. More recently, SMSG has begun distributing some of its materials through regular commercial publishers, and utilizing different publishers for different kinds of materials.

The BSCS, for its versions, felt that unless its materials were issued through commercial channels, their use would be limited. Further, if BSCS materials were placed in the public domain, it would be possible for publishers wanting to issue them to leave out those materials dealing with sensitive subjects—sections relating to evolution and human reproduction, for example—thereby distorting the presentation.

Each of the versions was written to develop a series of themes. Unless the material was presented as a sequential and continuing development of these themes, the purpose of the BSCS would not be reflected, and the results obtained by the BSCS would not be replicated. If materials were in the public domain, it would be possible to take parts of each version—to reflect the best of each version—and produce a new composite that would defeat the thematic development of the versions, even though the subject-matter coverage might be comparable, and each individual chapter and exercise, exemplary. Also, the BSCS felt that the American schools had a right to have access to the versions exactly as designed by the writers with public funds; this could not be guaranteed if the books were in the public domain. Thus, commercial publication and distribution were the avenues for releasing the completed materials.

The BSCS invited publishers interested in the high school level to submit bids on the versions, and an advance provision was made that no publisher could be awarded the contract for more than one version. Similar procedures were used for contract awards for other BSCS classroom materials developed later, and for those teacher materials with a sizable potential audience. Materials with more limited audiences—materials for teacher training and for administrators implementing BSCS—were published and distributed by the BSCS itself.

Distribution rights to the BSCS *Techniques Films* were given to the single distributor who produced the series; he was chosen on the basis of proximity to the writing conference, at a time when an unexpected decision to prepare the films was made, and such proximity seemed necessary if the work was to be completed during the writing conference. The *Single Topic Film Series* is distributed through several sources including the version publishers. The BSCS *Comprehension Final Examinations* for the versions are distributed through the testing agency that assisted in test preparation during the developmental period, and tests for each version are distributed through the version publishers.

There has been no official BSCS supplier of laboratory materials. The BSCS has issued official lists of recommended and required equipment and supplies, and has made available through its *NEWSLETTER* the names of companies that state they can supply these.

Thus, a variety of distribution channels have been used, reflecting kind of material, size of potential market, and convenience. All BSCS materials were copyrighted, and none are in the public domain. And the broadest possible type of competitive bidding was used for selecting the publishers of many of the materials, but has not been used in every case.[2]

---

[2]All royalties and returns on all sales of materials have gone to the United States Treasury, regardless of the way in which release has been arranged. This has been true of other NSF-financed projects releasing materials commercially.

The publishing arrangements for IME and other materials from the Interaction Project are part of the initial arrangements setting up the project. A single publisher sponsored the project, financed it, and at the very start of the developmental work, made contractual arrangements to publish final materials. However, even here, the authors retain control over content, with the publisher retaining control over format. Rand McNally also has equipment kits available to accompany the materials, but none of the equipment is unique to Rand McNally; the same items or comparable ones are available elsewhere, and many can be constructed by the teacher himself.

Projects financed in part or in full by Office of Education funds have very different publishing arrangements. While OE-funded materials may be copyrighted during the developmental period to preclude premature dissemination, for some time, the OE did not permit an exclusive copyright for any of the completed materials developed with its fund grants. Thus, any completed project materials were automatically in the public domain. Often, this meant that the completed project materials were not published in their entirety by anyone, since no publisher could afford the investment in publishing a textbook, advertising, and marketing it, when his competitors could publish a duplicate edition; and often the authors who had worked on project materials rewrote them, on their own time, and produced a different edition of the same materials a year or so later.

More recently, there have been some modifications of the OE policy on copyrights.The following is the statement of the Office of Education as of March 1, 1968, concerning copyrights.

> It is the policy of the Office of Education that the results of activities supported by it should be utilized in the manner which would best serve the public interest. It is believed that the public interest will, in general, best be served if materials produced under project grants or contracts from the Office of Education are made freely available to the Government, the education community, and to the general public. Ordinarily, this objective will be accomplished by placing such materials in the public domain. In some situations, however, it is recognized that limited copyright protection [generally not to exceed five years] may be necessary during development or as an incentive to promote the effective dissemination of such materials. At the request of a grantee or contractor, arrangements for copyright of such materials for a limited period of time may be authorized under appropriate conditions upon a showing satisfactory to the Office of Education that such protection will result in more effective development or dissemination of the materials and would otherwise be in the public interest.
>
> FEDERAL REGISTER, March 1, 1968

According to the OE Guidelines (USOE, 1968), such exceptions are made where suitable arrangements for dissemination cannot be made unless copyright protection is extended. Pursuant to this newer policy, HPP has a copyright on its experimental editions, and the final edition will be prepared by several of the HPP staff on their own time, copyrighted by them, and issued through commercial channels, with royalties paid to the copyright holders.

The problems of whether materials should be in the public domain, who should get royalties, and manner of distribution of materials are difficult ones. There are many questions involved. Should only a limited group profit from expenditure of public funds? Is it fair to give a single publisher exclusive rights to publish materials developed with public funds? If a single publisher is not awarded these rights, will it be possible to achieve the public purpose—the change in education—which is dependent on diffusion of the materials produced? In the long run, will competent and gifted individuals be willing to work with curriculum projects without the financial rewards of royalties? If royalties are paid to some of the staff members of a project who prepare a new adaptation of materials that they may copyright personally, who should share in the royalties, and to what extent? That is, in a team project to which hundreds contributed, should royalties go to only those few individuals working on the final edition?

If projects themselves cannot receive royalties, but must turn over all income for sales of materials to the federal Treasury, projects will be completely dependent on repeated appropriations of public funds. Should some of the royalties be returned to the project to continue the task of curriculum improvement? If developers cannot copyright project materials, the materials eventually copyrighted by the individual authors will not be the material tested during the experimental period. Will this mean that the materials generally available will be less effective than would be the case if projects could copyright materials and then arrange for them to be issued commercially?

The current policies developed by both NSF and OE represent compromises which do not completely satisfy anyone. They reflect a variety of pressures—from educators, from projects, from Congress, and from publishers. Educational considerations have not necessarily been the determinants in setting these policies. The policies will probably be modified in the future, but the direction of change cannot be predicted.

One modification, recently developed by the BSCS and NSF after consultation with the publishers of the BSCS materials, may provide a useful pattern. The BSCS, the NSF, and the publishers of the BSCS versions have agreed that for the current (revised) edition of BSCS materials, the royalty rate previously paid by the publisher—a rate higher than the standard royalty payment usually made to authors—would be reduced to a normal royalty rate, with the payment forwarded to the U.S. Treasury. The publisher will provide funds to the BSCS for the preparation of a second revised edition when it is needed. And the NSF will have no vesting in that future edition. All royalties which the second revised edition earns will go to the BSCS for further developmental work.

Thus, as the BSCS materials need modification, they can be made by the project without dependence on new financing from NSF. This guarantees some continuity to the project materials; it insures schools that the materials will continue to be available in an up-to-date form for some time; and the publisher knows he will have revised editions of the materials when they are considered needed, without having to depend on the uncertainties of an NSF grant. However, these funds will not be sufficient to carry out a broad writing and tryout effort, or to finance an extensive, systematic evaluation of the revised, 1968 editions of BSCS biology materials currently in use to prepare for such rewriting efforts. Thus, while providing a method of financing the future editions, the new financing arrangements clearly modify the process that can be used in their development.

CHEM Study has taken a different approach both to the initial release of its completed materials and to the problem of financing revised editions. CHEM Study arranged for private publication of materials, and it distributed the books itself. Thus, it did not have the promotional facilities of a commercial publisher at its disposal. It handled promotion by sending a sample copy to every high school chemistry teacher in the United States, with the assumption that the materials would sell themselves without the usual promotional campaign, and without salesmen visiting schools.

For the revision several years after the initial edition of CHEM Study materials was released, the project announced that it would not prepare a revision itself. Rather, it would authorize writing teams sponsored by three publishers to prepare three different revisions. Selection of the three teams would be based on a prospectus submitted to CHEM Study, including names of the writers to be involved and a general outline of the book to be prepared. CHEM Study also reserved the right to review final manuscripts. The three revised editions appeared in 1968 and 1969.

This method has advantages and disadvantages. It permits the project to cease materials preparation and phase out most of its activity at the same time that continuation of project materials in some form is guaranteed. However, it does not guarantee that revised materials will implement the theory developed by CHEM Study, or capitalize on the ideas developed earlier. Review of a general outline prior to work, and review of the final product, may not guarantee sufficient quality control; and the ensuing product, which, by implication, carries the CHEM Study lable, may not be as satisfactory as a product produced directly under the auspices of CHEM Study. While CHEM

Study announced it would keep the old edition prepared by CHEM Study itself in print as long as the demand warranted this, now, the choice given potential users is between a somewhat outdated volume, and three new volumes prepared under other auspices—volumes that may not reflect the best of the CHEM Study work.

In the balance, perhaps the approach which appears to have produced the most satisfactory results to date permits copyright of materials by projects, and revisions by them financed by income from the publications. Yet, this policy too has limitations in terms of providing sufficient funding for a developmental-type effort.

FORMAT OF MATERIALS

Until relatively recently, the textbook, perhaps supplemented by some kind of workbook, was usually regarded as the typical course material for schools. Particularly in the last few years, there has been greater diversity in curriculum materials, and the trend apparently is toward still greater diversity in the future. The choice of medium for the developmental materials is an important one, since some media or formats may facilitate or may preclude achievement of some desired outcomes. Format also influences cost of development of materials, selling price of materials, and equipment and facilities needed to use the materials.

Materials may be expendable (one-time use) or relatively permanent. If printed, they may be loose-leaf or regularly bound. They may be bound in hard or soft cover; they may be printed in one color or multicolor; they may be bound in units, or in sections (as with text in one book, laboratory manual in another). Where films are used, these may be black-and-white or in color, with or without sound, on standard, 16mm., or on short, 8 mm., four-minute loops. They may be in a format usable by the student himself or they may be used by an entire classroom at one time. Audio materials may be on phonograph records, or on tapes, either usable by individual students or by the class as a whole.

The format of some materials requires a given type of presentation, while the format of others permits various kinds of treatment. For example, when the *Invitations to Inquiry,* used in BSCS and IME, are given only in the teacher handbook, and the student does not have a copy, he cannot look ahead for clues to the questions he is to answer. The same materials, when programmed by one user, not only permit the student to look ahead for clues, but also permit him to find the answers he is supposed to be developing himself. The same is the case with the BSCS *Single Topic Films.* When the teacher directs the use and asks the accompanying questions, the later questions or pictures cannot give clues to the student; when programmed, with the student holding the entire list of questions and free to go ahead in the film before answering any, later information gives him clues.

Some curriculum materials can be used by the student himself. Some require teacher intervention. Some require rather expensive equipment to permit their use, as for example, the individual carrell needed for some language laboratories. And for some programmed or individual progress programs, where the student requires a variety of equipment to carry out his learning assignment.

The problems involved in deciding on format are not only educational ones—questions concerning what will promote the most learning—but also, matters of practicality, in terms of expense, in terms of commercial publishing constraints, and in terms of school system laws, regulations, or practices. Some of the questions in selection of format of materials appear to be merchandising questions only, rather than basic educational considerations, but often, what appear to be publishing or sales questions have strong educational implications.[3]

Schools may be more attracted to materials that cost less per student and materials that may be purchased under state textbook subsidies or federal funds for equipment. They may be precluded from using state funds to purchase paper-cover, expendable materials; for some states, the law does not permit state funds to be used by schools for "workbooks," and in others, such expenditures are viewed with extreme disfavor by the state or local authorities.

While color in photographs and for headings is more expensive than a black-and-white presentation, both in producing original artwork and in its reproduction, the use of color may make a book more acceptable to textbook purchasers, regardless of the educational value of color.[4] The argument that the school could buy three paperback, black-and-white books for the cost of one four-color, hardbound book may not influence the purchaser.

Some projects may want to encourage students to make marginal notes in their books. Some may want to give the students only a portion of the year's materials at one time, so that the student who is not verbally oriented will not be unduly discouraged by the sheer bulk of what he will be assigned during the year. Even if these are effective strategies in enhancing learning, they may be impractical, since schools will not buy the materials readily.

---

[3]Many projects specify in their contracts for commercial publication that content decisions are the prerogative of the project and format decisions are the prerogative of the publisher.

[4]There is no conclusive evidence that use of color in illustrations enhances learning.

The title of the book can influence its acceptance and the reaction of students to it. For example, when the materials for the lowest ability classes are clearly identifiable as such, some negative reactions may be anticipated. For some books, the title precludes their use at a level where they might be suitable; for example, some colleges, whose students come with little background in biology, commented that the *BSCS High School Biology—Green Version* would be eminently suited for incoming freshmen, but could not be used because of the words "high school" in the title.

The ways in which materials are combined in one package or binding may encourage use of the materials in the manner intended by the project. Binding laboratory exercises and textbook in one volume can be justified by the arguments that they are complementary and comprise parts of an integrated presentation, and that neither is complete alone. Such a binding procedure encourages use of both parts rather than of one part only. However, the laboratory manual may easily become soiled during laboratory work and need replacement more often than the text; the dual volume is heavy to carry; and if the two parts are bound together, the students cannot use the laboratory section of the volume as a laboratory report book for entering experimental observations, since the total volume is not expendable. If the text and laboratory manual are bound separately—even though they complement each other, and educationally, neither can stand alone—can the project be assured that they will both be used, that schools will buy and distribute both?

Some projects consider the tests used for evaluative purposes as a basic part of the curriculum materials, since tests are an excellent means of communicating the intent of the authors to both teacher and student. In purchasing books, school bidding procedures may require that the texts or text-laboratory manual materials be priced and offered separately from any other materials. Thus, the project cannot require that materials be sold as a complete package of text, laboratory manual, and tests. Yet, to fail to do so may jeopardize full implementation of the program.

If the project materials include a series of discrete units, and any single unit can be used, whether or not the others are—as in the case with SRSS and HSGP materials—separate packaging of individual units may encourage wide use of at least some of the materials. However, sale of complete packages, especially if they are bound together, might encourage use of the complete series, though by a smaller audience.

Binding the teacher's manual with student materials in a special teacher edition so that the teacher uses two volumes together, rather than a single volume, is more expensive than issuing a separate teacher volume, including only the materials directed to the teacher. However, not only is the interleaved volume more convenient for the teacher, but it increases the likelihood that the teacher will have these materials available and will use them as they are pertinent.

TEACHER TRAINING FOR USE OF MATERIALS

A major decision concerning the nature of the materials to be prepared is whether teachers will require special preparation prior to their use and, where such preparation is indicated, what kind of special preparation will be needed. While the extent of this problem may not be clear prior to some pilot testing of materials, if the content coverage is quite new, or if many of the prospective teachers of the materials have had no specific training in the particular discipline—for example, physics or astronomy for elementary teachers, economics for senior high history teachers, organic chemistry for biology teachers—obviously, some kind of special teacher orientation specific to the new materials and/or discipline will be needed.

If special training is needed, what kind should it be? Of what duration? Who should teach the teachers? What should the content be? Under whose auspices should the training take place? Should training proceed or be concomitant with teaching the new course?

Training sessions may be instituted by the project itself, by colleges and universities, teacher associations, state, county, and local school districts, or some combination of these. The project may help in actually providing staff or may advise on staffing for training given under other auspices. It may run training sessions for such training institute staff members, as well as for college personnel involved in teacher preparation. Some projects have also prepared materials for such teacher-preparation personnel, to guide them in organizing suitable courses, and to call to their attention existing resources for assisting in their implementation.

Need for special orientation. Some curricula delimit the teacher role to the point where no teacher preparation is needed beyond relatively brief instructions. For example, in some of the simulated games,[5] in effect, the teacher has few alternatives, since his activities are programmed. He may simply assign students to roles and read instructions to them, and then the students are more or less on their own. This may also be the case with some programmed or CAI course materials.

In some instances, a teacher handbook or guide to the materials, along with a list of useful references, will provide the requisite teacher orientation.

---

[5]These provide structured situations where students are given in-class assignments to act out a given role in a situation within predetermined constraints of the role and the structured situation (See Boocock, 1968).

Brief training films can illustrate unfamiliar techniques; 8 mm. cartridge-type films have been produced to provide teachers with such laboratory techniques as weighing and measuring accurately, removing the frog pituitary (a procedure required of the teacher if students are to carry out certain exercises), and handling fruit flies (which are widely used in laboratory experiments).[6] A few projects have produced films illustrating various teaching techniques—such as an inquiry approach—that are particularly appropriate to their materials.

For some kinds of materials, the teacher manual or training film is the only practical kind of orientation. If the project is preparing relatively short units, only one or two of which may be used in the course of a year—as is the case with the SRSS two-week sociology units—the materials must be self-explanatory, since special training may be impractical for many of the users. School systems are less likely to inaugurate special training courses for a two-or four-week unit than for a semester or full-year course. Furthermore, schools may want to use a variety of units with different classes or in different years. In such cases, if more training than can be obtained through a handbook or film is a requisite to suitable implementation of the curriculum, widespread use of the materials may be precluded.

For many materials, some organized kind of course work orientation for teachers is indicated. Some projects have assumed early in the materials preparation that special teacher-preparation activities will be necessary and possible. Others have tried written teacher materials during the field tryouts and have found that this is not sufficient. Thus, providing an elementary school teacher or high school teacher with a college text in economics will not prepare him to teach economics at his grade level.

Even where the subject-matter background does not present a serious problem, the problems of classroom management may be new, and so a brief, special training session could be useful. This may be the case where laboratory exercises are introduced at the grade level for the first time; where the teacher may have to improvise in the absence of a science laboratory facility; or where the emphasis of materials has changed to the point where teachers may feel hesitant about the approach.

Sponsorship of teacher training. The sponsorship of the teacher training for a given developmental curriculum in large part determines the extent of the project's influence on the training. Training requires funding. The projects funded by publishers may include such training in the project budget for the developmental period only, or for both the developmental and dissemination

---

[6]The 8 mm. cartridge-type film, which runs for four minutes, permits use of a relatively inexpensive and easy-to-operate projector, and reduces cost of film considerably. It permits stopping the film at any point, as well as rerunning the film with no rewinding or threading of the projector.

phases. Here, the project directs its own training. Some private foundations also include teacher-training funds in grants to developmental projects. Public funds are available from the National Science Foundation, the Office of Education, and state and local education departments for teacher training.

Sometimes, a project can obtain funds to plan and operate its own teacher-training sessions. At other times, funds are available to others who work in close consultation with the project, or who call the project in to do the actual training, although the scheduling and other arrangements may be handled by the individual receiving the funds. Thus, a school system may ask a project to provide staff for a teacher workshop or course concerned with the project's materials. Or the training may be independent of the project. For example, a professor of biology, chemistry, or geography at a college or university, may, on his own initiative, obtain a grant from the institute division of NSF to implement a training program which will prepare teachers to use a new curriculum in his field.

During the period when materials are being developed, it is relatively easier for projects to obtain grants for training teachers who will be involved in the experimental tryouts in the schools, since such teacher training is an essential part of the materials-development process. In such instances, the training can be included in the developmental grant. However, after the developmental period, often grants are available only from a different source. For example, in the NSF, the Curriculum Improvement Division handles materials development, and provides teacher-training funds only during the developmental period. The Institute Division, a completely separate branch of NSF, handles training funds.

A major portion of the public funds for teacher training for developmental curricula comes from NSF and OE. In awarding grants, the developmental project that has prepared materials is not necessarily involved in any way with the selection, approval, or guidance of institutes funded specifically to prepare teachers for its new curriculum materials. And grants to such projects for teacher training may be contrary to the general policy of the funding agency.

While some projects have been able to obtain training funds beyond the period of materials development, or have been instrumental in selecting recipients of grants or in making recommendations for staffing the training, this is not always the case. Criteria used in awarding grants do not always reflect the recipient's competence for the specific purpose of the training involved. Often, there seems to be an implicit, though unwarranted, assumption that any reputable scholar in a given discipline, simply because of his general professional eminence, is an appropriate director of an institute to train teachers for use of new developmental materials in that discipline.

One of the problems public granting agencies face in making grants for curriculum materials developed with public funds is that such agencies do not want to appear to be promoting their own product. Thus, the NSF does not wish to appear to be pushing use of PSSC or BSCS or SMSG materials.

This creates a difficult situation, since without special training, teachers cannot properly implement these materials. Most funds for such special training are governmental funds. For instance, when money is allocated for institutes for teachers of high school physics, the institutes use either traditional physics or PSSC physics materials. To use PSSC is, in a sense, to promote a government-financed project. To use traditional physics is to defeat the very purpose for which PSSC was created. And to combine the two, as some have tried to do, again may be defeating PSSC purposes. Thus, while the granting agency policies on teacher training may be open to some criticism, the situation in which they are operating is a difficult and sensitive one, where the issues have not yet been clearly resolved.

The BSCS experience is similar to that of a number of large projects. The BSCS operated its own teacher training exclusively for the first year of its experimental program; the second experimental year, it conducted its own sessions, but teachers in the experimental program were also permitted to obtain training from other NSF summer institutes or academic year institutes which had designated in their proposals that they would be training teachers for BSCS biology. In later years, the BSCS received no funds for teacher training, although it did hold meetings and prepare materials for interested persons who were doing such training, and it was asked to suggest staff, or on occasion to run a training session for a school system.

Unfortunately, there have been no comparative studies on the relative effectiveness of the BSCS and nonBSCS training. BSCS staff members have been convinced that the training under BSCS auspices was more effective than other training, since, in many instances which they could document, the training by outsiders—even though announced as training specific for BSCS—was a traditional biology course that had simply been relabeled or slightly modified. In other instances, the training consisted of subject-matter lectures with no opportunity to practice new laboratory exercises or inquiry techniques, and with no discussion of possible problems in implementing the BSCS classroom materials.

Participants in orientation. Some courses, in order to prepare teachers for new materials, take all teachers who will be using the materials. Thus, the courses run for experimental teachers during the formative period of the materials, would include all teachers in the experimental classroom tryouts.

Courses provided by textbook publishers include teachers who will be using the materials, and sometimes, anyone who is considering their use, with the training course used as a medium for helping the participant make up his mind.

The institutes under university or collegiate auspices—including NSF summer institutes or academic year institutes—may be limited to persons with several years teaching experience. They may specialize in persons from the geographic area, or persons with strong or weak academic backgrounds. And they may exclude persons who have attended other institutes recently. The decision concerning qualification of participants may be up to the institute director, or it may be a requisite of the funding.

In any event, the kind of training provided should be geared to the background of the participants, as well as to the unique demands of the curriculum. Thus, for some situations, it may be desirable and possible to provide different types of orientation for participants with different backgrounds and qualifications.

In some instances, the trainees are paid to attend sessions, as in the case of the NSF institutes. In some, their expenses are paid, as has sometimes been the case when experimental teachers try out project materials during the formative period. In some, the teachers pay tuition, as, for example, in university graduate courses and extension courses. In other situations, trainees are required to come, or may volunteer to come, with tuition paid, but no expenses paid, and with or without college credit.[7]

Training techniques, timing, and content. Orientation of teachers for the new developmental materials has taken many forms including: briefing sessions or short courses before the teacher uses the materials; cluster grouping of teachers in a geographic area; in-service institutes or workshops held prior to the opening of school, during the school year, or before and during the school year with some sessions possibly after the end of the school year; academic year institutes sponsored by the NSF; summer institutes sponsored by NSF or OE, and held on college campuses; regular college courses during the summer or school year; and college extension courses offered off campus during the year. Some of these carry academic credit; some carry in-service credit that can be used toward pay increments or maintenance of teaching certification.

Some training has been available to teachers at home through open-circuit television, with the possibility of academic credit as an option. Some training has been through filmed courses, such as the JCEE film series, *The American*

---

[7]Where no college or in-service credit toward maintaining certification or for promotion purposes is granted, and the training is extensive and no released time is given, the training can become quite burdensome and result in a negative attitude towards the new program.

Economy. In addition to being shown on open-circuit television, this film series has also been used in some school systems on a systemwide or a school-to-school basis for teacher training in economics. The *AIBS Film Series* has been similarly used for teacher preparation in subject matter.

In both of these instances, while the films provide the teacher with some coverage of subject matter in the discipline, they are not specifically geared to any developmental course. Neither series is concerned with teaching techniques. And neither provides useful exemplars of the kinds of discussion and inquiry techniques strongly urged by the various developmental projects in economics and biology as integral to the appropriate presentation of the projects' curricula.

There are some films specifically designed for teacher training in the new curricula. SMSG has thirty half-hour films for in-service elementary teachers, to provide a foundation in mathematics for any of the newer elementary school mathematics programs. The first sixteen films are for teachers from kindergarten to grade three. The rest build on mathematics normally taught in grades four to six. The BSCS has proposed developing teacher-training films to focus on teaching techniques appropriate to the implementation of BSCS biology, but funds have not been obtained.

Briefing sessions. A widely used and apparently successful technique for orienting teachers to new developmental curricula for the experimental tryouts is the intensive short course or briefing session, held before the start of the school year. Some sessions last only one or two days, some seven to ten days, the length depending on how much preparation appears needed, and the amount of funds available. These sessions have the advantage of giving the teacher advance exposure to the materials and techniques needed, where often in-service or extension courses do not start until after the teacher has already begun using the materials in school classes. In some instances, briefing sessions have been followed up by one or more meetings during the school year to answer further questions and to clear up any difficulties.[8]

Briefing sessions held by the project may be at one location, bringing teachers from various parts of the country to project headquarters, or at some other convenient site. In other instances, sessions are scheduled at various locations around the country, as travel convenience and demand indicate. The single location, while more expensive in terms of participant travel, permits

---

[8]Although briefing sessions have been a very useful technique for teacher preparation during the tryout stages of developmental project work, they have had only limited use after materials are generally available. Perhaps the reason is that projects have not been able to obtain funding for this activity after the end of the formative period for materials development, and the briefing session schedule may not lend itself equally well to other kinds of training situations, since it may not fit into college or school system schedules as well as a regular course or more extended training period.

greater staff flexibility and better advance preparation of materials needed for the institute. Thus, for a science briefing session, a number of demonstrations may be set up, and preparations may be made for teachers to perform some laboratory experiments themselves. Access to needed audiovisual equipment may also be simpler. However, some of the briefing sessions held away from project headquarters have had quite suitable facilities and arrangements in schools and colleges.

One of the characteristics of the briefings operated by projects has been the actual involvement of teachers in the kinds of activities they will be doing later in the classroom. Thus, teachers may carry out experiments, present films, lead discussions, etc. In addition, there are generally some subject-matter specialists on the briefing staff to assist with the subject-matter presentation.

Because of tight printing schedules during the experimental period, it is often not possible prior to the briefing for participating teachers to see copies of the experimental editions of the materials they will be studying in the briefing and using in their schools. This makes the briefing less efficient than would be the case if teachers could scan the materials in advance. This is one of the constraints resulting from the tight schedules on which many projects operate. In fact, on many occasions, only the first quarter or half of the year's materials may be available for the briefing, in those situations where student materials of experimental editions are published in several parts in order to get some materials to the schools by the opening date of school.

Projects may find it effective to use some of the writers on the briefing session staff. While not every writer would be suited to this role, some may be, and this is an effective way of communicating the intent of the writers to the teachers. It also gives the teachers who can say they met the writers a prestige that may be helpful for the project's public relations. After the first year of experimental use of materials, a teacher who has used them in his classes is a useful member of the briefing staff. Particularly where the materials represent a radical departure from previous practice, and teachers are skeptical of their practicality, the testimony of someone who has used them in a similar situation is reassuring. Also, such a teacher knows from firsthand experience what the problems will be, and he may have figured out some ways of avoiding them.

Briefing sessions are generally rather tightly scheduled, since there is a lot to do and very limited time in which to do it. Nonetheless, it is important for teachers to have time to talk with others who will be using the materials. This is particularly helpful when there may be several in the same locality who can talk with each other when problems arise during the year.

Briefings are rarely long enough to cover an entire new course. Thus, perhaps the best approach provides a sampling of the various kinds of activities that the teacher will face, and subject-matter coverage of unfamiliar materials in the first half of the course, with the hope that once the teacher gets off to a confident, informed start, he will have the opportunity to fill in the remaining subject-matter gaps later in the year. These gaps may be handled by the cluster groups where these exist.

Cluster grouping.   One technique, pioneered by PSSC and used extensively by other projects during their developmental period, is the cluster concept. Here, experimental teachers are selected in such a manner that there are at least half-dozen teachers within driving distance, so that teachers can meet on a regular basis (weekly, biweekly, or monthly) for a few hours to discuss their experience with the course. While this arrangement was initially set up to provide feedback to the course developers, it is an extremely useful training device, since this gives teachers an opportunity to discuss their problems, and to obtain information on those aspects of the curriculum where their background is incomplete.

In some instances, a subject-matter specialist—who is familiar with the new curriculum, both in terms of its intent and coverage —meets with the cluster group to serve as a resource person. For the BSCS, during the pilot tryouts of its first materials, the resource person was an author involved in materials development. Other groups that have not had a resource person present at each meeting may have one in from time to time as needed for expert help on subject matter.

Content of orientation.   To date, much of the teacher briefing for developmental curricula has either focused deliberately or inadvertently on subject-matter training or retraining, despite the emphasis in many of the developmental programs on developing new skills in students—skills which are expected to be mastered as a result of a different approach by the teacher. This may reflect a tacit assumption that a teacher who knows the subject matter, and is told to use discussion or inquiry methods, can and will do so; however, studies of teaching have provided clear evidence that this is not a warranted assumption.

If changes in methods of teaching are desired, then training in new methods—involving both demonstration and practice—is indicated. Thus, lectures on the discussion or inquiry techniques will not be very effective in changing the listener's teaching patterns. Obvious as this may seem, hundreds of summer and academic year institutes are still dominated by lecturing on the need for inquiry, while they focus on subject matter.

Some teacher-training sessions for the new developmental materials have consisted of an introductory course in the discipline. They may provide a standard college course in ecology, economics, geography, or biochemistry. Or they may be watered-down courses in one of these disciplines. But often, they have failed to concern themselves with the way in which the principles being taught apply to the new developmental curriculum which the teacher, supposedly, is being prepared to use. A first or second grade teacher may be expected to master *Economics* (Samuelson, 1967), the standard collegiate text in "Principles of Economics," in order to teach the concepts of scarcity and specialization of labor to his six- or seven-year-old students. And there may be no effort in the course to apply the ideas of Samuelson to the first or second grade curriculum. Such courses may cause a great deal of teacher hostility, not only towards the course, but also towards the curriculum in question.

A number of projects that have handled their own teacher training have built in the opportunity for teachers actually to work with the materials. In science, this may involve carrying out some basic experiments. Here and elsewhere, it may involve observing classes being taught with the materials, and teaching some of the materials either to demonstration classes or to other class participants. This is a basic part of Instituto Brasileiro de Educacão, Ciencia e Cultura (IBBEC) teacher training.

A limited number of teacher-training films, geared to a specific developmental program, have been prepared. This resource has not been explored very fully to date; however, it holds promise for alleviating some of the situations where the course staff is limited, or is not highly skilled in the teaching techniques which, it is hoped, the teachers will be using in the classroom. The BSCS developed a series of pamphlets, the *BSCS Special Publications Series* for persons concerned with teacher training for BSCS biology. The individual pamphlets deal with different curricular materials, and some represent updating of earlier issues, in order to reflect greater experience with training activities. In part, this series represents an attempt to influence teacher-training activities in a situation where funds were not available to the project to provide its own training, where funds were not available to prepare teacher-training films, and where dozens of NSF institutes were funded at universities and colleges each year, sometimes under the direction of persons not conversant with the BSCS basic purposes or with the problems facing the high school teacher.

Evaluation of orientation. Orientation specific to a developmental curriculum is directed towards improving the way the teacher handles materials in the classroom. While these courses may have some general intellectual benefits, unless some change occurs in the teacher's classroom behavior as a result of taking the course, the training has not made the teacher a more effective implementer of that curriculum. Despite this, there have been remarkably few instances where teacher behavior has been observed in the classroom before and after the special course orientation, to determine whether desired behavior changes have occurred, and whether some types of training are more effective than others in bringing about such changes.

Most of the testing during orientation courses has been of subject-matter recall. Since past research in education indicates no necessary correlation between the teacher's subject-matter recall and either the manner in which this knowledge is communicated in the classroom or the students' performance, it is obvious that such tests provide an inappropriate gauge of course success.

Several projects have changed their techniques for teacher preparation or their recommendations and guidelines for such training. For example, the BSCS keeps updating its recommendations in the *Special Publications Series*. Yet, such changes are generally based on nonsystematic and highly subjective criteria, rather than on systematic studies of the effects of various teacher-training methods.

In large part, preparation for teaching developmental materials has been crude and inefficient. There has often been inadequate consideration of precisely what new skills and understandings the teachers need, and what are the most effective ways of achieving these. Many courses for orienting teachers are taught as though there had been no definitive research whatsoever on teaching in that subject area. And there has been little systematic research on the effectiveness of any of those teacher-training efforts, or on their comparative outcomes. As a result, the implementation of new curricula may be seriously hampered.

IMPLEMENTATION OF MATERIALS

What happens to the developmental materials following their completion depends largely on the intent of the project. If the purpose of the project is the preparation of good or better materials than previously existed, or of materials that include coverage of activities not covered in previous materials, then completion of materials is completion of the project's mission. Given some arrangements for making the materials available—for example, putting them in the public domain so that anyone may publish them, or turning them over to a commercial publisher for printing and distribution through normal commercial channels—a project that took as its mission simply the preparation of materials may consider its job completed.

Such a decision may reflect an academic approach to the task—that is, the successful testing of a hypothesis that it is possible to prepare such a course.

It may reflect a lack of interest in the problems of dissemination. It may reflect the tacit assumption that the existence of good materials will result in their use and in a change of teaching and learning in the schools.

Many people feel that problems of diffusion are outside the domain of the developers and call for different skills, different techniques and even a different type of organizational structure. Such individuals see diffusion as a process separate from and independent of the developmental activities.

However, in many projects, either initially or after some experience with materials preparation, there has been active concern with implementation of materials in the schools. Such projects may take as a criterion of their success the extent to which education has actually been changed, rather than the extent to which change could theoretically occur through use of its curricula.

In this latter case, there may be a concern with whether there are enough materials to fill all course needs; thus, additional teachers materials, films, supplemental resource materials, laboratory equipment, etc. may be produced. There may be concern with widespread distribution of materials, with dissemination of information about the materials to various audiences, including school superintendents, supervisors, teachers, parents, persons in the discipline and in schools of education. The project may be concerned with availability of appropriate teacher preservice and in-service training. It may decide to undertake teacher training itself. Or it may take steps to see that those responsible for teacher training are informed, and have necessary materials for such training.

The project may be concerned with what happens to the materials after they reach schools. It may want to know whether the implementation is appropriate—that is, whether teachers are using them in an appropriate manner. The project may want to know whether teachers use all the materials or some of them. If only some are used, what other materials are used to fill the gaps? Are the materials adapted or used intact? Does the school adopting the materials continue to use them, or discard them after one or two years of use? What are the most appropriate conditions for their use? What are some of the problems teachers face in use of the materials? What are some of the problems the school systems face in use of the materials? To what extent do the materials fit into the rest of the school program? And to what extent are the materials compatible with the philosophy of the schools using them?

A school system preparing its own developmental materials may not have diffusion problems, since its materials were prepared for use in that school system and the school system may not be interested in disseminating them beyond the system. The same may be true in a state, where a state syllabus is prepared and becomes the official curriculum for that state. However, even here there may be problems, as is obvious in the many instances where the state syllabus is the official curriculum in form rather than in substance, and local schools continue doing what they did before the syllabus was adopted. Furthermore, some school systems have been interested in wider diffusion, both in terms of the educational and financial considerations. Thus, the Educational Research Council of Greater Cleveland initially prepared materials for use in the member school systems of the council, and more recently, has arranged for wider distribution.

While some projects wait until materials are nearing completion before exhibiting a concern with implementation problems and strategies, others have been concerned about the problems of implementation from a relatively early period. Some have set up large-scale information programs, and widely disseminated information on the anticipated program through newsletters, articles, speeches, news releases, formal and informal contacts, and simply through involving large numbers of people in the various stages of their work. Several have set up area consultants; generally these are classroom teachers who have used project materials and who are available within a region to provide information on the program.

Whether or not the project sees the diffusion activities and the investigation of diffusion as its own job or that of others, varies from project to project. Even for projects interested in diffusion, no single project can carry out a complete survey of implementation. But without some investigation of what happens to their materials, the project really has no measure of its success in bringing about change in American education, the purpose for which the developmental process was initiated in most instances.

Simply a figure for sales of books, films, or other instructional materials is not an adequate gauge of diffusion and of successful implementation. For example, in the last decade, there has been a change in exhibit displays by biological supply houses at professional meetings. Such exhibits have changed from emphasis on plaster models, charts, and specimens pickled in formaldehyde to live specimens. This shift is a better indicator of a change in student activities in science than are sales figures of new laboratory manuals or of textbooks including different kinds of laboratory exercises.

Such information is important, since to change the book is not necessarily to change the curriculum. There are a number of well-documented instances where different books have been used but the basic activities of students and their learnings have remained the same. There are developmental materials which have been purchased but not used, or that are used only in part, or used in ways directly opposed to the intents of the developers and the underlying philosophy of the new curriculum. Even supposedly teacherproof materials can be used in ways that defeat the specific intent of the materials.

When there were only a limited number of curriculum projects, with only one in a single subject area at a given school level, in one sense, diffusion problems were simpler than is now the case, but in another sense, they were more difficult. There was then no confusion in the public mind between experimental projects and their experimental products. There was no question of whose new math was better, or which third grade developmental science was best. The comparison was generally between the traditional materials and a single developmental product.

Today, for many subject areas, there are numerous developmental products for a given grade level, and there may be similar products for different grade levels. This raises problems not only of which materials to use at a given grade level, but of what the grade level placement should be.[9] When a dozen or more projects are working in the social studies, it is more difficult to disseminate information about each to the potential audience than it was for PSSC or BSCS—the only studies at their grade level and subject area at the time they were preparing initial materials—to command an audience. Yet, when there is only one relatively new project in an area, the dissemination task may be hampered by a lack of readiness by that part of the audience that has not thought much about the idea of change, that has not become accustomed to the need for teacher reeducation, or for retooling classrooms at considerable expense prior to adoption of new materials.

The problems of diffusion are becoming increasingly complex as increasing numbers of new developmental materials are coming into the general market. Various individuals and groups have expressed a concern with the lack of current comparative data about the plethora of materials, both developmental and other, coming onto the market.

There have been several recent attempts to systematize the diffusion of information about new curriculum materials, as, for example, through special publications devoted to such materials (Goodlad, 1966; Lockard, 1968; *The EPIE Forum,* now called *Educational Product Report,* 1967 — current), through institutes for school supervisors and college educators to keep them

---

[9]Unfortunately, in today's schools, the tendency is to move material down to a lower grade, not on the basis of research findings which indicate that this is suitable, or of studies of the relative advantages and disadvantages of changed grade placement, but simply because of the prestige advantage in teaching something as early as possible. Not only do the new curriculum materials tend to move subjects to earlier grades, but materials specifically prepared for one grade are often used one or two grades lower, with no research done to determine what is lost and what is gained. Thus, the project preparing ninth grade physical science materials will find these materials in use not only in the eighth grade, but also in the seventh grade. The project preparing sophisticated tenth grade biology material will find it used not only with ninth grade average and below-average students, but even with eighth graders.

abreast of new materials, and through the training of diffusion agents.[10] However, certainly, the projects cannot depend entirely on such activities yet, in place of some diffusion activities of their own. With the potential increased activity by publishers in sponsoring developmental curriculum work and in publishing developmental materials produced under other auspices, the problems of diffusion will increase both from the point of view of the project and the public.

How can the public compare parallel but dissimilar products? Whose data about a product should be accepted? How can a potential adopter identify all materials available before making a decision? How can he obtain comparable information on all? While such characteristics of the competing products as price, grade level, publication date, and facilities required, can be described in comparable terms, these may not be the most basic characteristics that should be considered in adopting a product. Such information does not reflect the contents, the philosophy, the extent of student learning in the subject area, in supporting subject areas, and in attitudes and values, that may be expected to come from use of the materials.

Given the concern with diffusion problems of school people and public agencies, doubtless there will be further advances in systematizing diffusion in the coming years. However, at the present time, to assume that diffusion may be adequately facilitated by sources outside the project, and whether these be the commercial distributor of materials of other facilities, would appear premature.

---

[10]A diffusion agent is a person whose job it is to make information available. In education, the job of the diffusion agent is often compared with that of the county agent, in agriculture, whose job it is to disseminate information about agricultural development.

VI

EVALUATION[1]

Evaluation of the wrong kind, at the wrong time, and for the wrong reasons has characterized too much of the current effort to appraise educational reforms.

NATIONAL ADVISORY COUNCIL ON EDUCATIONAL
PROFESSIONS DEVELOPMENT (1969)

SOME CONSTRAINTS ON EVALUATION OF DEVELOPMENTAL MATERIALS

According to the dictionary definition, to evaluate is to "determine the worth of." Taken in this sense, projects and project personnel are constantly evaluating, in each decision they make, as well when there is simply a tacit judgment that things are all right—where no overt decision is made, where things are permitted to go on as usual, where there is no intervention in the day-to-day *modus operandi* of the project in terms of a change of policy, process, or personnel.

As the project director appoints, assigns, and reassigns personnel, as one process or strategy is used rather than another, as materials are revised or not revised, someone is making evaluative decisions. Often, these are not deliberate, systematic decisions. But they are decisions and are evaluative nonetheless. However, systematic evaluation does have a large, though not clearly defined, role in developmental curricular projects.

Projects vary widely in the scope and intensity of their evaluation activities. Some tend to base decision making on systematic, evaluative feedback more than others. Some gather one kind of evaluative information, some another. Some collect more evaluative evidence than others. Some are concerned with the measurement of desirable consequences, and some are also concerned with possible undesirable consequences of the curriculum. And some use the available evaluative information more effectively than others.

---

[1] The author has written at greater length on evaluation activities of curriculum projects elsewhere (H. Grobman, 1968; H. Grobman and Hines, forthcoming), and these sources provide additional background on many of the points made here. Also see Stake (1968), Tyler *et al.* (1967), and Popham *et al.* (1969) for additional bibliographies on evaluation of developmental curriculum projects.

Thus, not only are there wide differences in the nature and extent of evaluative data gathered, but there are also wide differences in the effectiveness of their use.

Many projects limit their systematic evaluation efforts to determining through objective tests[2] whether students are learning the subject matter being presented—with learning defined as being able to recall material and apply it in situations comparable to those already taught. Such testing may be during the period when materials are being prepared (formative evaluation activities) and/or after they are completed (summative evaluation activities). Or the project may be concerned with counting things either during the formative or summative period—counting people involved, teachers trained, or adoptions by schools. As Suchman (1967) points out, in program evaluation, countable activities are often substituted for achievement, so that the evaluation is of the amount of effort expended rather than of the actual outcome.

Such activities are only a very limited part of the systematic evaluation appropriate and necessary to developmental curriculum activities. In developmental projects, a broader evaluation is imperative if the project is to avoid the dilemma of knowing that students have or have not mastered the desired materials but not knowing why or how this happened, not being able to identify the reasons for success or failure, and not being able to replicate the results. Unless the project can describe with some accuracy and detail the preexisting situation, what happened during the use of the material, and what the outcomes were—what Stake (1967) calls the antecedents, the transactions, and the outcomes—the project does not have the information it needs to determine if the project was successful, or to advise potential users of the materials how the project materials can best be used, and the nature of the constraints if materials are to be used optimally.

Herzog (1959) suggests that a satisfactory evaluation effort implies determining: the kind of change desired; the means by which change is to be brought about; the evidence that the changes observed are due to the means employed; the meaning of the changes found; and whether there are unexpected consequences.

Another view of program evaluation includes six essential steps (U.S. Public Health Service, 1955): identification of the goals to be evaluated; analysis of the problems with which the activity must cope; description and standarization of the activity; measurement of the degree of change that takes

---

[2]"An *objective test* is one which can be provided with a simple predetermined list of correct answers, so that subjective opinion or judgment in the scoring procedure is eliminated. The scoring of true-false, multiple-choice, or matching exercises is completely objective. The scoring of short-answer or completion items is partly objective." (Ebel, 1965)

place; determination of whether the observed change is due to the activity or to some other cause; and some indication of the durability of the effects.

These seem reasonable foci and procedures. Why, then, have they not been followed in the developmental curriculum work of most projects?

There are probably a number of contributing factors. In the United States, there has been no tradition of systematic evaluation of curriculum. In fact, the effectiveness of educational curricula has rarely been investigated systematically and thoroughly in the past. The Eight-Year Study (Chamberlin, 1942) of the 1930's was a landmark, since it not only was the first reasonably complete, large-scale evaluation of a curriculum, but until the early 1960's, it was the sole example of such an evaluation. Thus, broad curriculum evaluation was not a customary activity, and there were few existing prototypes for the developmental projects to follow.

Furthermore, the developmental process involves new kinds of evaluation problems. The limited curriculum evaluation efforts before the 1960's were of completed curricula—of materials that had already been published and were in the schools. These materials were not particularly new. They were materials to which teachers were accustomed, and for which teachers had been trained in their collegiate programs. And they did not venture into entirely new subject areas.

In contrast, the developmental process requires evaluation during the embryonic stages of the curriculum, since the whole point of the developmental process is to build, to check for flaws and successes, to rebuild and supplement, and to test out again. Without some systematic evaluation during the building and revising process, the revising is merely on hunch. Thus, systematic evaluation has an integral role during the building of developmental materials. This role of evaluation is one that is unique to the developmental process of curriculum preparation. And this is a type of evaluation in which there was little experience and for which few precedents had been set before the 1960's.

Thus, the circumstances for evaluation and the purposes of evaluation in developmental curriculum work are quite different than is usually the case in research on curriculum. Projects were not sure to what extent they were expected to systematize evaluation or to what extent systematic evaluation was desirable. There were no appropriate preexisting systems they could adopt. There was no authority or reference book to guide them. And so, the developmental projects had to set their own expectations for evaluation.

In fact, particularly for the first developmental projects, the traditions in educational research often constituted a hindrance rather than a help to project-evaluation activities. The new evaluation approaches, utilized to meet the evaluation needs of the developmental projects, often conflicted with some time-honored procedures in educational research.

There are a number of differences in the approach and methods of traditional educational research and those appropriate and practical for developmental curricula. In traditional educational research, the evaluation problem under consideration reflects the interests and concerns of the researcher or his research organization. In developmental projects, the evaluation reflects the needs of the project for quick answers—answers that may have to be incomplete and highly imperfect, but answers that cannot be delayed, since the decisions to which they are germane will be made on schedule whether or not the data are available. This often means compromise in research design, in instrument development, and in analysis.

In traditional research, the requirements of the research design determine the constraints of the evaluation. The scope of the research, the timetable, the instruments, are all those appropriate to the hypotheses the particular researcher is concerned with testing. In developmental curricula, the convenience and the requirements of the project set the constraints on the evaluation. The timetable is based on the needs and convenience of those developing the curriculum, not those planning and implementing the evaluation.

The project's systematic evaluation of developmental materials is one interdependent part of a large scheme, and the evaluation must fit into the scheme without too much disturbance. The major focus of the project is the development of materials, and evaluation is generally secondary. Where systematic evaluation becomes too onerous for the project, it is relegated to a smaller role or ignored altogether. Thus, if it is to be usable, evaluation of developmental material often sacrifices some of the niceties of traditional research because of time constraints. Compromises must also be made because the evaluation must be acceptable and usable by nonresearchers. It must answer those questions nonresearchers want answered, and both the research prospectus and the findings must be appropriate for this audience.

Often, developmental projects are expected to use existing standardized tests[3] to measure student achievement. When they do not, they are accused of being afraid their students will not match up to the performance of students in the norm groups[4] for the tests. Yet, because project goals and content differ

---

[3]"A *standarized test* is one which has been constructed in accord with detailed specifications, one for which the items have been selected after tryout for appropriateness in difficulty and discriminating power, one which is accompanied by a manual giving definite directions for uniform administration and scoring, and one which is provided with relevant and dependable norms for score interpretation. . . . Unfortunately not all tests offered as standardized tests have been prepared as carefully as the foregoing description suggests." (Ebel, 1965)

[4]"A *norm,* as the term is used in relation to test scores, is the average or typical test score (or other measure) for members of a specific group. Norms are often presented in tables giving typical score values for a series of different homogeneous groups such as students in a given grade or students of a given age." (Ebel, 1965)

from previous subject-matter coverage and expectations, existing subject-matter tests are often inappropriate. Thus, many projects prepared new tests for use during the formative period, both as part of the formative materials (since they consider tests as a basic part of the curriculum) and also to serve as evaluation devices.

Such new project tests are often prepared on a hurried schedule, after materials preparation is complete, and during the time of the school tryout of formative materials, so that the tests can be used as a source of feedback on the classroom trial use of materials. Where experimental materials are prepared during a summer writing period and tried out in classes during the school year starting the following September, tests generally are not prepared until fall and winter of the year in which they are to be used.

This schedule is far from optimal in terms of elegance of test preparation. But generally, it is the only feasible schedule in terms of the project writing and tryout calendar. Thus, the tests used in project formative evaluation are often imperfect. And they can not be normed before their use in the project evaluation. (Even if there is time to pretest the new instruments, there is often no suitable audience for such pretesting, since the tests generally reflect skills not taught in previous curricula. But again, projects have been criticized for using nonstandarized tests.)

On whatever tests are used in project evaluation, projects are expected to compare achievement of their experimental students with achievement of students in control groups—parallel groups set up for comparison purposes and taught with conventional curricula—with the same tests. These expectations are wholly unrealistic, yet they often prevail; where they do not prevail, the evaluation is criticized as lacking in rigor, and as being unscientific and unscholarly.[5]

Often, the developmental materials are in areas not previously included in the school curriculum at all, as is the case with sociology and anthropology; or the developmental materials might include subject-matter coverage that is completely new, as biochemistry in tenth grade biology, or laboratory skills and ecosystems in seventh or eighth grade biology. To compare subject-matter achievement of students in traditional courses with those in developmental curricula in such cases is meaningless, since the coverage of subject matter in each of the courses may be discrete, with little or no overlap, or with completely different emphases. For example, it is meaningless to test a control group on the developmental curriculum's test on anthropology when the control group has spent its time studying conventional civics, with no an-

---

[5]An extreme view has been taken by some scholars (e.g., Guba, 1969) that evaluation is not research, and to consider it that is to dilute the meaning of research.

thropology included. And to test the experimental curriculum students on the civics materials which has been replaced by anthropology is equally inappropriate.

The inappropriateness of such parallel testing on identical tests is less apparent, but nonetheless real, when the subject has been taught previously, but with different coverage and emphases. Thus, twelfth grade students were studying physics before PSSC; eleventh grade students were studying chemistry before CHEM Study and CBA; and tenth grade students were studying biology before BSCS. And there is doubtless some overlap in coverage in the old and new materials. But in each of these cases, the new emphases, coverage, and sequencing are somewhat different.

The whole point in the creation of the new developmental materials is to permit and promote such drastic differences. If the tests to be used as a criterion measure for experimental and control groups are at all content-oriented, then the same tests can not be appropriate to those in the new courses as well as those in the old courses. It is only where more general skills and attitudes are involved—creative thinking, critical thinking, reading ability in the subject area, attitude toward the subject and the school—that a single test might be appropriate for both groups. Thus, comparison of experimental groups with traditional groups is often inappropriate, though failure of developmental projects to make such comparisons has been widely criticized.

For the most part, project directors and personnel and even project policy boards include few educational research persons. Such policy boards are often dominated by persons from the discipline and practitioners of that discipline in the schools. While project participants sometimes include faculty members from schools of education, such educators often are not highly research-oriented in terms of curriculum evaluation. Even when they are research-oriented, their voices are in a very small minority.

The directive given most of the projects is to effect change in the teaching of a discipline; it is not to do research. Unless the project sees very clearly exactly how the evaluation activity contributes immediately and directly to this major goal—the immediate improvement of the teaching of the discipline —the evaluation activity is not espoused, or if carried on at all, becomes a supplementary activity. Even where this is not a project reaction, it is sometimes the reaction of the funding agency.

Perhaps a basic problem in planning and executing the systematic evaluation activities of developmental materials is that no one familiar with evaluation in or outside of developmental projects has taken the responsibility for determining precisely how evaluation at various points can be directly useful to the project in improving its product. While some efforts are made by project personnel, many areas of potential usefulness of evaluative data are over-looked. And educational researchers outside of projects have not developed clear suggestions or guidelines for projects to follow.

Even where developmental projects involve trained research people in evaluation work, and evaluative data are collected, the researchers often take for granted that the project people understand the data that is given them from testing activities, and will know how to use it. Often, this is not the case, and much data go unused simply because their implications and relevance are apparent only to the researchers collecting them.

Further, the research people working with project evaluation are often used to a relatively leisurely kind of scheduling, a scheduling that permits more elegance in reporting. As a result, data from testing of students using formative materials might appear six months after the testing is completed—in January of the school year following the testing of the previous spring. By the time the data are available, the experimental materials on which they are based and which they are supposed to test have already been completely revised during the intervening summer, so that they can again be tested in the fall. In such instances, the only formative purpose these data can serve is in the revision of the tests themselves.

Often, the people directing projects do not know that they need help on a variety of phases of evaluation. Many are not even aware of the potential usefulness of many kinds of evaluative data. When they seek expert help in these matters, they often have trouble finding useful sources. The research profession is slow in becoming interested in the rather special problems in-volved in developmental work. Often, the lag in evaluation reflects a lack of a clear sense of what is needed, and an inability to find anyone who can give direction, rather than the project's lack of interest in evaluation. More re-cently, some of the projects—UICSM and IPI, for example—have taken a clearer research orientation, with a number of highly specialized research people on the staff, and considerable basic as well as applied research carried out on the curriculum.

A further difficulty in effecting an evaluation of the developmental materi-als is the nature of evaluation, the fact that evaluation looks not just at success, but at limitations and at failures. Evaluation not only supports self-esteem; evaluation can erode self-esteem. It is a natural tendency for projects to wel-come evaluation when it tells the project that materials are successful, and it is easy for recipients of evaluative feedback to focus on that aspect.

But, particularly during the formative period, evaluation focuses not only on what was successful, but also on how the work can be made more success-ful. Thus, the formative evaluation may be most useful not when it identifies the successful ideas and aspects, but when it pinpoints what is not optimal. Even for the most honest person, for the person who genuinely wants to improve his product, this is a difficult kind of feedback to accept fully and to weigh fairly. Furthermore, receiving critical feedback is not the kind of experience successful professionals have had before, and for many, it takes a while to get used to it. Unfortunately, some people connected with developmental projects have never gotten used to accepting feedback productively.

Perhaps as the materials developer is able to evaluate directly, by himself, it is easier for him to use the data productively. Thus, as the developer of materials tries them out in a programmed format and identifies for himself inefficient sequencing, or materials that are not learned in a satisfactory manner, he is more willing to adapt materials in the light of these experiences, than is the case where an outsider is trying out the materials or identifying the ineffective aspects.

Similarly, the writer who tries teaching the materials in the classroom himself, as Suchman of the Inquiry Project and Beberman of UICSM have done, may not experience the same trauma or disbelief from their own direct experience that many writers have experienced when they see feedback from an unknown teacher. However, this practice also has limitations. It does not provide information on whether anyone else can achieve such results. Beberman's teaching is legendary, and when the classroom teaching of new math is discussed, often someone will suggest that Beberman could teach anything effectively, and students would love it, with the implication that no one else could obtain the same results. Thus, while face-to-face confrontation by the writers with students is useful, it is not a sufficient test of materials. Also, with the complete involvement needed for good teaching, there are kinds of observation that cannot be done by the person doing the teaching. At times, UICSM had one writer teaching while a second writer observed, a practice that would bypass this difficulty.

An alternate method that is effective for some purposes is for writers to visit classrooms of a variety of teachers, to observe what happens when the materials are used in classes, and perhaps this experience makes feedback more acceptable than is the case with feedback received secondhand. But, since this means a large drain on the time of the writers, the usefulness of the procedure is limited. And so, the problem of how evaluation can be acceptable and still useful is a pervasive one, and one that has limited the usefulness of evaluative information collected, and the effectiveness of the evaluation itself.

To appraise the evaluation efforts of developmental projects—particularly those before 1965—in today's terms is unrealistic, since the climate of educational research even as late as 1960 was far different from that by the end of the 1960's. There were far fewer education researchers, and there had been relatively little in the way of grant funds available for educational research. In 1960, educational research was not thinking big. It was not thinking in a highly practical context. And limited though the activities very clearly were, the evaluation activities of the BSCS in 1960-63 probably constituted the most extensive curriculum appraisal venture since the Eight-Year Study, not simply in size, but also in complexity.

Thus, the first developmental projects were caught in a difficult evaluation situation, with few appropriate precedents, several inappropriate expectations, and with a need to develop some new strategies and evaluation instruments. The development of such strategies is a time-consuming activity, and might take as long as the entire developmental period of the curriculum. This is one area of developmental work where the first evaluation efforts of the early projects could not do the kinds of things that are possible now, since a number of evaluation strategies had not yet been developed, and no one project could have developed enough strategies, quickly enough, to do the evaluation job that is possible today.

Some projects have used a seat-of-the-pants evaluation strategy, with evaluation almost entirely unsystematic and intuitive. Fortunately, the people in some of these projects had good intuitive instincts. Other projects tried a number of different evaluation approaches, some quite unsuccessfully, some relatively useful. As more experience has become available, the evaluation picture and the alternatives have become clearer and the possibility of an exemplary evaluation is improved; and even though there is no single adequate evaluation prototype, a number of prototypes for various aspects of evaluation are becoming available.[6]

KINDS OF EVALUATION ACTIVITIES

Evaluation always reflects compromises. There are so many questions that could be asked, that not all can be answered satisfactorily. Only a limited number of things can be investigated. Choices must be made. While it is easy to suggest that the "important" things be done first, until the research is completed, it is not always easy to determine what facet is most important. Herrnstein (1968) points out that "What looks 'important' at any time reflects a consensus based on what is already known. Thus, it should come as no surprise that many potent discoveries arise from the study of the apparently 'unimportant'. . . . " And regardless of the choices made and the priorities set, some criticism will follow.

---

[6]These include the systems reported by Stevens and Morrissett (1967-68), Easley, Jenkins, and Ashenfelter (1967), and Farr, Laffey, and Smith (1969).

Further, the circumstances for curriculum evaluation are never optimal. To determine whether curricula are appropriate for schools, one must use naturalistic settings—settings similar to those where the materials are intended for use. Further, schools are complex social systems. In even the most cooperative schools, all possible sources of variation in experimental conditions cannot be controlled. Evaluators must take the schools largely as they find them and must work within these constraints.

> Planning an experiment is always a matter of allocating scarce resources. We must decide, therefore, which sources of error . . . should deliberately be ignored, and which should be given care and attention; and for these we must ascertain the extent to which it is worthwhile to take the trouble to diminish their magnitude. It is pointless to conceive of a good experiment as one which takes account of every possible source of error. Such perfection is not to be found even in Heaven; whatever God was trying to prove by the creation of man, I rather imagine that the results are inconclusive.
>
> KAPLAN (1964)

In developmental project work, the formative and summative periods of materials development overlap and many of the activities are similar. But, in discussing evaluation, often these periods are viewed separately for convenience, and because the functions of evaluation and the problems involved differ to some extent in the period of materials preparation and in the period after materials are completed. Thus, formative evaluation is the evaluation during the period of materials preparation; and summative evaluation is the evaluation following completion of materials (Scriven, 1967).

During formative evaluation, the evaluation may be primarily for internal use, with the focus on whether the materials are feasible, and if so, how they can be improved. In the summative period, there may be additional audiences for the evaluation—including the research community and the target publics—and the focus may be on describing the effect of the use of the materials, and the student body and circumstances in which this use took place. This may be in terms of the immediate effect at the end of a unit, semester, or school year, or the long-range effect, involving follow-up (longitudinal) studies over a period of years.

Both formative and summative studies may deal entirely with the finite product developed by the project—with the curriculum materials developed—and focus on whether students do or do not learn them. The evaluation may consider whether all the materials are learned, or it may be concerned with which parts are most effectively learned. It may examine materials for validity to determine whether the content and methods involved are valid reflections of the intent of the project. It may also consider the processes involved in development of the materials and in their introduction and use.

The evaluation may be concerned with broad, general, overall aspects, i.e., with such questions as whether most students learn most of the materials successfully (macroevaluation). Or it may concentrate on discrete segments or events, for example, on whether specific parts of the curriculum, particular ideas, or particular project activities or parts of activities related to curriculum use—e.g., the teacher training or the implementation of materials—are handled effectively (microevaluation).

Some curriculum studies have restricted their systematic evaluation largely to the materials produced, and have focused on whether or not students score well on an achievement test. Unfortunately, this is usually a very gross testing—that is, an evaluation in terms of overall scores on a written achievement test—of very limited objectives, and often, the objectives tested are not the major objectives of the project. Through such an evaluation, the project will simply learn that students attain a particular score on an achievement test, but will not know which items were answered correctly, which ideas and skills were mastered and which were not, and what skills and ideas were not even tested.

Projects often measure what is most easily measurable, and assume that achievement of the other objectives follows as a matter of course. Some projects do use highly imaginative measures to broaden the scope of the information obtained. Some use new approaches that produce useful nonquantifiable information, where the problem does not readily lend itself to quantification. However, others simply ignore what they cannot easily quantify.

Thus, a project may wish to increase critical thinking skills and stimulate inquiry. It may wish to communicate the professional's view of anthropology, sociology, or history, and increase the accuracy of the student's view of the discipline. It may hope to encourage and stimulate self-education in the discipline and lay a groundwork for further education. Yet, the project's evaluation of student achievement may be nothing more than the measure of student performance at the end of the course on an achievement test that requires little but recall. For example, one of the most extensive and costly facets of the DEEP evaluation was the administration of the *Test of Economic Understanding* (Committee for the Measurement of Economic Understanding, 1963), which is largely a test of recall of specific economic facts and concepts, to thousands of students and teachers.[7]

Even where tests are newly designed by the developmental project for evaluation of project materials, they may not be appropriate. Such tests may cover different facts than were required in previous courses or tests, but there

---

[7]Maher, Symmes, and Green (1968) report the administration of this test to some 70,000 students from 1964 to 1967.

is often the same dependence on recall that the developmental projects deplore in curricula they hope to supersede. Thus, at times, project evaluation seems largely unrelated to the aims of the project. In contrast, some projects have taken a highly imaginative and extensive view of evaluation, and developed some new techniques that are highly appropriate to the job to be done.

FORMATIVE EVALUATION

During the formative period, the major function of evaluation is to improve materials. This means that data are needed rapidly, and they are needed in a form appropriate to the user—the developer of the materials.

Content Analysis

Content analysis is a major phase of formative evaluation. One of the facets of content analysis is the general review by persons in the discipline, as well as reviews by psychologists and educators, hopefully representing different areas of specialization, and different points of view. Regardless of diversity of backgrounds, it is important that all of the reviewers understand the purpose of the materials and of the project, and conduct their reviews in this context.

Some suggest that this is not an important constraint, and that perhaps the project is best served by reviewers who come to the work without an understanding of, or a sympathy with, the project intent. This attitude may be appropriate for the summative evaluation, when the project is compared with external criteria—for example, with school system aims—but for formative evaluation, once the project aims have been formulated by the project and have been subjected to evaluation, they provide the context of the review, since the primary purpose of such review is to determine whether the project is implementing its aims. The purpose is not to measure the project's materials against goals not necessarily of concern to the project.

Thus, while a review of goals is certainly a legitimate part of evaluation, it is discrete from the review of materials to determine the extent to which the project aims are implemented. In testing an automobile for performance, the decision of whether production of cars that can go 100 or 140 miles per hour may be evaluated in terms of desirability and propriety. However, when looking at the test models, the question is not whether cars should be designed to attain this speed, but rather whether the test car design is compatible with achieving the goal that has been set.

Similarly, in curriculum evaluation, the goals should be reviewed at an early point. But given the goals, the review of the materials for validity should be within the constraints of those goals. The question of whether biology should be a tenth or twelfth grade course is open to legitimate debate, as is the question of whether or not there should be prerequisites. After the problem has been carefully considered and a decision made that biology should be a general education course for tenth grade students, with no prerequisites, a reviewer who does not accept these constraints when making his review is simply not in a position to contribute to the development of materials which attempt to reflect these aims.

Thus, as new anthropology materials are developed for the sixth or eighth grade, after project agreement on this grade level goal, and after evaluation of this goal, the reviewer, during the formative period, is not serving the evaluation needs if he is hostile to the idea of teaching anthropology at this grade level, or is unsympathetic with the idea of using anthropology as the primary vehicle for teaching certain skills in the social studies. Questions about choice of subject area and grade placement are legitimate as part of evaluation of the project aims which hopefully precedes the preparation of materials. Once these aims become the accepted guidelines for the curriculum, the formative review is concerned with the extent to which these aims are implemented or can be implemented.

It is equally important that the reviewers during the formative period represent a variety of approaches or concerns. Thus, reviewers from various subspecialty areas may review for accuracy of presentation in these areas. Such specialists may also provide suggestions for new content or more appropriate illustrative materials than are included in the materials they review. There may be a psychologist reviewing materials from the child development standpoint. Another psychologist might be concerned about values communicated by the materials. And a third might be concerned about learning theory.

A different kind of review may be provided by those persons assigned to prepare new tests to accompany the curriculum materials. This is a kind of review that often is not sought. Particularly where test writers are not in close contact with other project writing and feedback staff, these reactions may not be volunteered, and a potentially valuable source of information may be untapped. Test writers often look for or notice different kinds of things than do persons reviewing materials for other purposes. For example, in preparing tests for a set of materials that was supposed to encourage an inquiring and analytical approach, test writers found they could not prepare questions measuring anything but memory and direct application skills, since to them, the curriculum did not seem to prepare students for anything but memory and direct application. The number and kinds of new words introduced or the absence of some key words used in the discipline may be noted by test writers when these aspects have been overlooked by other reviewers. As the experimental editions proceed from one edition to the next, the test questions that can no longer be asked, and those that must be modified if they are still to be used, may indicate some of the changes in materials that the writers themselves may not be aware of. Such reactions by the test writers should be encouraged, since they throw a different, and often useful, perspective on the developmental materials.

Content reviews may be relatively unstructured. However, other, more structured analyses are also desirable. These might include examining some of the following: difficulty level of words, and the number and nature of new words introduced (e.g., are new words esoteric, or will they be useful in improving general vocabulary, and is a new word used more than once?); extent to which the purposes of the project are implemented in various portions of the curriculum; kinds of activities indicated or implied; relative subject-matter emphases; extent to which the various portions of the curriculum are mutually supportive and consistent (e.g., whether the intent of developing inquiry is supported by all the materials, or by just some portions); and whether the stated intent to build on ideas is implemented so that the program is sequential rather than piecemeal.

Scriven (1967) points to three connected matching problems which might provide a framework for systematic review: the match between goals and course content; the match between goals and examination content; and the match between course content and examination content. Materials may also be examined from the point of view of the nature of the value assumptions of the curriculum, in terms of what is important—for example, what is a good society and a good life—questions which are often overlooked in subject-matter curricula reviews, even though most curricula include many underlying value assumptions (H. Grobman, to appear 1971).

It is a natural tendency for developers of materials to be confident that they have implemented their own goals and have included no activities or content that will have unfortunate side effects. However, this is not always the case. Thus, a specific systematic review for each such facet is highly desirable and often surprising in its results.

While general reviews, particularly those by subject-matter experts, have been widely used in developmental project formative evaluation, systematic reviews of other aspects of the materials have been far less frequent. Recently, there has been considerable attention given to various kinds of systematic analysis, and a number of useful analysis systems have been developed or proposed.[8] Some of these systems are appropriate for a single project or

---

[8] A general discussion of content analysis techniques is included in Fox (1969); specific systems for types of content analysis are included in Easley, Jenkins and Ashenfelter (1967); Farr, Laffey, and Smith (1969); H. Grobman (forthcoming); Klinckmann (1961); Stevens and Morrissett (1967–68).

subject area; other systems can be used with a wide variety of materials in various contexts.

Classroom Tryouts

Another aspect of the formative evaluation is the classroom tryout of materials, on a pilot basis or on a large-scale basis. This may involve tryout by project staff; tryout by specially trained teachers; or tryout by untrained teachers. It may involve volunteers, including only those teachers volunteering, or it may include nonvolunteers. The classroom tryout may involve optimal teaching situations or a variety of teaching situations. It may involve heterogeneous student groups, or student groups selected in terms of ability, socioeconomic background, and motivation. In any case, the classroom tryout can produce a variety of kinds of feedback on the classroom, the teacher, the students, and the learning outcomes.

Once the tryouts are set up, some projects proceed to determining outcomes, to the total neglect of antecedents and transactions. They look at results, without looking at the circumstances in which the evaluation is taking place (the antecedents) and what is being done in the course of the experimental treatment (transactions). Such a course of action is shortsighted, since without some knowledge of the antecedents and transactions, the results are relatively meaningless. They cannot be put into context, so that the interpretation includes the relevant factors. While research on instruction has demonstrated the influence of various factors in the learning situation in study after study, often these factors are ignored in curriculum evaluation. Yet, curriculum evaluation cannot realistically be divorced from instruction. And the ecological factors relevant to research on instruction are also relevant to curriculum evaluation.[9]

Antecedents. Regardless of the extent and nature of the tryout of experimental materials by the developmental project, the circumstances which constitute the antecedents of the curriculum experiment should be described. In effect, the antecedents include the past history and ecology of the experimental group. Some projects have ignored the antecedents in planning evaluation activities. This may reflect a tacit assumption that all schools are more or less alike, an assumption that all students have the same start-of-the-program achievement and skills in the curriculum area under study, or an assumption that if the sample is large enough, differences among groups will not be important. None of these assumptions is necessarily valid.

---

[9]Wittrock (in press) indicates some of the interactive relationships in such situations.

The teachers, school, students, and classroom situation of the evaluation population can be described generally or in some detail, including the adequacy of the classroom and the classroom equipment, the class size, its ability and achievement levels, sex of students, length of class period, class norms, teacher background, and previous exposure of students and teacher to the subject area. All these provide important bench marks if the results of the evaluation are to be placed in a proper perspective. Such descriptive data are sometimes obtained by questionnaire—either a highly structured questionnaire or an open-end one—or by classroom visits.

Some facets of the tryout situation can best be described with a checklist type of instrument. Such instruments are most useful when they are objective —that is, when the use of the instrument does not require subjective judgment. This does not eliminate the role of judgment from evaluative descriptions; rather, it restricts the role of judgment to deciding what is to be described and how this is to be described, and, after the description is completed, to interpreting the results obtained. However, for the description itself, it is far more useful for evaluative purposes to know whether a laboratory for thirty students has five or fifteen microscopes than to know that an observer considers the laboratory "fair" or of "high quality." It is more important to know that on a reading test, the students score at grade level with a range of reading levels of 1.5 years, than to have an observer's statement that the class is "about average in ability."

For many situations, objective checklists can be developed to give rather precise descriptions of the classrooms where evaluation is taking place. For example, the BSCS designed an objective checklist to describe the physical circumstances in which BSCS materials were being used during the formative evaluation (see Illustration 5). That obtaining detailed and precise information of this sort is important in curriculum evaluation is indicated by the BSCS findings that adequacy of laboratory facilities was a significant variable in student achievement (H. Grobman, 1963).[10]

Many other facets of evaluation situations lend themselves to such precise descriptions. However, in using data on the teaching situation, it is important to distinguish between availability and use of equipment. Many schools have the equipment; not all use it. The same is true of other variables. Small class size may permit a different kind of teaching than is possible in large classes. It does not necessarily follow that such teaching actually takes place. Thus,

---

[10]In addition to the usefulness of the BSCS checklist for evaluation purposes, it provided teachers and school administrators with an objective standard for their laboratories. This was useful in local efforts to upgrade biology laboratories in these schools, since the checklist provided an external, authoritative standard. Also, it became possible for any school to compare its facilities with those of other schools, since the BSCS evaluation reports provided a profile of the participating schools in terms of each equipment item, as well as for the overall ratings. The net result was a general upgrading of laboratory facilities in participating schools.

description of antecedents is an essential but not a sufficient indication of the circumstances in which the curriculum is being implemented. How the curriculum is implemented (the transactions) and the interaction between antecedents and transactions are critical to an understanding of outcomes.

Transactions. The descriptions of the transactions—what goes on in the classroom—can include: what the teacher does with the materials; how they are taught; where emphasis is given; to what extent the teacher departs from the materials, supplements, deletes, or modifies; whether mode of presentation is compatible with intent of the project and the materials; whether the teacher is mentally convinced that the materials are too difficult for the students, or that the student will have difficulty with them; whether the teacher is able to set aside previous notions or experiences concerning coverage and method and whether he is able to ignore the pending end-of-year systemwide traditional tests; the timing used; the problems faced; and the general atmosphere and attitude of students and teacher. This information can be derived from periodic reports from the experimental teachers, from interviews with teachers, students and supervisory staff, and from classroom visits with unstructured, somewhat structured, or highly structured observations.

Thus, the classroom visitor can observe experimental classes and report general observations. He can have a general observation sheet where he enters general information about interest level, adequacy of presentation, etc. Or he can use a highly structured and detailed system of observation, such as a classroom interaction system, where each statement by teacher and student is carefully coded in terms of content or purpose, and a record is kept of who talks, and whether this initiates a discussion or is in reply to the question raised by someone else.[11]

Such data as these are part of transactions. But they may also be part of the reporting of outcomes, since some of the classroom observations report not just the conditions of the teaching-learning situation, but also the skills learned. For example, an observation report may include the kinds of questions asked by students and the frequency with which questions are asked; in a project concerned with teaching students to ask insightful questions or to develop creative thinking, these data reflect some of the outcomes.

Another kind of feedback on the classroom tryout of materials is the reports of teachers—both written and oral—on their experience. Such reports also feed into both transactions and outcomes. Teachers trying out experimental editions of developmental materials are often asked to write reports reacting to the materials either weekly and/or at the end of each chapter or unit. Such

---

[11]Simon and Boyer (1967) is a reference source for instruments developed for such classroom observation purposes.

ILLUSTRATION 5

1964 Revised BSCS Biology Laboratory Facilities Checklist

To facilitate comparative evaluation of present biology laboratory facilities in a school, a Checklist is proposed for a laboratory used daily by four classes of 28 students each. This Checklist is *not* to be construed as the definitive standard; it is simply a means of permitting a general comparison of a school's facilities with optimal facilities.

In the Checklist, facilities have been grouped in categories to permit a separate evaluation of each category, since the pedagogic and monetary values of the various categories cannot be equated. For example, the Fixed Laboratory Installations category is the most costly and is of paramount importance. A high rating in this category would be more significant than a high rating in the Demonstration Aids category.

The Checklist may be used in the following manner:

For each facility listed, *circle* the category that best describes your laboratory. In the last column on that line, write in the point value for the circled item; i.e., the point value at the head of the column in which the circled item appears, e.g., under Fixed Laboratory Installations, if you have 200 square feet of shelf storage space, circle 200, and in the column at the extreme right put down 8 points, the value assigned to that item.

—Where the laboratory has none of the facility mentioned, do not circle any item and enter a zero in the *Your School* column, since the response value is zero.

—Find the category sub-totals for your school in each of the seven areas, and compare these with the maximum possible scores for each area.

—Obtain a grand total for all areas and compare it with the rating scale below:

RATING SCALE

Rating	Points	Per Cent of Optimal
A	460-541	85-100
B	379-459	70-84
C	298-378	55-69
D	216-297	40-54
E	135-215	25-39
F	8-134	0-24

SOURCE: Biological Sciences Curriculum Study, *Newsletter,* No. 21, April 1964. Reprinted by permission of the BSCS.

ILLUSTRATION 5 continued

Table 1-1964 Revised Laboratory Facilities Checklist
(Based on 28 students)

Facility	Point Value				
Category A	16 pts.	12 pts.	8 pts.	4 pts.	Your School
Fixed laboratory installations—*maximum possible score 216 pts.*					
Demonstration table	1	—	—	—	_____
Work counter (peripheral)—linear feet	120	60	30	15	_____
Sinks—regular	4	3	2	1	_____
—laundry	—	—	2	1	_____
Water—cold	4 taps	3 taps	2 taps	1 tap	_____
—hot	—	—	2 taps	1 tap	_____
Outlets—gas	7	5	3	2	_____
—electrical	7	5	3	2	_____
Compressed air	—	—	—	Yes	_____
Garbage disposal	—	—	—	Yes	_____
Shelf storage sq. ft.	450	300	200	100	_____
Preparation room	large	medium	small	—	_____
Life alcove	large	medium	small	—	_____
Project work area	large	medium	small	—	_____
Science library/min. 50 vols.	large	medium	small	—	_____
Display cases (in halls)	—	—	2	1	_____
Light and ventilation	good	fair	poor	—	_____
Sub-total points					_____
Budget considerations—*maximum possible score 48 pts.*					
Funds for perishables, glassware, chemicals, specimens, etc.	$500/yr.	$250/yr.	$125/yr.	$50/yr.	_____
Funds available *during* year as needed	yes	—	—	—	_____
Capital outlay funds	$500/yr.	$250/yr.	$125/yr.	$50/yr.	_____
Sub-total points					_____
Microscopes—*maximum possible score 32 pts.*					
Compound microscopes	28	14	7	4	_____
Binocular stereo microscopes	28	14	7	4	_____
Sub-total points					_____
Lab assistants—*maximum possible score 16 pts.*					
Paid lab assistants—5 hrs. per week per section	1	—	—	—	_____
Sub-total points					_____
Category B	12 pts.	9 pts.	6 pts.	3 pts.	Your School
Major equipment—*maximum possible 111 pts.*					
Refrigerator	1	—	—	—	_____
Gas range/oven	1	—	—	—	_____
Incubator	2	1	—	—	_____
Balances (.01 g)	4	3	2	1	_____
Autoclave	1	—	—	—	_____
Pressure cooker	2	1	—	—	_____
Centrifuge	—	—	2	1	_____
Temp., humidity & light controlled chamber	—	—	1	—	_____
Fume hood	—	1	—	—	_____
Laboratory cart	2	1	—	—	_____
Power supply units (AC/DC portable)	—	—	2	1	_____
Sub-total points					_____
Category C	8 pts	6 pts.	4 pts.	2 pts.	Your School
Small equipment—*maximum possible 70 pts.*					
Basic laboratory equipment*	many	adeq.	few	sparse	_____
Aquaria	4	3	2	1	_____
Terraria	4	3	2	1	_____
Glassware	many	adeq.	few	sparse	_____
Collecting equipment	many	adeq.	few	sparse	_____
Animal cages	8	6	4	2	_____
Covered disposal containers	2	1	—	—	_____
Electric hot plates	—	2	1	—	_____
Chemicals	many	adeq.	few	sparse	_____
Sub-total points					_____
Demonstration aids—*maximum possible 48 pts.*					
Specimen sets	many	adeq.	few	sparse	_____
Models and charts	many	adeq.	few	sparse	_____
Prepared microscope slides	many	adeq.	few	sparse	_____
Overhead projector	—	1	—	—	_____
Cartridge projector	—	—	—	—	_____
Slide projector	—	1	—	—	_____
Microprojector	—	—	1	—	_____
Sub-total points					_____

All facilities--maximum possible score 541 pts.
Your school—total score

*Includes items such as centigrade thermometers, pipettes, Bunsen burners, dissecting sets, tripod stands, ring stands, etc.

reports may be structured, with a checklist indicating time required to complete specified activities, difficulty level, problems in teaching and in learning, and a general positive or negative reaction. Often, the structured report forms have a space at the end of the form for other comments. Some projects prefer an open-ended teacher reaction, since they want to avoid suggesting to the teacher the kinds of things to look for. Structured reports are easier to tabulate and analyze. Also, they can reduce the problem of such overgeneral teacher comments as "needs improvement" that often are given on completely unstructured reports. However, structured reports may unduly restrict the teacher's response, and the most valuable insights may not be reported.

To facilitate feedback, some projects have provided feedback books for teachers. Each blank, tear-out page is coded to a chapter and section. And the teacher is asked to enter his comments as his class finishes the appropriate chapter or section. Other projects provide the teacher with an extra set of classroom materials. (This may include both teacher and student materials, interleaved for greater convenience.) In the extra volume of the project materials that is provided for reporting purposes, the pages may be perforated for easy removal. The teacher is asked to make marginal notes in this copy, so that these comments can be easily tied to specific sections, exercises, and even specific sentences.

In either of these feedback situations, the teacher can enter comments as they occur to him, then tear out the appropriate pages and send them in, perhaps accompanied by other, more general notes on an accompanying sheet. In both situations, the hope is that by making the mechanics of the feedback process as convenient as possible, the teacher will be encouraged to make notes promptly, as ideas occur to him, and will be encouraged to send them in.[12]

Requesting written feedback from teachers is a fairly common practice for those projects that are testing materials over a geographic area too large to permit frequent face-to-face contacts. For some projects—IME for example—written teacher reports constitute a major source of feedback, and reports are read and considered very carefully. Other projects use these reports less systematically. And some projects stack them in a corner and consider such teacher reports somewhat superfluous. In the latter case, it is not clear why the reports were ever obtained.

A number of projects have considered the teacher reports quite basic to the feedback and revision processes. Some projects have also used the reports as a method of identifying individuals for helping in project activities, includ-

---

[12]Even such a simple thing as providing preaddressed, stamped envelopes for feedback mailings can make a decided difference in proportion of teachers sending in feedback and in the promptness with which this feedback is returned to the project.

ing teacher training. In this case, teacher feedback reports are used to locate people who seem to understand the intents and strategies of the project, and who are analytical and creative in suggesting new approaches.

Feedback from teachers may also be obtained from periodic teacher meetings. In some cases, materials are tried out in schools near the project headquarters and teachers are invited in, or project staff may meet from time to time with teachers in a central location to discuss teacher reactions on classroom use of the materials. In other instances, where tryout teachers are spread over a larger geographic area, teachers within a given area may meet together periodically.

In some instances, there has been a deliberate policy of selecting tryout teachers in geographic clusters so that such meetings are possible. For example, the teachers who were to try out version materials for BSCS in 1960–61 and 1961–62 were selected in geographic clusters so that there were at least six experimental teachers within a radius of twenty or thirty miles at most.

Projects may ask teachers to attend feedback meetings as a contribution to the project. In some projects, the teachers are paid a standard fee for the time devoted to this activity. For example, during one of its tryout years, the BSCS paid teachers a fee equal to 10 percent of their regular school salaries for the work they were doing for the BSCS in providing feedback. (This fee was not for teaching experimental materials or for attending the initial preparation sessions to learn how to teach the materials. It was paid for the specific services involved in providing feedback through written reports and through contributing ideas at weekly two-hour feedback meetings.) For each cluster or center, the teacher-designated center leader conducted the weekly meetings and wrote reports of these meetings. He also checked on the sending in of individual teacher reports. The center leader was paid an extra 5 percent for the additional services he performed for the BSCS.

In looking at transactions, projects generally have some classroom visiting. They also often have teacher reports, and meetings between selected teachers and writers. But there has been relatively little done in the way of precise descriptions of what is occurring in the classroom. Thus, the projects often do not know whether all the materials provided were used. They may not know how these were used. They may not know by whom they were used, in terms of the characteristics of the users. And they are often completely unaware of the interaction of antecedents with transactions. In such cases, the project may have a great deal of data, often on very extensive samples, with little idea of what the implications of the data are. Data on student achievement can be interpreted adequately only when they are interpreted within the context of the situation in which the achievement took place.

Outcomes. Almost all projects use some kind of outcomes measure. Most projects use achievement tests, though some attitude testing has been done. There has been heavy dependence on written, objective tests. Achievement testing has also included some essay and short answer tests; however, these have been minor facets of the evaluation effort. The dependence on objective testing reflects the convenience of such testing for large groups of students. Also, the problems of interpreting answers are minimized. And subject-matter tests are often developed as part of the curriculum materials, so they are available to serve a dual purpose.

While it is easy to decry the objective test as unimaginative and inappropriate for measuring many kinds of skills, and certainly, many objective tests have been limited in this way, this need not necessarily be the case. Objective tests can be based on a presentation of data or situations by movies, transparencies, or slides, and by tapes and records. HPP and the SSCP have used photographs to present data and problem situations. Another possibility is the programmed test, permitting the student to follow a unique pathway in answering a series of questions, so that students need not answer in the same sequence in order to arrive at the eventual solution to a complex problem (McGuire, undated; McGuire, 1967; McGuire and Babbott, 1967).

With few exceptions, evaluation has depended on written testing to see if the student has learned certain skills. This has several clear limitations. First, that the student can do something on a test does not mean he will do it in practice; *can do* and *will do* are not synonymous. Thus, while some projects have tested to determine whether the student is able to evaluate data in a formal testing situation, there has been little investigation of whether the student does, in fact, evaluate data systematically and accurately when arriving at decisions outside the testing, which takes place in the classroom where the appropriate subject is taught.

Further, written tests often merely reflect the students' verbal ability or verbal limitations. Students with low verbal ability may be handicapped in answering, even though they have mastered the skills. For example, in the first pilot year of IMB, a few teachers reported that relatively low-ability seventh grade students were able to handle the readings and the activities in class, but that the tests were beyond them—that even when questions were read aloud, such students could not cope with them. The tests were not at a particularly high reading or difficulty level, as was indicated by the high scores (43 of the 45 items correct) achieved by a number of students, and a relatively high average score (65 percent correct) for the experimental group as a whole. Yet, these tests did not permit some low-ability students to indicate what they had learned and, in fact, were evidently quite disturbing to some of the slower students.

A comparable situation may exist in multilingual cultures—for example, in working with Puerto Rican or Mexican-American children. Here, the student may master the content, but the mastery of English may not be sufficiently sophisticated for him to give test answers that reflect mastery of the desired skills.

Also, on written tests, the scores obtained may indicate only a total number of items correct, with little or no indication of the areas in which the student has scored high or low. Thus, most projects review only total test data, rather than reviewing subscore data. And, even if individual scores on items in the test and subscores on sections of the test are examined, this merely shows what answers the student gave, and does not necessarily indicate the process by which he arrived at the answers (Kropp and Stoker, 1966). There should be an investigation of the ways in which the answer was chosen—that is, the reasoning used by the student in selecting the answer.

Written tests often assume that being able to describe a task is the same as being able to do a task. Thus, a question may ask whether a microscope slide must be moved left or right, or the lens moved up or down to bring the image of an object on the slide into focus. The assumption is that anyone who can use a microscope correctly can answer this question, that failure to answer means inability to focus a microscope, and that this test question will distinguish between those who can operate a microscope and those who cannot. Yet, this is not necessarily the case. Not only can some people use a microscope without being able to visualize the operation on a diagram, but they may do this more efficiently than some who can give the correct answer on the written question.

Despite these limitations of written tests in developmental projects, there has been little testing which requires actual performance in a real situation, or in a simulated situation which approaches reality.[13] This is an area where testing is difficult and expensive, yet since the long-run primary aims of projects generally involve doing something rather than writing about something, this is an area which should not be neglected in evaluation of curricula.

Thus, there has been relatively little performance testing to determine not whether the student can verbalize a correct response, but whether he can perform an operation—e.g., a laboratory experiment or an analysis of a complex problem. An exception is the AAAS project which has relied to a major degree on individual performance testing, presenting the student with a problem and asking him to do something to solve it. The student may be asked to

---

[13]A classic in this area is the *Assessment of Men* (OSS Assessment Staff, 1948). McGuire (undated), McGuire (1967) and McGuire and Babbott (1967) illustrate some of the possibilities in this area.

carry out a simple function or a more complex one, but answering depends on doing, rather than on verbalizing.

For the junior and senior high school developmental science curricula, even though there is a stated emphasis on laboratory skills, there has been little effort to measure the ability of students to perform even the basic laboratory tasks, much less to carry out more complex laboratory experiments. It is assumed that the written achievement examinations will reflect this skill, since the student who performs laboratory work should have a better understanding of the principles of the science. IME and IMB have suggested such testing of the basic laboratory skills involved in their programs, but for IME, this was not part of the evaluation program.

Most project testing has been done in the context of the subject area classroom. Thus, problems in which the student is asked to recognize the biological implications of public issues are presented in the biology classroom on a test labeled "biology." Situations where it is hoped that the student will recognize the mathematical problems involved in a nonmathematical situation are presented in a math class on a test labeled "mathematics." The same is true in the social studies.

In other words, in the curriculum evaluations, the tests that have been used to measure student achievement of skills have been in the context of the subject area itself. This fact provides a cue to the student that the problem presented does, in fact, involve that subject area and something he has learned there. Yet, biologists are concerned not so much with the in-class performance of the student, as with his long-run ability to recognize the biological implications of public problems in new and unfamiliar contexts, in out-of-school situations.

Thus, it might be appropriate to do some of the testing for such skills outside the biology class, perhaps in study hall, homeroom, English, or social studies. To present a problem with no clues to the student as to which items he has learned should be applied in solving the problem—to present it without subject-area identification—would be a far better indicator of student ability to apply biological concepts to new and unfamiliar situations than has been provided by most of the tests used to evaluate biology curricula in the past. The same can be said of testing in mathematics, social studies, and English, where the projects are concerned with long-run, out-of-school use of skills, rather than with immediate, direct application of skills in the subject area.

One of the most difficult questions concerning evaluation of developmental curricula concerns the selection of appropriate standards or criteria for evaluation, and the problems of target audience acceptance of these standards. The product of the developmental work may be radically different from earlier intents in coverage or in skill to be mastered. The purposes of projects are generally long-term rather than immediate.

What is an appropriate criterion for adequate performance? Quite clearly, many of the old standards are not relevant. A test measuring student's mastery of a science vocabulary is inappropriate for materials aimed at problem solving in science, rather than mastery of content. The student's ability to write a foreign language correctly is inappropriate to a language program focusing on fluency in speech. Similarly, in situations where students are self-directing— as in IPI—it is entirely inappropriate to use such standard criteria as validity of teacher- student group interaction in rating teacher performance.

All these are clearly inappropriate measures. Yet, these are criteria that have been used to judge the relative effectiveness of new curricula. And in using such inappropriate standards, either because they are traditional, or because no other standards are available, the implementation of a new curriculum may be damaged.

Particularly in achievement testing, there has been inadequate consideration given to precisely what the tests being used are measuring. Too often, validity of the tests used has been automatically assumed. Or statistical data on test validity have been the sole aspect of validity considered, with little systematic consideration of content validity and construct validity.[14] *The appropriateness or validity of any test must be considered in terms of the context in which the test is to be used.* Thus, the appropriateness of a test in the social studies for measuring achievement in a social studies curriculum depends on whether or not the test is measuring what the curriculum purports to be teaching—that is, whether the facets of the test are relevant to the course.

Test driving a car across a desert is not an appropriate guide to its cross-country performance in mountains or in swampy terrain. In these three instances, an automotive vehicle is needed. But the criteria for operation and the standards of performance in the first instance are not necessarily germane to the performance in the two latter instances. It would be the height of folly to assume that a car is suitable for mountain and/or marshland driving because it meets criteria appropriate for desert driving. Similarly, just because a test is labeled "skills in social science" or "American history" does not mean that the skills measured by the test are germane to the curriculum prepared by a developmental project. In fact, what is being measured by the existing test may reflect precisely the approach to the social studies or to history that the developmental project deplores.

---

[14]Ebel (1965) and Fox (1969) include cogent discussions of various aspects of test validity. A more technical discussion is found in French and Michael (1966).

There is some evidence that the criteria used to evaluate performance influence that performance. An example is provided in a study by Blau (1963) of the operation of a state employment office. Blau reports that when the number of job referrals made by an employee was used as a criterion of employee effectiveness, the initial purpose of the organization—to make the most appropriate job referrals and job placements—was sacrificed to the goal of making the greatest number of job referrals. This involved considerable human cost, since the fastest referral to jobs was made, rather than the most appropriate referral. Thus, when a request for a referral was received from an employer, the interviewer tended to refer any job seeker who was in the employment office at the time, rather than to take the time to check his files of job applicants and call in someone who might be more qualified and more appropriate for the job opening. The organization never systematically decided to sacrifice the humans involved. But the criterion measure of efficiency—high job referrals—became an end in itself, an end which conflicted with the basic, stated purpose of the organization.

The situation described by Blau may well have its parallel in education. In education, one might anticipate that the use of inappropriate criterion measures of studying performance when using development materials not only might be irrelevant to the goals of the developmental project, but may be detrimental to the attainment of those goals. If a curriculum is to be judged by the student scores on a criterion measure, the achievement of high scores might become an end in itself, and replace the initial purpose when these two purposes are conflicting. For example, in an intensive program to improve reading skills of the disadvantaged, the City of New York has used school and class averages as criterion measures, and data on schools have been released publicly. Such a policy is intended to improve the reading of the school-age students. However, it may well result in schools encouraging students to drop out, or in the failure by school authorities to follow up on truancy reports. Both are practices which increase the likelihood that school reading scores will be improved, since it is more likely that poor readers will not be included in the school's final reports on reading achievement. While this contravenes the basic purpose of the citywide testing program of reading ability, it may supersede this purpose.

A similar situation may develop in New York State. The New York State Department of Education has announced that all test data on file in the department (except individual pupil test scores) must be made available on demand to reporters and other interested persons (*Education Recaps,* July 1969). This supposedly will permit the public to know how well or poorly the schools in the state are performing. Use of such criterion measures, particularly in a situation where there are statewide testing programs, can well preclude attainment of other objectives in the subject areas in which the testing is done.

The question of the appropriateness of any evaluative measure is not an absolute one. A measure may be appropriate for one curriculum when it is inappropriate for another. For example, a school system may use as its criterion the dollar cost of materials and time, while a project may be concerned with achievement of cognitive or affective goals. A school system may be concerned with achievement on CEEB (College Entrance Examination Board) tests, while a project may not be concerned with such achievement, since its purpose is not reflected in the skills being tested on the CEEB tests. Schools may be concerned with the extent to which one year's curriculum materials prepare the student for the next year's work at that school; the project may not have this concern.

The validity of criterion measures is not something that can be assumed. Validity must be developed in a context, and a criterion measure that is valid in one context may not be valid in another. Further, a measure valid at one point in time may not be valid at another. It may be valid for one group of students and not for another. Or a criterion measure valid for one set of materials in a discipline may not be valid for another set of materials with a different purpose. Or it may not be appropriate to ability or ethnic or linguistic background of the students.

Because an instrument has been used in a systematic study, one may not safely assume that it is valid for that study. In teaching and testing foreign languages, Lado (1961) points out that tests of direct translation ability do not reflect mastery of the language, despite the widespread use of this means of testing in order to determine mastery. Translation tests are particularly inappropriate when literal translation is required. In fact, one might speculate that the requirement of translation from the language being learned into the native tongue—or the reverse—would hinder the development of the student's ability to think in the foreign language (an aim of many foreign language curricula) since it reinforces a behavior that is contrary to the aim. Robinson (1969) indicates that there is a low correlation between student performance on tests where the student is actually using the laboratory, and paper-and-pencil tests of achievement in a laboratory-oriented biology course.

Even such a straightforward method as asking a child his name to determine whether or not he knows it may be open to serious question, as is indicated by Zigler (1969):

> When asked his name by the teacher, the first thought that probably comes to the [disadvantaged] child's mind is: "Why does she want to know? Is she a police lady? Does all of this have something to do with the welfare check?

She looks friendly enough—maybe I should tell her . . . but, no, it might cause trouble. What did I learn in the slums; what's a good safe gambit when dealing with strangers . . . 'Keep your mouth shut.' "What you then get out of such a child is "I don't know." If your orientation is simply a cognitive one, your conclusion is that this child . . . doesn't even know his own name. He knows his name probably as well as you know yours. . . . [In the New Haven Head Start program] We did find a small number of children who, upon entering the program, stated that they did not know their own names. . . . When the child said he didn't know his name, the teacher was to say to the child: "My name is Mrs. ———, and it must be very scary to have somebody you don't know ask your name. You're probably wondering why I want to know your name. Well, you see, a little later we're going to have juice and cookies and if I don't know your name, I might not be able to call you and you'll miss out on your juice and cookies." Following this, all but one child immediately told the teacher their names. . . . This child not only didn't seem to know her own name, but as the year progressed was found to be very withdrawn and participated minimally in the program. One day, an older child from the neighborhood came to pick up . . . [this child] and the teacher said to the older child: "You know, this little girl doesn't know her name. I bet you know her name and could tell me." The little girl in question immediately grabbed the older child's arm and frantically shouted "Don't you tell her!" What we had here was a child whose motivational structure was too hardened by the age of 5 to be circumvented by the promise of juice and cookies. She was more interested in protecting herself than to receive the good things of the little society in which she found herself.

Zigler points out that failure to appreciate the importance of motivational and emotional factors in the child's performance has led us to overemphasize, misinterpret, and misunderstand the implications of data which report increased IQ in deprived children following a nursery school appearance, and that competing motivational responses may result in a performance far below that dictated by the cognitive and achievement abilities of the child. Basically, this is a question of the validity of the measures used, and the interpretation of the data obtained by standards that are inappropriate to the test population. This problem is not limited to the testing of very young disadvantaged students.

Before using an existing test or even one the project itself develops, there should be a systematic consideration of what the test is measuring, and its appropriateness in terms of project goals and the test population. Such consideration is often given in a casual way. Such casual, unsystematic assessment is not a sufficient guarantee of the appropriateness of tests. The test analysis systems developed by Klinckmann (1961) and by Easley *et al.* (1967) are well worth the time involved, since they provide a sounder basis for test selection than sole reliance on existing data about previous uses of the test, or general review of the instruments under consideration.

In evaluation, there may be a temptation to test the obvious, to prove what we already know or what is quite obvious without testing. Some projects have administered traditional tests covering old subject matter and new tests covering new subject matter to students in the traditional and in the developmental curriculum. Since the traditional program students did not study the new subject coverage, and the developmental program students did not study the traditional subject matter, it was obvious that the traditional students would do better on the traditional test and the developmental students would do better on the developmental test. The comparison was not an appropriate one.

To compare both groups on general skills, such as critical thinking in science, or ability to interpret graphs, charts, and maps—skills common to both programs, or skills common to objectives of both programs—is germane. To test on skills not common to both programs and, in the case of the traditional test, skills the developmental program is not concerned with developing, results only in describing differences between programs; it does not provide information on whether the developmental program is successful or unsuccessful.

Given the data collected from testing and other evaluative instruments, there is often a preoccupation with complex, sophisticated analysis. At the same time, there should also be consideration of what has been overlooked, what data exist that have not been noticed or recognized (Webb *et al.,* 1966) and whether the data on hand are being studied in the most profitable ways —in the ways that will provide the most useful information. Often, conventional analyses of data are the only uses to which the evaluative data are put, when new relationships and new trends might be observed if anyone thought to look for them. Simply the scanning of answer sheets or of raw data often gives leads to new ways of looking at data that are already on hand.

Project objectives often reflect some concern with attitudes and values, yet, there has been relatively little systematic evaluation of these. A few projects have used a variety of general attitude scales with teachers and students. Some have attempted to measure increase in critical thinking ability, general problem-solving ability, and change in degree of stereotyped thinking relevant to the discipline and in a general social context. But such efforts have not been widespread. At least one reason for this lack is the difficulty of obtaining accurate reliable measures of these dimensions. Also, for many projects, the skills in the discipline are the primary concern, and the attitude questions are of relatively low priority. Few projects ever consider to what extent the curriculum increases the anxiety level of students. Consideration should be given to whether some of the basic education-related problems of children may be aggravated, rather than diminished, by the developmental curriculum efforts.

Even where appropriate criterion measures are used in the evaluation of developmental materials, and the analyses of data are imaginative, the question may be raised during the formative and the summative periods as to whether the positive outcomes resulting from the use of the developmental materials reflect the Hawthorne effect.[15] That is, when comparisons between experimental students using developmental materials and control groups using traditional materials have been made, to what extent are any differences in favor of the experimental group ascribable simply to the psychological effect of participating in an experiment? Based on a review of the research literature and on his own research, Cook (1967) concludes that:

> It appears unlikely that one can employ a Hawthorne effect concept to explain differences or lack of differences between experimental and control groups in educational research studies in so far as the variables commonly believed to generate the effect such as direct and indirect cues, the duration of a study, and mechanical changes introduced in an experiment are considered to be of sufficient potency to produce the effect.

Outcome measures generally focus on expected change, on the change that is desired. Often overlooked is the fact that not all the effects of a curriculum program are expected effects, and not all are necessarily desirable. And the focus on the desired outcomes may divert attention from the undesired outcomes. As Halpin (1969) points out, "obviously no social change of any kind can be completely or equally desirable for all the parties concerned." Yet, there had been a clear tendency to assume that all change is good, and that some good outcomes are all that must be sought. Suchman (1967), Blau (1963), Savin (1969), and H. Grobman (to appear 1971) have been concerned with dysfunctional outcomes in programs, outcomes that are unanticipated and that may be far more detrimental than is generally realized. The effects of such dysfunctional outcomes may outweigh any gains that are achieved. This is a vital, although neglected aspect of curriculum evaluation.

For the most part, the testing discussed thus far is macroevaluation—evaluation to answer broad questions. It is evaluation in rather general terms, although some aspects of such testing can lend themselves to a more precise look at individual segments or small parts of materials or specific aspects of learning—to microevaluation.

---

[15]Hawthorne effect is the name given the beneficial effect that may be produced in experimental situations because the subject realizes that he is a participant in an experiment, and so, is the object of special attention. The term arose from a study in the 1920's in the Hawthorne Plant of the Western Electric Company, where such an experimental effect was observed.

However, microevaluation has a different focus than macroevaluation. This focus is reflected in the efforts of a number of projects to examine parts of materials, to determine optimal sequencing, or the most effective teaching medium for given skills or concepts, or for teaching particular kinds of students. Or the question may focus on progress of the individual student rather than the group, or on the individual teacher rather than on groups of teachers. Here, the evaluation may use only a small pilot group—perhaps five or ten students, or classes of five or ten teachers—and it examines performance in detail, often through systematic classroom observation, through branched programming, or computer-assisted instruction (CAI) with a careful record kept of successes, failures, and trial times (Gallagher, 1967; Anderson, 1969).

Macroevaluation has received far more attention from developmental projects than microevaluation. Perhaps this emphasis is reasonable when the problem being faced is radical, overall change to be effected rather rapidly. However, as the developmental curriculum efforts mature, feedback from more sensitive microevaluation, which provides appropriate information on parts of materials, on sequencing, or on kinds of populations or techniques used, as well as on broader questions, is indicated.

Despite the need for more microevaluation, the increase of such efforts may constitute a potential threat to the achievement of some of the long-run global objectives of the project. Microevaluation may reflect just a part or a small facet of the curriculum. And the kinds of outcomes that can be measured in such a limited sphere may reflect far more limited goals—goals that are more immediate and at lower cognitive levels—than those with which the curriculum is concerned.

In evaluating an experience that requires ten minutes, thirty minutes or even an hour—a film, a program, a sequencing of questions—it would be unrealistic to expect dramatic changes in a student's manner of problem solving, use of higher cognitive skills, or value system. Thus, for small parts of materials or teaching segments, it is possible and desirable to determine whether knowledge is obtained more rapidly in one manner than in another. But the extent to which the activity contributes to the more substantive long-run goals probably cannot be determined.

It is simply not possible in most circumstances to determine the long-run contribution of any single activity, carried on for a relatively short period of time, to a long-run, global aim. Yet, as evaluation focuses on short-run aims, success in achievement of these may be taken to imply a contribution to success in the long run. Unfortunately, some short-run successes may deter rather than enhance achievement of long-run goals.

The Use of Evaluative Data

What happens to the information obtained in the formative evaluation—the test scores of various-kinds, reports from various experts, reports from teachers, reports of interviews with teachers? Are they used? And if so, how are they used?

Generally, data are collected with a purpose in mind. This may be a vague idea of their usefulness, or the project may have highly specific plans for the use of the data. But with few exceptions, those who collect data intend to use them. However, there is little doubt that some projects do not use the data collected, and that few effectively use all the data they amass. Despite the very sincere intent of most projects to use feedback, often, it is not used efficiently or effectively. For most projects, it seems likely that many of the revisions made in experimental materials during the formative period are not based on systematic reaction to feedback.

There may be no intent to ignore the data, but the project may not get around to using it. Or project personnel may be so sure things are working well that they simply do not take the time to systematize and collate the feedback and check it against the materials. In a few cases, there has been a conviction that the project knows more than the person sending in the feedback—a conviction that is sometimes justified, other times not—and so, the project deliberately does not use the feedback effectively.[16]

There are a number of problems involved in using feedback. One is the sheer magnitude of the job of reviewing, collating, and digesting the feedback. Even the task of interpreting test data from three or four objective-type tests is time-consuming. Given testing schedules with a final exam administered in June, answer sheets arriving back from the schools in late June or early July, and the time required for processing them, meaningful feedback from these tests to the writers working during July and August becomes difficult, if not impossible.

Another problem is the form in which feedback is presented. Research experts are often not used to dealing with people who are not at home with statistical data; they are also unused to dealing with people who demand specific answers to specific questions. They tend to view their findings as relative and tentative, and they often find it difficult to go from their data to specific recommendations for project direction. Yet, this is the very purpose of evaluative efforts in the formative period.

---

[16]When a project considers feedback systematically, and then rejects a suggestion or decides to continue a practice despite evidence that might indicate a problem, this is a use of feedback. While the project's decision may not be a wise one, this is a quite different situation than the failure of a project to consider such evidence systematically.

The problem may be particularly severe in the case of statistical feedback which must be interpreted for writers if it is to be useful to them. Unless this interpretation job is done with clarity and in a manner that does not offend the writers, the feedback may be largely wasted. Again, the human element perhaps should not enter, but it does, and it must be taken into account. For example, a reaction given to writers in one project—that a given presentation was "stupid"—perhaps was accurate, but hardly endeared the reviewer to the writers, and certainly was not conducive to encouraging them to accept suggested changes.

Another limitation in use of feedback is the problem of determining the appropriateness of the feedback and its implications—that is, whether it comes from a source qualified to comment on that particular aspect of the presentation, or whether the feedback is affected by some bias or unusual circumstances. For example, for some of the BSCS materials, the staff consultants responsible for collating the feedback entered comments on a master copy of the materials, so that for a given section or even page, the writer could rapidly scan comments. Even after the staff consultant screened comments that, in his view, were inappropriate, the feedback was difficult to use, because the identity of the commenter was lost. The writer could not determine whether a given comment was from someone who was simply unfamiliar with the discipline and so, thought a statement of technique improper, whether it was from someone who was a suitable judge in that particular area, or whether inappropriate teaching circumstances—a poorly prepared teacher, too large a class, poor equipment, or a deviation from suggested schedules or materials—resulted in problems that would not arise in more adequate circumstances. Thus, there is a basic problem in determining what the feedback means.

To facilitate interpretation of teacher feedback, the BSCS coded teacher reports according to the kind of classroom and the general background of the teacher and students, so that the writer, trying to use the feedback, could judge whether a reported difficulty might be a reflection of a problem in teacher background, equipment available, size of class, ability level of students, or some problem intrinsic in the materials. The collating and summarizing of feedback in this manner saves time of the user and permits the review of a variety of views. But it also segments feedback to the point where suggestions may be inappropriate.

For example, appreciation of a given suggestion late in the course, or at the end of a chapter, may be contingent on understanding the reviewer's suggestion in an earlier chapter or section; but, presented out of this context, the later comment may not seem logical. Further, to accept all the valid suggestions on a given section or chapter may so change the chapter that the essence of the original, which all the commentators approved, is lost.

A further problem in use of feedback arises from the very natural tendency to look with greater favor on comments by persons of higher status. In one project, teachers complained for two years about one aspect of a developmental program with no results; but when a high-status, outside consultant pointed out the same defect, the problem was readily, though regretfully, recognized. To avoid this problem of differential treatment of feedback, the identification of the source of the feedback could be removed. However, this raises equally troublesome difficulties. Without some knowledge of the source of the comment, it is difficult to weigh its validity. It is important for the user of the feedback to know that the reviewer who considers the biology in the program inadequate is a psychologist, invited to review materials from a learning standpoint, rather than a Nobel Laureate in biology. It is important for the user of the feedback to know that the reviewer who says that the materials are at an inappropriate level for the intended student group is a research biologist, whose only contact with this age group occurred thirty years earlier, not a teacher at that grade level. One strategy would be to code feedback by nature of source rather than by individual, but this too is not an entirely satisfactory answer.

One knowledgeable observer of the developmental curriculum field has suggested that during the formative period of materials preparation, it would be interesting to determine the proportion of changes made that reflect feedback, in comparison with the proportion of changes made based on hunch. His hypothesis is that for most projects, the latter far outweigh the former. It seems likely that the projects using CAI or other programmed techniques to improve sequencing or presentation of segments of materials use feedback from students more effectively. Yet, here the feedback from CAI may produce a product appropriate for CAI, but not for conventional textbook or classroom presentation, even though the sequencing that is being evaluated through CAI is intended for conventional text or class use. Further, such feedback is limited to student-performance information and does not reflect considerations of content validity—of the extent to which the materials adequately reflect the discipline being presented.

The development of feedback mechanisms for obtaining information on developmental materials and their use, and the use of feedback in formative evaluation, are still highly imperfect, even in those projects which have had the most serious intentions of using it. For the most part, this is not a matter of project dishonesty, of becoming used to the process of analyzing such feedback systematically, or of reluctance to take advice. Rather, it is a problem of overcoming prejudices about some sources, of obtaining needed information in usable form, in time for use, and of devising mechanisms and routines for interpreting and using a large volume of information.

Evaluation of Process

Most evaluation activities of developmental projects are concerned with evaluation of product. The content analyses, the reports from teachers, the student testing, and even to some extent, the classroom visits and observations by project staff are concerned with looking at the product and determining whether the outcome in terms of the product is satisfactory. There has been relatively little attention given to evaluation of process.

Process evaluation can have two facets: first, the process of the developmental project itself; and second, the process involved in introduction and use of the curricula in the schools. Both aspects are important. Both have been largely neglected to date. Examination of the project's processes is part of improving operations and permitting replication by the project, or by other projects, of the successful processes and avoiding the unsuccessful ones. Examination of the process of diffusion of materials and their use is important if materials are to be used optimally. Blum and Leonard (1963) point out that if a demonstration or experiment accomplishes its objectives, "the key to its adoption and usefulness elsewhere may not be so much in the proof of effectiveness as in knowledge of the steps that resulted in its development and secured participation and acceptance."

Project self-study. Few projects are systematically introspective about how they operate and what procedures work well and which do not. True, as projects mature, some ways of doing things are discarded and others are modified, based either on hunches, or on a feeling that they were not particularly successful. But there has been little systematic examination of the process involved in the various facets of curriculum work.

The problem discussed earlier of the effective use of feedback is one example, When feedback is coming into the project in such quantities that the data cannot be adequately handled, the system may be modified in some way. But once volume is under control, projects do not ask whether changes in program materials or in teacher training reflect a systematic consideration of feedback, whether such changes reflect feedback from just a few sources, or whether the changes are relatively independent of feedback.

For many projects, an investigation of the extent to which the large volume of data obtained from analyses of tests or observation schedules is used in revising materials would have surprising results. It is not that the feedback data are not potentially useful; it is that they are rarely used effectively. And by and large, projects do not realize how ineffectively these data are being used.

The developmental method of preparing curricula is becoming one of the accepted methods for preparing new curricular materials. The internal processes of the projects undoubtedly influence the project outcomes—the materials developed and their dissemination. The examination of administrative processes is a growing field of research in industry and in public education, but not yet in curriculum projects. The systematic evaluation of procedures—and even the careful description of these—has not been a facet of the evaluation programs of the developmental projects to date.

That the sociology of a writing conference, and the differences in interaction patterns between writing conferences would be a fascinating area of study, is often mentioned by participants and observers in writing conferences. Yet, the projects have not undertaken the systematic study of such writing conferences and the relation between writing conference processes and project outcomes.

The systematic study of decision making as a discipline has not been applied to developmental projects, notwithstanding the fact that the process of decision making may be the most important single factor in the success of projects. Smith (1966) and Hills (1966) indicate how patterns of communication affect organizational procedures and products. Maguire (1969) suggests a study of decision making in curriculum building. A. Grobman (1969) describes much of the processes of the BSCS and the circumstances of many of the decisions made, and he documents the ultimate authority for many of these decisions, in what is perhaps the most detailed description of the process of developmental curriculum projects to date. Yet, even here, the description is incomplete and often does not reflect the dynamics of project communication and operation, and the values involved in the decision making.

Study of diffusion and use of materials. There have been hundreds of millions of dollars spent on OE and NSF teacher-training institutes in the last decade. Some of these are intended to upgrade broad subject-matter skills, but others are specifically geared to help teachers use the products of developmental curriculum studies. Yet, there have been few systematic evaluations of such teacher training in terms of the process of the training—what goes on during the sessions, who is involved, and how they interact. Those institute evaluations that have been effected are generally concerned with changes in subject-matter mastery or with descriptions of the attitudes of staff and participants. Even though available evidence from other areas indicates that increase in subject-matter mastery does not necessarily change teacher classroom behavior or produce more effective teaching, there appears to be little interest in observing the performance of the teacher before and after the institute training, or in comparing change in on-the-job performance of teachers from different kinds of institutes preparing teachers for a given curriculum.

During 1961-62 and 1962-63, both the BSCS and collegiate institutions conducted teacher-preparation activities, to orient teachers to the BSCS versions. Several BSCS staff members who visited BSCS classrooms commented that there were observable differences between classrooms of teachers oriented by the BSCS in its short briefing sessions, and those of teachers prepared elsewhere. In later years, there were also comments from visitors to BSCS institutes and classrooms about the comparative adequacy of the types of institutes and also of the kind of leadership of the institutes. As a result, the BSCS has published a series of manuals for persons conducting institutes.[17] They include recommendations on scheduling, coverage, and presentation. The manuals are based on informal evaluation only, with no systematic evaluation of the results of any of the methods recommended. This information gap is not unique with the BSCS; it is the general rule rather than the exception.

There have been relatively few studies by projects of what happens to materials once they are produced. Book sales are quite properly cited as one index of success, but relatively few other indices are used. There are inadequate data available on: why schools adopt program materials; which kinds of schools adopt them; whether the adoptions are lasting or temporary, and when temporary, the reasons or circumstances for the change away from project materials; and what happens in the classroom after project materials are adopted.

There have been many casual comments about several of the older curriculum study materials, to the effect that even though books have been adopted, the teachers are not teaching the course fully—that they are using only parts of the new courses, and are introducing a great deal of traditional materials in place of much of the developmental materials. There have been few attempts to document this.

Many projects, when faced with a direct question concerning the importance of manner of implementation of materials, agree that their materials do not teach themselves, that a given mode of presentation is desirable. Nonetheless, there seems to be a tacit assumption that if there is a teacher's manual accompanying the materials, or if teachers attend some kind of institute in the subject area, classroom handling of the materials will be implemented in a reasonably satisfactory manner, evidence to the contrary notwithstanding.

One important aspect of change concerns the concomitants of the planned change, of the adoption of the developmental curriculum. Such study may address itself to several questions. Is there a ripple effect from the introduction

---

[17]This *BSCS Special Publications Series* is concerned with various aspects of teacher training. The most recent in the series is No. 6, *New Materials and Techniques in the Preparation of High School Biology Teachers* (BSCS, 1969).

of materials? What other parts of the school system are affected, either favorably or unfavorably? Schools are complex, interrelated systems. A single change may have many repercussions. What are these? And are these desirable and enhancing to the total school effort and to the aims of the new curriculum practice? Concern is often given to the need for new facilities or resources for program implementation, but more subtle changes may be equally important. Carlson (1965) in documenting the effect of introducing programmed instruction on instructional supervision concludes that:

> . . . it is clear that programmed instruction created a classroom situation with which principals were not prepared to deal. The principal's training in supervision is built around the standard classroom setting in which the teacher is presenting ideas, discussing material with students, setting their tasks, and directing their group activities.
>
> As far as classroom observation is concerned, programmed instruction is characterized by two features which throw the principal and his supervisory tactics off stride. One has to do with the teaching goals . . . this strategy [of teacher submission of daily lesson plans] is rendered irrelevant with programmed instruction because there are no daily lesson plans to be submitted. In fact the program sets the over-all goals, and the daily activities cannot be controlled by the teacher because the students no longer work together with the teacher.
>
> The second characteristic feature of programmed instruction which undermines the standard practice of classroom observation is that it breaks down the group . . . into a mere collection of individuals. . . . Current supervisory tactics are geared to the group setting. . . .
>
> Without daily lesson plans and without seeing the teacher work with a group, the principals either ignored the classroom observation functions, resorted to asking students to judge the teacher, or merely noted her clerical-like abilities.

Such concomitant ripple effects of introducing project materials generally are unstudied and often are unnoticed.

The evaluation of process is an integral part of the evaluation of developmental projects, from the time the project is initiated, throughout its life. Without an understanding of the ways the project itself is operating and of the process in classrooms, in teacher training, in school system adoptions and use of the product, evaluation data cannot be placed in proper perspective and the project may not be able to build on past experience in planning future activities. Yet, this area has been largely neglected.

The DEEP evaluation of the processes used by the thirty DEEP systems, with a view to identifying the critical facets in successful developmental efforts, is a noteworthy exception. Here, there is a systematic evaluation effort to find out what techniques and circumstances are most conducive to a developmental effort at the local school level. Such efforts to evaluate process should be the rule rather than the exception.

In recent years, there has been a developing literature on the science of effecting planned change in institutions, with much of the literature germane to education, and some specifically geared to problems of educational change. (Rogers, 1962; Bennis, Benne and Chin, 1969; Goldhammer, 1965; Pellegrin, 1966 are a few such studies.) Such research and theory building have largely been independent of the curriculum studies. Where research on change processes involves developmental project materials, these activities have mostly been done outside the project by investigators interested in change, and the investigation is generally entirely independent of the project, and is uncoordinated with other investigations germane to the project.

SUMMATIVE EVALUATION

Generally speaking, summative evaluation serves two purposes: to describe the product or activities of the project, and to indicate the extent to which project goals have been achieved. However, before it is possible to answer the question, "Was the project successful?" it is necessary to specify the criteria for success.

What constitutes success? Is it in terms of producing good materials? Having materials adopted in many schools? Having materials adapted and copied in many schools? Having a lasting impact on education through continued long-term use of the materials, as well as change in the way the subject and other subjects are taught? Training a new generation of research and development people? Identifying and developing a new generation of gifted teachers? Changing methods of teacher training? Developing new processes for development or implementation of curriculum?

Unless success is clearly defined, one cannot say whether or not a project was successful. Thus, as is the case in formative evaluation, there must be a clear indication of what outcomes are to be examined.

In part, formative evaluation and summative evaluation overlap, both in time and in activity. As Scriven (1967) points out, formative evaluation does not come to an abrupt stop before summative evaluation begins. Many of the evaluation questions to be asked, and the types of evaluative activities carried on, are not unique to one period or the other, although the emphasis on a given technique may be greater during one period than another.

For both periods, evaluation of product and of process are appropriate. For both, macroevaluation and microevaluation are appropriate. For formative evaluation, the pressure of time is generally greater, since developmental activities often have tight time schedules, and the formative evaluation must fit into these, if the ensuing data are to be effectively used. For summative evaluation, timetables may be less rigid, and less dependent on other project activities.

Where in formative evaluation, the focus is on evaluation to improve materials in terms of meeting the goals of the project, in summative evaluation, the focus is on describing the materials, with the descriptions useful not only to potential adopters of the materials, but also to the project, and other projects, to permit the improvement of later materials. Thus, some evaluation activities in the summative period have a formative evaluation aspect. The summative data may be useful to similar projects preparing parallel materials and to the same project, or other projects, preparing sequential materials, or materials to supplement the initial curriculum. These data may also be used in planning change strategies, in implementing further teacher-preparation activities, and in learning more about learning.

Summative evaluative questions may focus on the single developmental curriculum, or they may compare several curricula in the same subject at one grade level, different curricula with similar purposes at different grade levels, or sequences or combinations of curricula. Thus, summative evaluation may focus on such questions as:

> Are the materials consistent with the intent of the project? Are the materials mutually supportive of this intent? For example, do all parts of the materials support the idea of inquiry, or do the end-of-chapter questions negate this idea?
>
> To what extent are the materials consistent with and enhancing to the aims of school systems adopting them?
>
> What philosophy of education and what theories of learning are reflected in the materials?
>
> What kinds of values are implicit in the materials—e.g., what view of a good society, of progress, of individual responsibility and the role of the individual in society do the materials communicate?
>
> Do the materials contribute to the general operating vocabulary of the student? Do they enhance his verbal abilities—both oral and written?
>
> For what kind of student—ability level, ethnic background, sex, age—are the materials most effective?
>
> What learning gains are made by using this curriculum, for what kinds of students, in what kinds of school situations (socioeconomic backgrounds, size and location)?
>
> What are the opportunity costs of using this curriculum? What is the cost in terms of alternative ways of spending the resources and time? What would students have been learning if they had not been studying this curriculum? And what else could the money and facilities have been used for?
>
> To what extent are the developed skills retained over a period of time? What is the relearning time for skills learned in the program but forgotten

over time—that is, are there any savings over the time required if the materials had not been taught before?

Is the sequencing of activities and ideas appropriate?

Are the media for presenting skills and ideas appropriate to all students? For some students?

What happens to the materials after they are released? Which schools adopt? Why do they adopt? Is the adoption a one-year or two-year adoption, or a more lasting adoption?

What happens in the classroom where the materials are being used? To what extent are classroom activities compatible with the goals of the project?

In what circumstances are the adoption and use most consistent with the project goals?

What are the unanticipated outcomes—both negative and positive—resulting from use of the materials? What kind of teacher orientation provides the classroom implementation most consistent with project goals? What kinds of staff and experiences are most appropriate for teacher preparation, in terms of optimal classroom implementation of materials?

Many of these questions have already been asked in the formative evaluation. However, they should be asked again in the summative evaluation because the end-product materials are different from the experimental materials used in the formative evaluation. While hopefully, the end product is better and achieves better results, this cannot be assumed. Data should be obtained to determine whether this is the case. Further, the population using the materials during the summative period may be different from the experimental populations of the formative periods in terms of kinds of schools, teachers, and pupils. And, with fewer time restrictions during the summative period, the research design can be more elegant since there is more time for developing and refining evaluative instruments and techniques.

In the formative evaluation, projects need information rapidly, and this must be obtained efficiently, often at the cost of rigor in methodology. Also, in the formative evaluation, the purpose may be more in terms of general feasibility, rather than what happens in the classroom not under project control. Some outcomes can be measured only after a significant time lapse. As indicated by The National Advisory Council on Educational Professions Development (1969),

> Probably nothing violates common sense more than evaluation of an educational venture before it is operating on a basis where there is any reasonable possibility of tangible results.

In connection with his experience with the Israeli adaptation of the BSCS biology materials and their introduction into schools, Jungwirth (1968) points out that, because of major changes required in the subject-matter coverage and presentation, it "would be plausible to assume a need for a period of readjustment of more than two years . . . for B.S.C.S. teachers or teachers of similar curricula to become effective." Thus, summative evaluation does provide information on classroom outcomes beyond that that can be obtained even in an optimal formative evaluation.

To date, the formative evaluation of developmental materials has received greater attention in curriculum projects than the summative evaluation of these materials. There are probably a number of contributing factors.

Formative evaluation is clearly a new kind of activity. For example, the field testing of experimental materials as they are being written is not a process that has been used in the development of classroom materials prior to the advent of the curriculum studies. Less obvious is the newness of the idea of effective summative evaluation. While there have been investigations of various curricula, the dearth of systematic, summative studies and even of systematic techniques for summative evaluation is clearly indicated in the many checklists that have been developed by school systems in the past for use in considering curriculum adoptions.

Such checklists are often concerned with such matters as size of print, presence of a glossary, and multicolored and/or transparent overlay illustrations, with a range of possible points assigned to each feature of the checklist, and the total score used as an indicator of goodness of the volume under consideration. In such lists, there is generally no place for evidence of relative student performance on the materials, or even of systematic descriptions of situations in which adequate learning is facilitated. And there is usually an assumption that the whole—the total score—is equal to the sum of the parts.

According to its Foreword, the 1963 *Guidelines for Textbook Selection* (Joint Committee of the National Education Association and the American Textbook Publishers Institute, 1963) is intended "to raise the standards and quality of the American Textbook." Although it uses the word "evaluation" many times, nowhere does the *Guidelines* refer to the desirability of summative research data to be used in the adoption decisions, or of the responsibility of the publisher for furnishing more than the materials themselves and "promotional material."

The 1967 revision of the *Guidelines* (Joint Committee of the National Education Association and the American Textbook Publishers Institute, 1967) again suggests that the publisher representatives assist textbook adoption committees in building criteria for evaluation, but again, no mention is made of the responsibility of publishers for providing summative research data or of the kinds of summative research data that should be considered in making textbook adoptions. In overlooking the fundamental role summative research findings should have in textbook selection, the NEA-ATPI committee has done a disservice to American education.

The idea of systematic, summative evaluation as a responsibility of those producing materials is new. In the past, producers of materials have not provided systematic data on classroom use, and the potential users have not expected them to do so. School decisions have not been made on the basis of rational evaluation, and schools are unaccustomed to having systematic data on curriculum on which to base educational decisions. Although there is still not general acceptance of the responsibility to provide summative data by projects, and the educational community does not generally demand or expect to receive such data, the research community is beginning to include this as an expectation for educational materials, and especially for those produced by projects.

The function of the formative evaluation is relatively clear—to improve the materials. As the evaluative data prove their worth during the formative period, the evaluation activities are more likely to be supported. It is harder to justify the summative evaluation in terms of their contribution to the project, and the contribution of this activity is less obvious both to projects and to project funders.

Funds for curriculum development generally come from agencies handling these. Thus, the curriculum development funds from the NSF are specifically for curriculum development and, for the most part, NSF course content improvement section funds have not been available for summative evaluation activities beyond norming of tests, which is considered part of materials preparation. For the Office of Education, formative and summative funds may come from different sections within OE; the developmental funds are supposed to be for curriculum development purposes, and summative evaluation is not generally considered as part of this.

For projects receiving developmental funds from NSF, at times NSF has suggested that summative evaluation be financed elsewhere—with the logical source being OE, which currently distributes the bulk of educational research funds available in the United States. OE has understandably been reluctant to give money to evaluate a project developed by another agency, an evaluation which might result in data critical of the expenditure of funds by another agency. Further, OE personnel have commented that if the NSF thought summative evaluation activities for the projects it finances were appropriate, it would finance such activities itself; since such financing has not been forthcoming, evidently the activity is considered inappropriate by NSF. The fact that NSF considered summative evaluation as basic educational research and not part of its proper sphere of activity was not an OE concern in such discussions.

There has been relatively little demand for summative evaluation data by the schools for which the materials are intended. While the formative evaluation data have often been made available by projects as an indication that materials will be usable and appropriate, the same has not generally been done with data on the final product. Schools have not asked for such data either from projects or from publishers of textbooks. Perhaps if schools demanded these data, projects would be responsive and more active in trying to obtain summative evaluation funds, and their arguments to potential funders supporting such activities might be more convincing.

A further limitation on summative evaluation activities to date may be the problem of who should do the summative evaluation. There has been some question concerning the proper location of formative evaluation activities— whether these should be carried on in the project or by outsiders in order to insure objectivity. But projects have generally done at least some of the formative evaluation themselves in order to guarantee the availability of the data they require when they need it, and the funders have recognized this need. On summative evaluation, the issue is less clear-cut, and a number of sources, including some funders, feel that the summative evaluation should be external to the project. Some even argue that the project should in no way guide the summative evaluation activities.

If summative evaluation is entirely external to the project, is it proper for the project to insure that there is such an evaluation? Can it do so with no control over the direction of the evaluation? How can it insure that the summative evaluation will be adequate and accurate? Who should initiate it and who should coordinate it?

To date, much of the summative work carried out external to projects has been in the form of individual doctoral studies. These, of necessity, have been of limited scope, and often are of very limited design, with the design reflecting the doctoral expectations of the collegiate institution and the availability of experimental classes, rather than the needs for answering broad questions about the project. Further, such a piecemeal approach to summative evaluation ignores the fact that evaluation today is an expensive and complex task, often requiring a number of complementary skills and considerable time, staff, and money. It often requires the development and validation of a number of complementary instruments. If a number of individual doctoral studies at a single institution were coordinated in order to contribute to a systematic, larger design, then perhaps this arrangement would be appropriate for the summative evaluation of project materials.

Where independent studies are undertaken by a variety of investigators, they may not be comparable. The National Longitudinal Study of Mathematical Abilities (NLSMA) is one of the few studies that provides somewhat comparable data on a variety of curricula. Here a five-year summative study of mathematics abilities of students in various mathematics curricula—including students in different "new math" curricula—investigated outcomes in mathematics skills in a way that student performance in each curriculum could be described and compared with performance in other curricula (Cahen, 1965; Romberg and Wilson, 1968). The effort of SSEC (Social Science Education Consortium) in content analysis, using a common system to compare a variety of curricula in the social studies, is also noteworthy (Stevens and Morrissett, 1967-68). *The EPIE Forum* has developed similar comparison systems, but with less emphasis on substantive aspects of the curriculum.

Despite these and other efforts in systematizing summative evaluation, the summative evaluation efforts to date have been far less extensive than the formative evaluation efforts. Americans are not used to having hard data about their curricula, and schools have been accepting or rejecting the products of the developmental projects on such bases as testimonials, prestige of the developmental group, formative evaluation data (data based on curricula which no longer exist, since the curricula on which they were based have been extensively revised), as well as on the usual sales attraction of four-color illustrations and transparencies, and the promotional activities of the publishers of the materials, when these are issued through regular commercial channels.

A look at the BSCS evaluation *vis-à-vis* formative and summative periods may illustrate some of the problems of relative emphases between the two periods. During the period 1960-63, a substantial portion of the total BSCS budget was devoted to evaluation, though the budget did not classify as evaluation all expenditures involved in evaluation. For example, the evaluation section of the budget did not include the cost of printing and distributing experimental editions of books, the training of experimental teachers, and the teacher-feedback meetings. The testing budget alone was a sizable one, and constituted perhaps one of the most extensive evaluation efforts of developmental projects at that time. The statistical data gathering was largely macro-evaluation, and a considerable effort went into the development of new instruments to test cognitive abilities.

The developmental period for BSCS tenth grade materials for average and above-average students came to a close for the most part with the issuing of books for fall, 1963, through commercial publishers. Rigorous classroom testing had closed in spring, 1963, when the final experimental year closed. Thus, the impetus for evaluation was slowing down and the staff evaluator's efforts were redirected to two other developmental projects of the BSCS—the materials for the lower-ability student and materials for a second, advanced course in high school biology.

In part, this reflects a problem of staff limitations. Perhaps, the BSCS should have looked for additional evaluation staff and had parallel evaluation activities pursued, with attention directed both to formative evaluation of new developmental activities, and to planning summative evaluation and developing new instruments for a summative evaluation of the completed version materials. Given the limited availability of evaluation personnel at the time and also the tightening-up of foundation funds, this probably was not feasible. At that time, the BSCS was one of the few projects having a person trained in education research on the staff, and the BSCS consultant who worked on evaluation was never assigned full-time to evaluation.

In 1963, there were few precedents on summative evaluation, and there had been little written about this function. In fact, the distinction between formative and summative evaluation, and the implications of each, had not yet appeared in the literature. The idea of the project evaluating its completed materials was new, and the BSCS policy committee was not enthusiastic, particularly since many of the members were not entirely happy about evaluation in general, and about some of the results of the formative evaluation that had been carried on.

Some felt that the formative evaluation expenditures for testing had been too high. A few were disillusioned by the outside criticisms by educators and psychologists about the inadequacy of the evaluation programs of all developmental studies. And a few were disappointed about the results that had been shown in the formative evaluation test programs.

Here, perhaps the people involved in the evaluation activities had been shortsighted in not anticipating the problem. The members of the policy committee were not generally familiar with educational measurement or with attempting to change the ways students think and act. Even though they were used to statistical tests of significance in their work in the biology laboratory, with small numerical differences indicating highly significant distinctions, they were not accustomed to this in educational statistics.

It did not occur to either the outside consultants working with the BSCS evaluation, or the staff member assigned to evaluation activities, that such a warning about the magnitude of expected differences was necessary. The test data, indicating differences between control and experimental groups on a fifty-item test of four or five points—more than one standard deviation—constituted a severe disappointment to a number of the biologists who had been working with incredible fervor for three or four years, while neglecting their personal research, for this cause.

Further, there had been a number of setbacks in the BSCS evaluation. A number of time-consuming and expensive problems had developed *vis-à-vis* some of the evaluation services for which contracts had been made (A. Grobman, 1969). There had been some data analyses that were never completed, since the needed expertise could not be obtained. There were interpretations about the BSCS materials, made in evaluation work done by outsiders, that the BSCS considered highly inaccurate and reflecting a lack of understanding of what the BSCS was all about.

There had been a number of serious disappointments about some evaluation activities—for example, the widespread circulation of a review of materials with unwarranted criticisms, the inappropriateness of other reviews, and the tardiness of several reviews which arrived too late to be considered. While the problems connected with reviews were minor and relatively inexpensive aspects of the formative evaluation program, they left considerable bitterness about evaluation and about educators and psychologists on the part of several biologists and biology educators, who had not been enthusiastic supporters of all aspects of evaluation in the first place.

The kinds of summative evaluation activities that were suggested to the BSCS policymakers required the development of some different kinds of instruments and techniques which the group felt would constitute basic educational research; they did not consider this a proper part of the BSCS work. Also, the situation was further complicated by a number of staff changes.

There had been relatively little questioning of evaluation budgeting by the NSF prior to 1963, perhaps because the NSF had had little experience with developmental projects, or because there were no evaluation experts on the NSF staff and probably few or none on the review panels screening proposals for the NSF course content improvement section, or because the NSF had little idea of what constituted evaluation. In 1964-65, NSF funds became tighter, as developmental projects proliferated, and nondefense spending by the government was curtailed. Other developmental projects financed by NSF had cut their budgets for evaluation after publication of materials, and there was no particular interest at NSF for summative evaluation. There was also no serious pressure on granting agencies by the education research community supporting the funding of summative evaluation. And schools did not ask for summative evaluation information.

Perhaps if the BSCS had been more interested in summative evaluation at the time, there would have been a more active seeking of funds, or BSCS budget cuts would not have hit evaluation more severely than other BSCS activities. At any rate, with the exception of studies by Gallagher (1967) and Anderson *et al.* (Anderson, 1969; Anderson, Faust, and Roderick, 1969) and the norming of the tests to accompany the BSCS versions, the BSCS was inactive on summative evaluation on the version materials.

The BSCS did continue to collect feedback data on a small scale for use in the anticipated revision of the books for the 1968 editions, but it did virtually nothing else on evaluation of the versions. A number of doctoral and independent studies have been done, but the scope of these has been limited, and there has not been much in the way of development of new instruments suitable for imagination thrusts in summative evaluation of biology materials.

One particularly unfortunate aspect of this BSCS inactivity in summative evaluation is related to comments by a number of educators to the effect that either BSCS is not being taught in the classes using BSCS books—that teachers are omitting parts of the materials and substituting traditional materials—or that the teachers are using a highly traditional approach with the books. There has also been the criticism voiced that the books are overly complex—that they are filled with minutiae and are as complex as the books that preceded BSCS. Yet, there has been no rigorous, systematic content analysis to determine whether the BSCS materials are valid in terms of the aims of the BSCS.

There have been no systematic, broad studies to indicate how BSCS is being taught. Gallagher's study (1967)—as well as individual studies, such as La Shier and Westmeyer (1967), Evans (1969), Balzer (1969), and Parakh (1968)in interaction patterns in classrooms — would tend to support the claim that BSCS is often taught in a manner not intended by the authors. Yet, while the BSCS has been concerned about this problem, it has done nothing to investigate the factors involved, or to attempt to identify systematically the cause-and-effect relationships.

There was virtually no feedback from testing on the 1963 commercial edition of the BSCS versions that could be used in preparing the revised edition in 1968. There was little systematic classroom visiting. There were some meetings held with a few teachers to obtain feedback for the materials. And there were reviews by biologists. But, there was relatively little summative evaluation data obtained beyond general testing one year.

For the third edition, to be prepared in the 1970's, it is unlikely that there will be systematic data available on the BSCS classroom experience, on relative successes and failures, on what is emphasized in the class, and on method of use of materials. As a result, it would appear that the BSCS process, insofar as the versions are concerned, is ceasing to be developmental and is coming more and more to resemble the process used in conventional textbook preparation.

The first commercial edition of the BSCS versions was truly an experimental product, and represented a developmental process. The second edition was less truly developmental. And, given the funding problems and the NSF-stated intent to cease support of the BSCS version activity, it appears that the third edition will, of necessity, be even less developmental.

This appears to be a less than optimal evaluation history of one developmental project. Unfortunately, it is not atypical. This is the general pattern of most developmental projects, where the project has a developmental orientation rather than a research orientation, and where the project has development funds rather than both development and research funds.

The problem is one of concern not only to the projects involved, but it should also be of concern to a broader group. As outsiders—the research profession and the schools—bring pressure on both developmental projects and on granting agencies for systematic, summative evaluation data, there will undoubtedly be more summative evaluation both by the projects and by outside groups, and there will be better coordination of these activities to enhance their usefulness.

RESPONSIBILITY FOR EVALUATION

Should evaluation decisions be made inside or outside the project? Should the evaluation be planned inside or outside the project? And should it be executed inside or outside the project? Different considerations are involved during the formative and summative periods.

There are a number of reasons for a closer, more direct involvement of the project in formative than in summative evaluation. During the formative period, there is certain information the project must have; it has a timetable to meet; and unless the project is satisfied with the methods and instruments for data collection, the results of the evaluation will not be useful to the project.

The project will have certain questions it wants to ask of the curriculum —for example, whether or not it can be taught to average students in the way the writers intend that it be taught. It may be concerned with a specific target group. And it may be concerned with a specific kind of learning. The choice of questions on which the evaluation should focus cannot be decided by outsiders, though such outsiders may be useful in making suggestions.

During the formative evaluation, the evaluation instruments must be satisfactory to the project. Unless the project feels that these reflect their purpose, the data collected with such instruments will not be useful in formative evaluation. Thus, if a project is concerned with certain kinds of cognitive skills—for example, the ability to analyze social science data—unless project personnel are convinced that the test experimental students take does in fact measure this ability, test data will not be considered germane to project needs and will not be useful for improving material.

It is quite possible that the outsider will be able to select tests more appropriately, or will be concerned with measuring more important facets of the program than those desired by the project. However, if a major purpose of formative evaluation is to feed back into materials and program for their improvement, the data collected must be those for which the project sees a need, is willing to use, and has on hand in time and in an appropriate form for project use. If evaluation is entirely turned over to outsiders, these conditions may not be met. During formative evaluation, some projects have had unfortunate experiences with failure of outsiders to meet deadlines, with the use by outsiders of evaluation instruments which the project considers inappropriate, and with data presented in inappropriate formats.

Some aspects of formative evaluation in particular—such as the visiting of classrooms and the reading of teacher reports—would be extremely difficult for nonproject staff to carry out. Testing has more often been farmed out, but even here, the degree of close, day-to-day contact and cooperation with the project appears to be a key factor in successful implementation of the evaluation and use of results.

This does not mean that the most successful formative evaluation efforts are handled completely inside the project. But unless there is one person in the project conversant with evaluation and responsible for the evaluation activities of the project and for liaison with any outside evaluators, and unless the project itself is the final arbiter of the direction of the evaluation, the formative evaluation activities are usually not notably successful.

In both formative and summative evaluations, the question of credibility of findings may be raised where the project entirely implements its own evaluation. It is unfortunate that there is not a greater respect for the reliability and basic honesty of persons carrying on such educational research. But whether or not such doubts are warranted, some have questioned whether data collected by the project itself can be trusted.

During formative evaluation, this question is not as important as during summative evaluation. In the former case, the major purpose of the data is to feed information back into the project, and much of the data are not in a form to be released generally, and would not be of general interest. There would be little gained by distortion. The project may release some formative data to the granting agency to indicate the progress of the project, and to the potential public to prepare it for materials that will appear later. But for these purposes, the really critical data are those collected during the summative period. Thus, during the formative period, the question of whether the project should be trusted to direct or conduct its own evaluation activities is really not germane.

During the summative evaluation, the argument favoring evaluation by outsiders as a way of gaining improved credibility and increased objectivity is more appropriate. Yet, if the project completely divorces itself from the summative evaluation, how can it be assured that there will be a summative evaluation which will include the appropriate facets? True, the project could hire an outsider and turn the evaluation over to him, with no project control over direction. However, the project could hardly secure funding on this basis. Further, the accuracy and objectivity of the evaluation of project materials are not necessarily guaranteed by the divorce of an evaluation from the project.

The project may be harmed by inaccurate outside investigations, with no way of determining the accuracy of the investigation. If there is some evaluation carried on within the project or in close cooperation with the project, perhaps the project is assured of some basic data it needs, is assured that there will be at least a minimum of summative evaluation, and also has some guidelines which can indicate the deviation of outside research from expectation, and so permit a replication of research where the results of outside research seem out of line.

Perhaps the project's direct role in formative evaluation should be larger than in summative evaluation, since, during formative evaluation, there is specific information needed by the project, and the project timetable must be met. However, though undoubtedly some summative evaluation should be done outside the project, it appears highly wasteful to have the summative evaluation research as widely dispersed and uncoordinated as has been the case to date.

Much of the summative research has been done in connection with doctoral dissertations. While dissertations at a single institution may cluster, this is not generally the case, and the data, even at a single institution, may not be comparable. Further, the results of the various summative studies are generally not collected and regarded as a whole.[18] This means that even where there is rigorous summative research done involving curriculum studies, such studies are generally not brought together and systematically and critically reviewed and summated.

Further, there is generally no coordination of the outside researchers' efforts among themselves or with research by the project, so that the data collected will be comparable. Often, in the independent studies, the description

---

[18]A. Lee (1967) provides a noteworthy exception to this.

of method and of study populations are so sparse that it is not possible to determine whether the studies are comparable. The idea of complementary research studies of developmental project materials has been largely untapped. For those projects with a research-oriented staff, as at IPI or HPP, and a number of doctoral students involved in project work, such complementary research has been more frequent. But the idea of complementary studies which are mutually supportive or of parallel studies constructed so that the data are comparable, has not been widely adopted.[19]

Projects would do well to assign to an individual or unit either in the project or outside the project, the specific task of identifying research related to the project's materials, collecting reports of such research, assessing these and then summarizing in some fashion the results of the variety of investigations. In this way, the existing summative research findings would be optimized; they would be in a form usable by both project and target audience, and the gaps to be filled by further research would be clearer.

Projects might also serve a clearinghouse function for research proposals, so that individuals interested in some aspect of summative research on the project could readily contact others interested in similar research, thus facilitating the organization of parallel or complementary research efforts. This area of coordinated research efforts has been largely unexplored by developmental projects, yet, it offers tremendous advantages in facilitating financing of research, implementation of research, and maximization of findings.

THE ACCOMPLISHMENT AND THE POTENTIAL

In one sense, the evaluation activities of curriculum projects have been remarkable in their scope, in their diversity, and in the completely new areas into which they have ventured. In another sense, the evaluation activities may

---

[19]Parallel research studies are those where there is an advance agreement by independent researchers on a problem in a similar curriculum area—e.g., first grade reading, seventh grade science, or twelfth grade world history—on some of the basic parameters of the study, on some of the antecedents and the manner of describing them, and on some of the instruments. This area of agreement is sufficient to permit comparability of data to some extent, while permitting some degree of flexibility for the individual researchers. Thus, it would be possible to study several methods of implementing one curriculum, or the comparative effectiveness of several curricula with data from half-dozen investigators contributing to the final analysis. The organization of parallel studies is discussed in more detail in H. Grobman (1970), and Bond and Dykstra (1967).

Complementary studies are those in which individual investigators select parts of a larger problem collecting data in such a way that while each study is investigating a problem or series of problems, data from several studies can be combined or studied together, so that the overall findings are more than the sum of discrete studies. For example, in the University of Florida Leadership Study of the 1950's, in a three-year field research project, there were some eighteen separate research studies, but there was sufficient interrelationship among these studies in terms of instruments used, population studied, and problems investigated that each of the final two studies consisted of a synthesis of data from all preceding studies (H. Grobman, 1958; Thomsen, 1956).

provide the least satisfactory aspect of the developmental projects' work to date. Much evaluation work has been done that had never been done before. The evaluation activities have certainly produced better products than would have been possible without these activities.

Yet, so much has not been done. Some projects have had virtually no systematic evaluation. In others, although evaluation activities were carried on, little was done with the results. The possible parameters of curriculum evaluation are broad. But the accomplishments to date have been relatively modest. And there are areas that have been virtually untouched thus far.

Whether the evaluation activities of projects in the coming years will have fewer limitations than those in the past depends on a number of things. Funding agencies—particularly those distributing public funds—like to have hard facts to prove their case to Congress. However, they are often not particularly receptive to substantial budgets for evaluation. And the more evaluation looks like research, the less favorable the reaction may be from a division or an agency concerned with development.

While testing preliminary materials in the schools makes obvious sense, even this evaluation activity has often been severely limited by the budget constraints imposed by the funder. Such activities as the development of new evaluation instruments for testing specific areas of outcomes, or experiments in microevaluation to develop new techniques for curriculum evaluation are less obviously useful. And so, they may find still less favor in the eyes of the funder.

As the potential users of the project materials demand more evaluation evidence—both formative and summative—projects may be inclined to devote greater energy and imagination to evaluation. There have been some efforts to educate the target publics to the kinds of questions they should ask (BSCS, 1963; Leeper, 1965; H. Grobman, 1965), as well as attempts to systematize some kinds of evaluative evidence to permit comparison among projects; to date, these have had limited success.

Many of the summations of data concerning projects presented in issues of *The EPIE Forum,* while useful in giving some base data on what is available, do not provide a basis for a substantive comparison among available project materials. Thus, a summary may list elementary mathematics programs currently available; but information about the program is limited to grade level, copyright date, prices, whether there is a workbook, and "other information," such as whether there are enrichment materials. The work of the SSEC (Stevens and Morrissett,1967-68), which has set up a system for analyzing materials, and has prepared a series of analyses of various current materials in the social studies using the same analysis system, is perhaps more promising;

but here, the analysis is a content analysis only, and does not venture into the area of outcomes.[20]

The temptation of the critic of project evaluations is to suggest the grandiose—to ask for a "complete" evaluation. The accomplishment of a complete evaluation is an impossibility. It would take too long. It would be too expensive. The materials being evaluated would be obsolete before such an evaluation could be completed. And there are insufficient trained staff available to perform evaluation tasks for all the developmental projects currently in existence.

It would appear more realistic to ask for more complete evaluations, for evaluations that are better geared to serve the purposes and needs of the individual projects, and for the development of more evaluation systems—for guidelines and structures that can be applied, with or without modification, to various aspects of curriculum evaluation. Despite the danger that an inappropriate system will be foisted on a project, or that unimaginative approaches to evaluation problems will be designed, such systems can provide starting points, and as a number of parallel systems are developed, projects. can be more easily aware of the evaluation choices they may make and the ramifications of these choices.

---

[20]The Social Science Education Consortium (1424 15th Street, Boulder, Colorado 80302) has a series of analyses of various social science curriculum materials using the Stevens-Morrisett system available. These are worth examining in terms of applicability of similar systems to other materials.

VII

A SUMMING-UP

In its first decade, the developmental process of curriculum building has made great strides in effecting change. While the developmental process had become accepted as an effective medium for building materials, the processes involved have not necessarily been refined in this period. The projects that have been in existence for a number of years have not always demonstrated a growth and refinement of techniques. The newer projects are not necessarily operating more effectively than the early ones. And some of the newer ones are clearly using less effective methods than did some earlier ones.

Perhaps a major contributing factor is the failure of project personnel and of outsiders to analyze systematically the processes used by projects, and to ask the questions, "What did we do wrong?" and "What should we do differently next time?" Not only are these questions infrequently asked, but even when asked, the answers are rarely made public. Greater attention to process and more sharing of information on process seem urgent.

Some of the factors that distinguish between successful and less successful projects are the scope of operations, the individuals involved, and the processes used in operating the project and in building materials. The mixture of discipline-oriented people and educators in materials preparation seems effective, providing the use of both groups is an honest collaborative effort, rather than a window dressing for materials produced by one group or the other. The involvement of large numbers of people and the openness of communication among them also characterize the most effective projects. Rigid, traditional administrative arrangements, with hierarchies of responsibility and authority, and the limited communication that results in such situations, are not conducive to productivity in the developmental effort.

Those projects that have been concerned with the development of complete programs for innovation, including not only preparation of complete student materials and equipment, but also the other concomitants related to change—teacher training, public relations programs, ready availibility of materials through commercial channels, and assistance for those adopting the materials—have effected greater actual change than those that have stopped with materials preparation.

Generally, projects have not been concerned with the factors in change, and have left problems of adoption and implementation of new programs to others. This has often created an unfilled gap, with the result that the change effort has fallen short. Projects also have not maximized the opportunities for evaluation and for feedback into the project of many of the kinds of information that would be useful.

Although initially, projects had considerable latitude in policymaking and manner of operation, public funding agencies have added restrictions, red tape, and delays. There has been no apparent need to remedy excesses in previous efforts, and the red tape and restrictions do not necessarily reflect areas in which funders have found improper or ineffective use of funds.

Perhaps the development of a plethora of rules and procedures reflects the natural tendency of mature organizations and programs to become more restrictive, for regulations to be added, and for freedom of action to be decreased. Regardless of the reason, such restrictions and the resulting delays constitute a serious threat to the future of the developmental process in terms of needed flexibility, untenable delays, and increased time involved in obtaining and administering funds. Such frustrations have already had a very clear adverse effect on the kinds of personnel that can be recruited for developmental project work, and they may further seriously diminish the attractiveness of such work in the future.

As the developmental process has continued, the problems of staffing have increased. Initially, the idea of project work attracted many outstanding individuals from scholarly disciplines and from education, some of them individuals who had had no prior experience with school curriculum work. For the scholars from the disciplines, developmental projects offered an exciting opportunity to work in a new area and, despite the fact that such work might interfere with scholarly research, the opportunity to make a difference—to really effect the schools—was sufficiently attractive that it was not difficult for projects to attract the desired personnel. Today, attracting personnel has become increasingly difficult and the working conditions are often not as desirable as was the case earlier. The red tape and restrictions on funding, the uncertainties of funding, the regulations and procedures for payment for expenses and services, and the limitations on copyrighting of the products have diminished the lure of project work for many people.

Why should an eminent scholar participate in a project activity at an out-of-pocket financial loss? Why should he give up scholarly work, that enhances his professional reputation, or highly remunerative consulting opportunities, to work on curricula for a modest compensation, when others doing similar work receive royalties? The initial enthusiasm of participants in the earliest projects could not possibly be sustained indefinitely, or when the idea of developmental work became less revolutionary. But the luster of project participation has diminished more than was necessary.

Working with projects is simply no longer as attractive in terms of what it is possible to do, in terms of amenities, and in terms of freedom from bureaucratic frustration. Unless some new arrangements can be made to improve this situation, publicly funded developmental work certainly will not be as effectively staffed as has been the case in the past. Since staffing is a key to project success, the implications are quite serious.

The developmental process has been useful and effective in producing engineered change in the schools. The successes to date have been unprecedented in American education. And yet, they have not been as great as some project participants and observers have desired or expected. In part, this may reflect unrealistic expectations and a simplistic view of change, in terms of the difficulty of effecting lasting change in organized systems, and the complexity of the change process.

Initially, there was some naïveté about change. Some early projects assumed that a change in the student's books and the mere availability of the changed books would result in changed teaching and in changed learning. There was also an assumption by some that the involvement of personnel from the discipline, of scholars, would automatically produce a product that would be adequate from a discipline standpoint, and also appropriate for use in schools. Some projects never got beyond these initial misconceptions of the curriculum and the change process.

There has also been a widespread misunderstanding of how people change, and of the potential effectiveness of a single curriculum, a set of materials for one discipline, for one year or part of a year. When the outcome of a developmental project's work has not been up to the initial expectation of its organizers, some project people have blamed the schools, the teachers, and the colleges of education. They have overlooked the fact that the more basic the desired change in behavior or values is, the more difficult it is to achieve.

While it is a commonplace that *Rome was not built in a day,* it is not as clear that basic behavior changes—changes in the way individuals think and act—are also not built overnight or even in a year. And when the stimuli for change are inconsistent, when the entire environment is not consistently supportive of the desired change, the change is less likely to be achieved.

Bloom (1964) points out that the older the individual, the greater the difficulty in effecting change in basic patterns. School children are more difficult to effect than preschool children. Adolescents are more difficult to change than younger children. And different types of change may require different degrees of effort.

> ... the more complex types of growth (emotional as well as intellectual) may be affected only where there is considerable consistency in the environment as different individuals and ideas interact with the subjects (or learners).
>
> BLOOM (1964)

Bloom uses the words *powerful, constancy,* and *consistency* in describing the environments where change is most likely to occur. Research of Dressel and Mayhew (1954) supports this view. But to date, it has rarely been possible for a single curriculum project to provide powerful, constant, and consistent environments. A single curriculum project, particularly at the junior and senior high school level, can hardly expect to achieve drastic changes in basic thinking and value patterns without the support of the other curricula to which the student is exposed.

Developmental projects have often worked at a single grade level in a single discipline, entirely independent of other student contacts at that grade level in and out of school, and other contacts in previous and subsequent schooling. They have expected to build inquiring minds and creativity in 180 forty-minute school periods (barring assemblies, pep rallies, and snow days), when the accumulated wisdom of the student they are attempting to change warns him that inquiry and creativity are generally not effective ways of operating either in or out of school.

The student who has learned for years that the way to get along with teachers is to give the expected answers, the answer that is usual and conforming, or the student who is tested on standardized or teacher-made tests that penalize imaginative thinking and reward the memorizer and parroter, will not discard this hard-won behavior pattern overnight. In fact, for him to do so, for him to be convinced that creativity is good and that sheer memorizing is bad, may place him in serious jeopardy in terms of concurrent and later educational experiences. As Tyler (1950) points out, a unified school environment where the same values are reinforced throughout is necessary to facilitate the development of desired attitudes.

For any developmental project, tackling the entire K-12 curriculum simultaneously, even in one discipline, is too large an endeavor to be manageable, and in the early years of developmental curriculum work, funding for all levels of schooling and all disciplines was not available. However, enough of the developmental curriculum work has been done to date, and enough experience has been gained to permit a greater coordination of efforts among developmental projects and among developmental curricula, so that the sequence within a discipline and among the disciplines presented at the same grade level would have greater consistency.

To date, most of the consideration of sequencing within a discipline has been concerned with coverage and development of prerequisite knowledge and knowledge-oriented skills, and there has been little consideration of the question of consistency among disciplines. What is needed now is a systematic concern with parallel and sequential development of consistent objectives. Until this is the case, no single curriculum can possibly be optimally effective.

Until all experiences in social studies from kindergarten through twelfth grade stress the same skills and values, and reward these, and until other disciplines also stress the same skills and values, and also reward them, the desired skills, if learned at all, will be used only in the single classroom where they are learned; and the values that the curriculum attempts to build will not be internalized by the student and accepted operationally. They will only be verbalized, and this verbalization will be limited to that classroom too.

Predictions are always hazardous. And predictions about the future of curriculum projects are not exceptions. It seems clear that the developmental method of preparing classroom materials through experimentation, trial use, further refining, and further trials will continue to be used. How future developmental work will be organized, sponsored, and funded is less clear. Also in question is the proportion of curriculum materials that will be produced in this manner.

The involvement of book publishers as sponsors of developmental work indicates that developmental products are attractive to schools. Whether developmental work will increasingly be taken over by publishers, and the extent to which developmental materials will continue to replace individual authorship and conventional methods of textbook writing are not clear. If projects are increasingly financed by publishers, their nature and scope will necessarily be somewhat different. While the materials produced may be of high quality, the extent of experimentation would, of necessity, be more limited.

Publishers are profitmaking enterprises. They cannot afford the large-scale and highly experimental, long-range activities that have been possible with public or private foundation funding. They need more assurance of a salable product with an adequate return on the investment—not merely a paying off of the investment, but a return beyond the initial cost—within not too long a period.

Several NSF-financed projects report millions of dollars in royalties turned over to the United States Treasury within ten years of the initiation of the project (A. Grobman, 1969; Merrill and Ridgway, 1969). The BSCS commands a major portion of the U.S. market for high school biology books, and in the first five years that its books were generally available, over 2.2 million books were sold. Yet, the royalties received by the BSCS and turned over to the U.S. Treasury did not repay the grants received by the BSCS from the NSF. It is unlikely that a commercial publisher would invest comparable funds and wait a decade for the repayment of only a part or even the whole sum.

Further, although some of the publishers funding projects have undertaken some evaluative activities, these have been far less extensive because of financial considerations than the admittedly limited evaluations undertaken by the foundation-financed projects. While public pressure for additional evaluative data would doubtless be reflected in increased evaluation activities by all projects, such increases for publisher-funded projects would hardly be of the scope possible with noncommercial funding. Thus, should financing for developmental work come increasingly from publishers, the work is likely to be more conservative, operate on a small scale, and include somewhat different activities.

Developmental curriculum work has changed the nature of the curriculum and of the curriculum-development process. The mark already made is indelible. There are many areas where the developmental process could be improved and could make a greater positive impact. Whether this potential will be fully realized is questionable, given today's educational and political climates. Unfortunately, the most productive and effective period of developmental work may be in the past rather than in the future.

APPENDIX A

IDENTIFICATION OF ABBREVIATIONS

AAAS	American Association for the Advancement of Science
AHA	American Historical Association
AIBS	American Institute of Biological Sciences
BSCS	Biological Sciences Curriculum Study
CAI	Computer-Assisted Instruction
CASEA	Center for Advanced Study of Educational Administration
CBA	Chemical Bond Approach
CHEM Study	Chemical Education Materials Study
CUE	Center for Urban Education
DEEP	Developmental Economic Education Program
EDC	Educational Development Center, Incorporated
ESI	Educational Services, Incorporated
ERC	Educational Research Council of America
ESCP	Earth Sciences Curriculum Project
ESSP	Elementary-School Science Project (in astronomy)
ETV	Educational Television
HPP	Harvard Project Physics
HSGP	High School Geography Project
IBECC	Instituto Brasileiro de Educacão, Ciencia e Cultura (São Paulo)
IMB	Interaction of Man and Biosphere
IME	Interaction of Matter and Energy
IPI	Individually Prescribed Instruction
JCEE	Joint Council on Economic Education
NIH	National Institutes of Health
NLSMA	National Longitudinal Study of Mathematical Abilities

NSF	National Science Foundation
OE	Office of Education
PSNS	Physical Science for Nonscience Students
PSSC	Physical Sciences Study Committee (later changed to ESI—Educational Services Incorporated, and then to EDC—Educational Development Center, Incorporated, which is a Regional Laboratory of the Office of Education)
R and D Center	Research and Development Center (established under the auspices of the USOE)
SMSG	School Mathematics Study Group
SRSS	Sociological Resources for Secondary Schools
SSCP	School Science Curriculum Project
SSEC	Social Science Education Consortium
UICSM	University of Illinois Committee on School Mathematics

APPENDIX B
SUMMARY OF THE CATEGORIES OF THE COGNITIVE, AFFECTIVE AND PSYCHOMOTOR DOMAINS

THE COGNITIVE DOMAIN

In considering the categories of the taxonomy, it is important to keep in mind that, by definition, the system is a taxonomy; that is, it is hierarchical, and so, for each ascending category, all lower categories must be included. Thus, a cognitive task cannot be categorized as analysis, level 4 of the hierarchy, unless it includes knowledge (level 1), comprehension (level 2), and application (level 3).[1]

Knowledge

1.0 *Knowledge* involves the recall of specifics and universals, the recall of methods and processes, or the recall of a pattern, structure, or setting. The recall situation involves little more than bringing to mind the appropriate material, although some alteration of the material may be required.

1.1 *Knowledge of specifics* is the recall of specific and isolatable bits of information, including knowledge of terminology and knowledge of specific facts.

1.2 *Knowledge of ways of dealing with specifics* involves the ways of organizing, studying, judging, and criticizing, including methods of inquiry, chronological sequences, standards of judgment, and patterns of organization, through which the areas of fields are determined and internally organized. This includes: knowledge of conventions, of ways of treating ideas and phenomena (e.g., correct form and usage in writing); knowledge of trends and sequences (e.g., continuity in American history of certain trends); knowledge of classifications and categories, or the arrangements or divisions fundamental to a given subject; knowledge of criteria, that is, the criteria by which judgments are made; knowledge of methodology, the methods of inquiry in a subject (e.g., the way of testing a hypothesis).

SOURCE: Adapted from Benjamin S. Bloom (Ed.) *Taxonomy of Educational Objectives, the Classification of Educational Goals, Handbook I: the Cognitive Domain.* New York: David McKay, Co., Inc., 1956. Adapted with permission of the publisher.
[1]The Taxonomy itself provides specific illustrations of test questions for each category and subcategory of the system.

1.3 *Knowledge of universals and abstractions in a field* involves the major patterns by which phenomena and ideas are organized, including knowledge of principles and generalizations and knowledge of theories and structures, such as the principles and generalizations that present a systematic view of a field, problem, or complex phenomenon (e.g., the seven organizing themes of biology, including genetic continuity, interrelation of structure and function, etc.; the major divisions into which physics is organized).

While the above categories range from the highly specific to the abstract, the tasks covered by these categories nonetheless involve only recall of knowledge.

Intellectual Abilities and Skills

Abilities and skills refer to modes of operation requiring more than knowledge, and emphasize mental processes of organizing and reorganizing materials, either given or remembered, to achieve a specific purpose.

2.0 *Comprehension* means that the individual knows what is being communicated and can make use of the idea without necessarily seeing its fullest implications. This includes what is commonly termed "direct application."

    2.1 *Translation* involves a paraphrasing or rephrasing from one language or form of communication to another, as from graph to prose, chart to graph, or prose material to formula or other symbolic statement (including art, cartoons, music, poetry).

    2.2 *Interpretation* is a reordering or rearrangement of material.

    2.3 *Extrapolation* is an extension of trends or tendencies, prediction, consequences, corollaries.

3.0 *Application* involves the use of abstractions in particular and concrete situations; it includes what is commonly termed "indirect application" and involves tasks not directly replicating those done earlier.

4.0 *Analysis* requires the breakdown of a communication into constituent elements so that the relative hierarchy of ideas and/or interrelationships is made explicit.

    4.1 *Analysis of elements* is the identification of the elements included in a communication (e.g., ability to distinguish fact from hypothesis).

    4.2 *Analysis of relationships* involves a recognition of the connections and interactions among parts (e.g., consistency of hypotheses with given assumptions or information).

4.3 *Analysis of organizational principles* is a recognition of the organization or structure, both explicit and implicit, in a unit (e.g., inferring an author's philosophy or biases from his writings).

5.0 *Synthesis* requires the putting together of elements and parts to form a whole, the rearranging or recombining of units into a new, unique (for that individual) product.

    5.1 *Production of a unique communication* does not include all new writing or plans, but requires a systematic, excellent organization of ideas and statements or an effective presentation.

    5.2 *Production of a plan or proposed set of operations* requires a plan or proposal that satisfies the requirements or specifications of the task, as, for example, the development of a new way for testing a hypothesis, the design of a new instrument, or a unique plan for solving a mathematics problem.

    5.3 *Derivation of a set of abstract relations* may be a new way of classifying things or an explanation of a phenomenon or the derivation of new (for that individual) propositions.

6.0 *Evaluation* involves making systematic qualitative or quantitative judgments based on criteria developed by the individual or given him.

    6.1 *Judgments in terms of internal evidence,* use internal criteria such as logical accuracy, consistency, absence of internal flaws, etc.

    6.2 *Judgments in terms of external criteria* require systematic judgment with selected or remembered criteria, as, for example, comparison with other materials, general standards of excellence, consistency with an arbitrary or nonarbitrary standard.

THE AFFECTIVE DOMAIN[2]

As is the case with the cognitive domain, the categories of the affective domain constitute a hierarchy. Thus, each ascending category includes the lower categories. The taxonomy of the affective domain is based on objectives that teachers hold. Thus, the categories are defined in positive, desirable terms, and the attitudes and values used as exemplars for each category reflect educationally desirable outcomes. It should be noted that a similar hierarchy could be built for all values and attitudes of students, not necessarily including those values and attitudes desired by educators, but those that are actually developed

SOURCE: Adapted from David Krathwohl, Benjamin S. Bloom, and Bertram B. Masia. *Taxonomy of Educational Objectives, the Classification of Educational Goals, Handbook II: the Affective Domain.* New York: David McKay Co., Inc., 1964. Adapted with permission of the publisher.

[2]The taxonomy itself provides specific illustrations of test questions for each category and subcategory of the system.

in students. Thus, the response in category 2 might be a response rising from fear rather than willingness, and the values actually developed in category 3, valuing, may be undesired rather than desired ones. In category 4, the hierarchy of values might indicate an undesired rather than a desired hierarchy.

1.0   *Receiving (attending)* means that the learner is sensitized to the existence of certain phenomena and stimuli; that is, he is willing to receive or to attend to them. Receiving has been divided into three subcategories to indicate three different levels of attending to phenomena; these levels represent a continuum from an extremely passive student role to a point where the student directs his attention, at least at a semiconscious level, toward the preferred stimuli.

1.1   *Awareness* means that given an appropriate opportunity, the learner will merely be conscious of something—he takes into account a situation, phenomenon, object, or stage of affairs. This does not imply an assessment of the qualities or nature of the stimulus and does not necessarily imply attention. There can be simple awareness without specific discrimination or recognition of the characteristics of the object, even though these characteristics must be deemed to have an effect. The individual may not be able to verbalize the aspects of the stimulus which cause the awareness.

1.2   *Willingness to receive,* at a minimum level, involves willingness to tolerate a given stimulus, not to avoid it. Like awareness, it involves a neutrality or suspended judgment toward the stimulus. At worst, the student may merely not actively seek to avoid the stimulus. At best, he is willing to take notice of the phenomenon and give it his attention.

1.3   *Controlled or selected attention* requires the differentiation of aspects of a stimulus which is perceived as clearly marked off from adjacent impressions. It may refer not only to the selectivity of attention, but also to the control of attention, so that the individual will attend to certain stimuli when they are present.

2.0   *Responding* is concerned with responses which go beyond merely attending to the phenomenon. The student is doing something with or about the phenomenon besides merely perceiving it. Most commonly, the student becomes sufficiently involved in or committed to a subject, phenomenon, or activity that he will seek it out and gain satisfaction from working with it or engaging in it.

2.1   *Acquiescence in responding* may be described as compliance. There is a passiveness so far as the initiation of the behavior is concerned, and the stimulus calling for this behavior is not subtle. Compliance is perhaps a better term than obedience, since there is more of the element of reaction to a suggestion and less of the implication of resistance or yielding unwillingly. The student makes the response, but he has not fully accepted the necessity for doing so.

2.2 *Willingness to respond* implies a voluntary activity. The element of resistance or of yielding unwillingly, which may be present at the previous level, is here replaced with consent or proceeding from one's own choice.

2.3 *Satisfaction in response* is behavior accompanied by a feeling of satisfaction—an emotional response, generally of pleasure, zest, or enjoyment.

3.0 *Valuing* means that a thing, phenomenon, or behavior has worth. This abstract concept of worth is, in part, a result of the individual's own valuing or assessment, but it is much more a social product that has been slowly internalized or accepted, and has come to be used by the student as his own criterion of worth.

Behavior categorized at this level is sufficiently consistent and stable to have taken on the characteristics of a belief or an attitude. The learner displays this behavior with sufficient consistency in appropriate situations that he comes to be perceived as holding a value. (At this level we are not concerned with the relationships among values.) An important element of behavior characterized by valuing is that it is not motivated by the desire to comply or obey, but by the individual's commitment to the underlying value guiding the behavior.

3.1 *Acceptance of a value* is concerned with ascribing worth to a phenomenon, behavior, object, etc. At this lowest level of valuing, we are concerned with the lowest levels of certainty—that is, there is more of a readiness to reevaluate one's position than at higher levels. It is a position that is somewhat tentative. One of the distinguishing characteristics of this behavior is consistency of response to the class of objects, phenomena, etc. with which the belief or attitude is identified.

3.2 *Preference for a value* reflects a level of internalization between the mere acceptance of a value and commitment in terms of deep involvement in an area. Behavior at this level implies not just the acceptance of a value to the point of being willing to be identified with it, but the individual will pursue the value, seek it out, want it.

3.3 *Commitment* involves a high degree of certainty in a belief. In some instances, this may border on faith, in the sense of a firm emotional acceptance of a belief upon admittedly nonrational grounds. Loyalty to a position, group, or cause would also be classified here.

4.0 *Organization* may occur as the learner encounters situations for which more than one of the values he has internalized is relevant. Thus, the necessity arises for (a) the organization of the values into a system, (b) the determination of the interrelationships among them, and (c) the establishment of the dominant and pervasive ones. Such a system is built gradually, subject to change as new values are incorporated.

4.1 *Conceptualization of a value* occurs when the individual sees how the value relates to those that he already holds or to new ones that he is coming to hold.

4.2 *Organization of a value system* begins when the learner brings together a complex of values, possibly disparate values, and brings these into an ordered relationship with one another. Ideally, the ordered relationship will be one which is harmonious and internally consistent. In actuality, the relationship is best described as a kind of dynamic equilibrium which is, in part, dependent upon those portions of the environment which are salient at any point in time.

5.0 *Characterization by a value or value complex* is reached when the values already internalized in the individual's value hierarchy, are organized into some kind of internally consistent system, and control the behavior of the individual for a sufficient time, that the individual acts consistently in accordance with the values he has internalized.

5.1 *Generalized set* is that which gives an internal consistency to the system of attitudes and values at any particular moment. It involves selective responding at a very high level. It may often be an unconscious set which guides action without conscious forethought. A generalized set is a basic orientation which enables the individual to reduce and order the complex world about him, and to act consistently and effectively on it.

5.2 *Characterization,* the peak of the internalization process, includes those objectives which are broadest with respect to both the phenomena covered and to the range of behavior which they comprise. Thus, here are found those objectives which concern one's view of the universe, one's philosophy of life, one's *Weltanschauung* —a value system having as its object the whole of what is known or knowable.

THE PSYCHOMOTOR DOMAIN

1.0 *Perception*—This is an essential first step in performing a motor act. It is the process of becoming aware of objects, qualities or relations by way of the sense organs. It is a necessary but not sufficient condition for motor activity. It is basic in the   situation - interpretation - action   chain leading to motor activity. The category of perception has been divided into three subcategories indicating three different levels of the perception process. This level is a parallel of the first category, receiving or attending, in the affective domain.

1.1 *Sensory stimulation* — Impingement of a stimulus (i) upon one or more of the sense organs.

1.11 *Auditory* — Hearing or the sense of organs of hearing.

1.12 *Visual* — Concerned with the mental pictures or images obtained through the eyes.

1.13 *Tactile* — Pertaining to the sense of touch.

1.14 *Taste* — Determine the relish or flavor of by taking a portion into the mouth.

1.15 *Smell* — To perceive by excitation of the olfactory nerves.

1.16 *Kinesthetic* — The muscle sense; pertaining to sensitivity from activation of receptors in muscles, tendons, and joints.

The preceding categories are not presented in any special order of importance, although, in Western cultures, the visual cues are said to have dominance, whereas in some cultures, the auditory and tactile clues may preempt the high position we give the visual. Probably no sensible ordering of these is possible at this time. It should also be pointed out that "the cues that guide action may change for a particular motor activity as learning progresses (e.g., kinesthetic cues replacing visual cues)" [51].[3]

1.1 *Sensory stimulation* — Illustrative educational objectives.

Sensitivity to auditory cues in playing a musical instrument as a member of a group.

Awareness of difference in "hand" of various fabrics.

Sensitivity to flavors in seasoning food.

1.2 *Cue selection* — Deciding to what cues one must respond in order to satisfy the particular requirements of task performance.

SOURCE: Simpson (1969). See Simpson (1966-67) for rationale and method of development of the classification system.

[3]Reference 51 not reprinted here.

This involves identification of the cue or cues and associating them with the task to be performed.

It may involve grouping of cues in terms of past experience and knowledge. Cues relevant to the situation are selected as a guide to action; irrelevant cues are ignored or discarded.

1.2   *Cue selection* — Illustrative educational objectives.

Recognition of operating difficulties with machinery through the sound of the machine in operation.

Sensing where the needle should be set in beginning machine stitching.

Recognizing factors to take into account in batting in a softball game.

1.3   *Translation* — Relating of perception to action in performing a motor act. This is the mental process of determining the meaning of the cues received for action. It involves symbolic translation, that is, having an image or being reminded of something, "having an idea," as a result of cues received.

It may involve insight which is essential in solving a problem through perceiving the relationships essential to solution. Sensory translation is an aspect of this level. It involves "feedback," that is, knowledge of the effects of the process. Translation is a continuous part of the motor act being performed.

1.3   *Translation* — Illustrative educational objectives.

Ability to relate music to dance form.

Ability to follow a recipe in preparing food.

Knowledge of the "feel" of operating a sewing machine successfully and use of this knowledge as a guide in stitching.

2.0 *Set* — Set is a preparatory adjustment or readiness for a particular kind of action or experience.

Three aspects of set have been identified: mental, physical, and emotional.

2.1   *Mental set* — Readiness, in the mental sense, to perform a certain motor act. This involves, as prerequisite, the level of perception and its subcategories. Discrimination, that is, using judgment in making distinctions, is an aspect of mental set.

2.1   *Mental set* — Illustrative educational objectives.

Knowledge of steps in setting the table.

Knowledge of tools appropriate to performance of various sewing operations.

2.2 *Physical set* — Readiness in the sense of having made the anatomical adjustments necessary for a motor act to be performed. Readiness, in the physical sense, involves receptor set, that is, sensory attending, or focusing the attention of the needed sensory organs and postural set, or positioning of the body.

   2.2 *Physical set* — Illustrative educational objectives.

   Achievement of bodily stance preparatory to bowling.

   Positioning of hands preparatory to typing.

2.3 *Emotional set* — Readiness in terms of attitudes favorable to the motor acts taking place. Willingness to respond is implied.

   2.3 *Emotional set* — Illustrative educational objectives.

   Disposition to perform sewing machine operation to best of ability.

   Desire to operate a production drill press with skill.

3.0 *Guided response* — This is an early step in the development of skill. Emphasis here is upon abilities which are components of the more complex skill. Guided response is the overt behavioral act of an individual under the guidance of the instructor or in response to self-evaluation where the student has a model or criteria against which he can judge his performance. Prerequisite to performance of the act are readiness to respond, in terms of set to produce the overt behavioral act and selection of the appropriate response. Selection of response may be defined as deciding what response must be made in order to satisfy the requirements of task performance. There appear to be two major subcategories, imitation and trial and error.

3.1 *Imitation* — Imitation is the execution of an act as a direct response to the perception of another person performing the act.

   3.1 *Imitation* — Illustrative educational objectives.

   Imitation of the process of stay-stitching the curved neck edge of a bodice.

   Performing a dance step as demonstrated.

   Debeaking a chick in the manner demonstrated.

3.2 *Trial and error* — Trying various responses, usually with some rationale for each response, until an appropriate response is achieved. The appropriate response is one which meets the requirements of task performance, that is, "gets the job done" or does it more efficiently. This level may be defined as multiple-response learning in which the proper response is selected out of varied behavior, possibly through the influence of reward and punishment.

3.2   *Trial and error* — Illustrative educational objectives.

Discovering the most efficient method of ironing a blouse through trial of various procedures.

Determining the sequence for cleaning a room through trial of several patterns.

4.0   *Mechanism* — Learned response has become habitual. At this level, the learner has achieved a certain confidence and degree of proficiency in the performance of the act. The act is a part of his repertoire of possible responses to stimuli and the demands of situations where the response is an appropriate one. The response may be more complex than at the preceding level; it may involve some patterning in carrying out the task.

4.0   *Mechanism* — Illustrative educational objectives.

Ability to perform a hand-hemming operation.

Ability to mix ingredients for butter cake.

Ability to pollinate an oat flower.

5.0   *Complex overt response* — At this level, the individual can perform a motor act that is considered complex because of the movement pattern required. At this level, skill has been attained. The act can be carried out smoothly and efficiently, that is, with minimum expenditure of time and energy. There are two subcategories: resolution of uncertainty and automatic performance.

5.1   *Resolution of uncertainty* — The act is performed without hesitation of the individual to get a mental picture of task sequence. That is, he knows the sequence required and so proceeds with confidence. The act is here defined as complex in nature.

5.1   *Resolution of uncertainty* — Illustrative educational objectives.

Skill in operating a milling machine.

Skill in setting up and operating a production band saw.

Skill in laying a pattern on fabric and cutting out a garment.

5.2   *Automatic performance* — At this level, the individual can perform a finely coordinated motor skill with a great deal of ease and muscle control.

5.2   *Automatic performance* — Illustrative educational objectives.

Skill in performing basic steps of national folk dances.

Skill in tailoring a suit.

Skill in performing on the violin.

6.0 *Adaptation* — Altering motor activities to meet the demands of new problematic situations requiring a physical response.

6.0 *Adaptation* — Illustrative educational objectives.

Developing a modern dance composition through adapting known abilities and skills in dance.

7.0 *Origination* — Creating new motor acts or ways of manipulating materials out of understandings, abilities, and skills developed in the psychomotor area.

7.0 *Origination* — Illustrative educational objectives.

Creation of a modern dance.

Creation of a new game requiring psychomotor response.

BIBLIOGRAPHY

AIKEN, WILFORD M. *The Story of the Eight-Year Study.* New York: Harper and Brothers, 1942.

AMERICAN ASSOCIATION FOR THE ADVANCEMENT OF SCIENCE. *Science—a Process Approach.* Part A–E. New York: Xerox Corp., 1969.

————. Part F–G. New York: Xerox Corp., 1970.

ANDERSON, RICHARD C. "The Comparative Field Experiment: an Illustration from High School Biology," *Proceedings of the 1968 Invitational Conference on Testing Problems.* Princeton, N.J.: Educational Testing Service (1969).

ANDERSON, RICHARD C., FAUST, GERALD W., AND RODERICK, MARIANNE C. "A Brief Report on the Field Test of a Program in Population Genetics," *BSCS Newsletter,* No. 35 (May, 1969).

ATKIN, MYRON. "Behavioral Objectives in Curriculum Design," *Science Teacher* (May, 1968).

BALZER, LE VON. "Nonverbal and Verbal Behaviors of Biology Teachers," *The American Biology Teacher* (April, 1969).

BENNIS, WARREN G. *Changing Organizations.* New York: McGraw-Hill Book Co., 1966.

BENNIS, WARREN G., AND SLATER, PHILIP E. *The Temporary Society.* New York: Harper & Row, Publishers, 1968.

BENNIS, WARREN G., BENNE, KENNETH D., AND CHIN, ROBERT. *The Planning of Change.* (2d ed.) New York: Holt, Rinehart & Winston, Inc., 1969.

BIOLOGICAL SCIENCES CURRICULUM STUDY. *BSCS Newsletter,* No. 17 (March, 1963). Boulder, Colorado: BSCS, P.O. Box 930, Boulder, Colorado, 80302.

————. "1964 Revised BSCS Biology Laboratory Facilities Checklist," *ibid.,* No. 21 (April, 1964).

————. *New Materials and Techniques in the Preparation of High School Biology Teachers.* (*BSCS Special Publication,* No. 6.) Boulder, Colo.: BSCS, 1969.

BLAU, PETER M. *The Dynamics of Bureaucracy.* Chicago, Ill.: University of Chicago Press, 1963.

BLOOM, BENJAMIN S. *Stability and Change in Human Characteristics.* New York: John Wiley & Sons, Inc., 1964.

———(ed.). *Taxonomy of Educational Objectives, the Classification of Educational Goals, Handbook I: the Cognitive Domain.* New York: David McKay Co., Inc., 1956.

BLUM, HENDRICK L. AND LEONARD, ALVIN R. *Public Administration: a Public Health Viewpoint.* New York: The Macmillan Co., 1963.

BOBBITT, F. *How to Make a Curriculum.* New York: Houghton Mifflin Co., 1924.

BODE, BOYD. *Modern Educational Theories.* New York: The Macmillan Co., 1927.

BOFFEY, PHILIP M. "Budget Trauma: NSF Funds Run Dry at University of Massachusetts. News and Commentary," *Science* (November 15, 1968).

BOND, GUY L., AND DYKSTRA, ROBERT. "The Cooperative Research Program in First Grade Reading Instruction," *Reading Research Quarterly,* II, No. 4 (Summer, 1967).

BOOCOCK, SARANE S., AND SCHILD, E.O. (ed.). *Simulation Games in Learning.* Beverly Hills, Calif.: Sage Publications, Inc., 1968.

BOYER, WILLIAM H. AND WALSH, PAUL. "Are Children Born Unequal?" *The Saturday Review* (October 19, 1968).

BRAMELD, THEODORE. *Education as Power.* New York: Holt, Rinehart & Winston, Inc., 1965.

BROUDY, H.S. "Research and the Dogma of Behavioral Objectives." Unpublished paper read at the annual meeting of the American Educational Research Association, Los Angeles, Calif., 1969.

BRUDNER, HARVEY J. "Computer-Managed Instruction," *Science* (November 29, 1968).

BRUNER, JEROME S. *The Process of Education.* New York: Random House, Inc., 1960.

———. *Toward a Theory of Instruction.* Cambridge, Mass.: The Belknap Press of Harvard University Press, 1966.

CAHEN, LEONARD S. "An Interim Report on the National Longitudinal Study of Mathematical Abilities," *Mathematics Teacher,* LVIII (October, 1965).

CARLSON, RICHARD O. *Adoption of Educational Innovations.* Eugene, Ore.: Center for the Advanced Study of Educational Administration, University of Oregon, 1965.

CARLSON, RICHARD O., GALLAHER, ART, JR., MILES, MATTHEW B., PELLE-GRIN, ROLAND J., AND ROGERS, EVERETT M. *Change Processes in the Public Schools.* Eugene, Ore.: Center for the Advanced Study of Educational Administration, University of Oregon, 1965.

CHAMBERLIN, C.D., CHAMBERLIN, ENID, DROUGHT, N.E., AND SCOTT, W.E. *Did They Succeed in College?* (*Adventure in American Education,* Vol. IV) New York: Harper and Brothers, 1942.

COMMITTEE FOR MEASUREMENT OF ECONOMIC UNDERSTANDING OF THE JOINT COUNCIL ON ECONOMIC EDUCATION. *Test of Economic Understanding.* Chicago, Ill.: Science Research Associates, 1963.

CONTRA COSTA COUNTY. *DEEP, 1964–67.* Unit 1 and Unit 2. Pleasant Hill, Calif.: Contra Costa County Department of Education, 1967.

COOK, DESMOND L. *The Impact of the Hawthorne Effect in Experimental Designs in Educational Research.* (OE Project No. 1757, Contract No. OE-3-10-041.) Columbus, Ohio: The Ohio State University, 1967.

DRESSEL, P., AND MAYHEW, L.B. *General Education: Explorations in Evaluation.* Washington, D.C.: American Council on Education, 1954.

EASLEY, J.A., JR., KENDZIOR, ELIZABETH, AND WALLACE, ROBERT. "A 'Bio-Assay' of Biology Tests," *The American Biology Teacher* (May, 1967).

EASLEY, JOHN A., JR., JENKINS, EDWARD S., AND ASHENFELTER, JOHN W. "A Scheme for the Analysis of Elementary Science Materials," *The EPIE Forum* (November, 1967).

EASTERN REGIONAL INSTITUTE FOR EDUCATION. *Improving Process-Oriented Education.* Syracuse, N.Y.: Eastern Regional Institute for Education, undated.

EBEL, ROBERT L. *Measuring Educational Achievement.* Englewood Cliffs, N.J.: Prentice-Hall, Inc., 1965. Reprinted by permission of Prentice-Hall, Inc.

Education Recaps. Princeton, N.J.: Educational Testing Service, 1969.

EVANS, T.P. "Category System for Teacher Behaviors," *The American Biology Teacher* (April, 1969).

FARR, ROGER, LAFFEY, JAMES, AND SMITH, CARL. "Taxonomy of Evaluation Techniques for Reading Programs." Mimeographed. Bloomington, Ind.: Measurement and Evaluation Center in Reading Education, School of Education, Indiana University, 1968.

FOX, DAVID J. "Techniques for the Analysis of Qualitative Data," In *The Research Process in Education* by David J. Fox, chapter 22. New York: Holt, Rinehart & Winston, Inc., 1969.

FREEMAN, IRA M., AND PATTON, A. RAE. *The Science of Chemistry.* New York: Random House, Inc., 1968.

FRENCH, JOHN W., AND MICHAEL, WILLIAM B. (cochairmen). *Standards for Educational and Psychological Tests and Manuals.* (Prepared by a Joint Committee of the American Psychological Association, American Educational Research Association, and National Council for Measurement in Education.) Washington, D.C.: American Psychological Association, Inc., 1966.

GAGNÉ, ROBERT M. *The Conditions of Learning.* New York: Holt, Rinehart & Winston, Inc., 1964.

GAGNÉ, ROBERT M. AND GEPHART, WILLIAM J. (ed.). *Learning Research and School Subjects.* Itasca, Ill.: F.E. Peacock Publishers, Inc., 1968.

GALLAGHER, JAMES J. "Teacher Variation in Concept Presentation in BSCS Curriculum Program," *BSCS Newsletter* (November 30, 1967).

GARDNER, JOHN W. *Excellence.* New York: Harper and Brothers, 1961.

GLASER, ROBERT. "Learning," *Encyclopedia of Educational Research,* ed. Robert Ebel (4th ed.). New York: The Macmillan Co., 1969.

GOLDHAMMER, KEITH. "Issues and Strategies in the Public Acceptance of Educational Change." Mimeographed. Eugene, Ore.: Center for the Advanced Study of Educational Administration, University of Oregon, 1965.

GOODLAD, JOHN. *School Curriculum Reform in the United States.* New York: The Fund for the Advancement of Education, 1964.

GOODLAD, JOHN, WITH VON STOEPHASIUS, RENATA, AND KLEIN, M. FRANCES. *The Changing School Curriculum.* New York: The Fund for the Advancement of Education, 1966.

GREENBERG, D.S. "American Institute of Biological Sciences Accused of Misuse of NSF Grant Funds," *Science* (January 25, 1963).

GROBMAN, ARNOLD B. *The Changing Classroom: the Role of the Biological Science Curriculum Study.* New York: Doubleday & Co., Inc., 1969.

GROBMAN, ARNOLD B., HURD, PAUL DEH., KLINGE, PAUL, LAWLER, MARGARET MCKIBBEN, AND PALMER, ELRA. *BSCS Biology—Implementation in the Schools.* (*Biological Sciences Curriculum Study Bulletin,* No. 3.) Boulder, Colo.: Biological Sciences Curriculum Study, 1964.

GROBMAN, HULDA. "The Public School Principal's Operational Behavior, Theory and Practice, and Related School and Community Interactions, Based on Data from the Investigations of the University of Florida CPEA Leadership Project." Unpublished dissertation, University of Florida, 1958.

————. "Comments on the Evaluation Program Findings and their Implications," *BSCS Newsletter,* No. 19 (September, 1963).

————. "Needed Research in High School Biology," *The American Biology Teacher* (November, 1965).

————. *Evaluation Activities of Curriculum Projects. (The American Educational Research Association Monograph Series on Curriculum Evaluation,* No. 2.) Chicago, Ill.: Rand McNally & Co., 1968.

————. "Cooperative Parallel Research in Science Education," *The Science Teacher* (February, 1970).

————. "Considerations Germane to the Identification of Nonspecified Functional Objectives and Dysfunctional Outcomes in Curriculum Evaluation." In *Readings on Curriculum Evaluation,* edited by Hulda Grobman and Vynce P. Hines. Itasca, Ill.: F.E. Peacock Publishers, Inc., forthcoming.

GROBMAN, HULDA AND HINES, VYNCE A.   "Teacher as Conservator of the Past versus Leader for Change." In *The Teacher's Role in American Society* (14th yearbook of the John Dewey Society), edited by Lindley J. Styles. New York: Harper and Brothers, 1957.

———— (eds.).   *Readings on Curriculum Evaluation.* Itasca, Ill.: F.E. Peacock Publishers, Inc., forthcoming.

GUBA, EGA.   "Significant Differences," *Educational Researcher.* (Newsletter of the American Educational Research Association) (March, 1969).

GUILFORD, J.P.   *The Nature of Human Intelligence.* New York: McGraw-Hill Book Co., 1967.

HALPIN, ANDREWS.   "Change—the Mythology," *Theory into Practice* (February, 1969).

HERRNSTEIN, R.J.   "Importance of Being Important." (Letter to the Editor.) *Science* (May 24, 1968).

HERZOG, ELIZABETH.   *Some Guidelines for Evaluative Research.* Washington, D.C.: U.S. Department of Health, Education and Welfare, Social Security Administration, Children's Bureau, 1959.

HILLS, R. JEAN.   *A Second Analysis of Communication and Status: the Dynamics of a Research Center.* (Occasional paper.) Eugene, Ore.: Center for the Advanced Study of Educational Administration, University of Oregon, 1966.

HINES, VYNCE A.   "A Critical Study of Certain Criteria for Selecting Curriculum Content." Unpublished dissertation, University of Illinois, 1950.

JOINT COMMITTEE OF THE NATIONAL EDUCATION ASSOCIATION AND THE AMERICAN TEXTBOOK PUBLISHERS INSTITUTE. *Guidelines for Textbook Selection.* Washington, D.C.: National Education Association, 1963.

―――. (Revised.) Washington, D.C.: National Education Association, 1967.

JOINT COUNCIL ON ECONOMIC EDUCATION. *DEEP 1969: Perspectives on a 5-year Experiment in Curriculum Change.* New York: Joint Council on Economic Education, 1969.

JUNGWIRTH, E. "Teaching for 'Understanding of Science.' " *Journal of Biological Education* (1968).

KAPLAN, ABRAHAM. *The Conduct of Inquiry.* San Francisco, Calif.: Chandler Publishing Company, copyright c 1964 by Chandler Publishing Company.

KLAUSMEIER, HERBERT J. "Transfer of Learning," *Encyclopedia of Educational Research,* ed. Robert Ebel (4th ed.). New York: The Macmillan Co., 1969.

KLINCKMANN, EVELYN. "Preparation of Test Items and Tests for BSCS Biology," *BSCS Newsletter,* No. 10 (November, 1961).

KRATHWOHL, DAVID R. "Stating Objectives Appropriately for Program, for Curriculum, and for Instructional Material Development," *Journal of Teacher Education,* 16, p. 83-92 (1965).

KRATHWOHL, DAVID R., BLOOM, BENJAMIN S., AND MASIA, BERTRAM B. *Taxonomy of Educational Objectives, the Classification of Educational Goals, Handbook II: Affective Domain.* New York: David McKay Co., Inc., 1964.

KROPP, RUSSELL P., AND STOKER, HOWARD W. "The Construction and Validation of Tests of the Cognitive Processes as Described in the *Taxonomy of Educational Objectives,"* *Cooperative Research Project,* No. 2117 (February, 1966).

KURTZ, EDWIN B., JR. "Biology in Science . . . a Process Approach," *The American Biology Teacher* (March, 1967).

LADO, ROBERT. *Language Testing.* New York: McGraw-Hill Book Co., 1961.

LA SHIER, W.S., JR., AND WESTMEYER, J.T. "Use of Interaction Analysis in BSCS Laboratory Block Classrooms," *Journal of Teacher Education* (Winter, 1967).

LEE, ADDISON E. (ed.). *Research and Curriculum Development in Science Education, New Programs in High School Biology.* Austin, Tex.: University of Texas Science Education Center, 1967.

LEE, KIM. *Chinese Cookbook.* New York: Harper & Row, Publishers, 1968.

LEEPER, ROBERT R. (ed.). *Assessing and Using Curriculum Content.* Washington, D.C.: Association for Supervision and Curriculum Development, 1965.

LIKERT, RENSIS. *The Human Organization, Its Management and Value.* New York: McGraw-Hill Book Co., 1967.

LOCKARD, J. DAVID. (ed.). *Sixth Report of the International Clearinghouse on Science and Mathematics Curricular Developments, 1968.* (A joint project of the Commission on Science Education, American Association for the Advancement of Science, and Science Teaching Center, University of Maryland.) College Park, Md.: University of Maryland, 1968.

MCCOY, ELEANOR. Untitled manuscript of UICSM history. Urbana, Ill.: Curriculum Laboratory, University of Illinois, forthcoming.

MCGUIRE, CHRISTINE. *Simulation Technique in the Evaluation of Clinical Judgment.* Chicago, Ill.: Evaluation Unit, Center for the Study of Medical Education, College of Medicine, University of Illinois, 1967.

————. "A Behavioral Approach to the Examination and Evaluation of Medical Students and Medical Curricula." Mimeographed. Chicago, Ill.: Evaluation Unit, Center for the Study of Medical Education, College of Medicine, University of Illinois, undated.

MCGUIRE, CHRISTINE, AND BABBOTT, DAVID. "Simulation Technique in the Measurement of Problem-Solving Skills," *Journal of Educational Measurement* (Spring, 1967).

MAGER, ROBERT F. *Preparing Instructional Objectives.* Palo Alto, Calif.: Fearon Publishers, Inc., 1962.

MAGUIRE, THOMAS O. "Decisions and Curriculum Objectives: a Methodology for Evaluation," *Alberta Journal of Educational Research* (March, 1969).

MAHER, JOHN E., SYMMES, S. STOWELL, AND GREEN, WILLIAM D. *DEEP '67.* New York: Joint Council on Economic Education, 1968.

MALLERY, DAVID. *High School Students Speak Out.* New York: Harper & Row, Publishers, 1962.

MASSIALAS, BYRON G., AND ZEVIN, JACK. *World History through Inquiry.* (A series of nine units, issued individually.) Chicago, Ill.: Rand McNally & Co., 1969–197_.

MERRILL, RICHARD J., AND RIDGWAY, DAVID W. *The CHEM Study Story.* San Francisco, Calif.: W.H. Freeman & Co. Publishers, 1969.

MORRISON, ROBERT S. "Where is Biology Taking Us?" *Science* (January 27, 1967).

NATIONAL ADVISORY COMMISSION ON CIVIL DISORDERS. *Report of the National Advisory Commission on Civil Disorders, March 1, 1968.* Washington, D.C.: U.S. Government Printing Office, 1968.

NATIONAL ADVISORY COUNCIL ON EDUCATIONAL PROFESSIONS DEVELOPMENT. "Evaluation of Educational Programs." Mimeographed. Washington, D.C.: National Advisory Council on Educational Professions Development, 1969.

OSS ASSESSMENT STAFF. *Assessment of Men.* New York: Rinehart, 1948.

PARAKH, J.S. "A Study of Teacher-Pupil Interaction in BSCS Yellow Version Biology Classes," *The American Biology Teacher* (December, 1968).

PELLEGRIN, ROLAND J. "An Analysis of Sources and Processes of Innovation in Education." Mimeographed. Eugene, Ore.: Center for the Advanced Study of Educational Administration, 1966.

PETER, LAWRENCE J., AND HULL, RAYMOND. *The Peter Principle.* New York: William Morrow & Co., Inc., 1969.

POPHAM, W. JAMES, EISNER, ELIOT S., SULLIVAN, HOWARD J., AND TYLER, LOUISE L. *Instructional Objectives.* (*The American Educational Research Association Monograph Series on Curriculum Evaluation,* No. 3.) Chicago, Ill.: Rand McNally & Co., 1969.

"Pressures on Children," *Theory into Practice* (February, 1968).

RATHS, JAMES D. "Specificity as a Threat to Curriculum Reform." (Paper read at the annual meeting of The American Educational Research Association.) Chicago, Ill.: February, 1968.

RIPLEY, ANTHONY. "A-Plants: Wealth and Worry," *The New York Times* (September 20, 1969).

ROBINSON, JAMES T. "Evaluating Laboratory Work in High School Biology," *The American Biology Teacher* (April, 1969).

ROGERS, EVERETT M. *Diffusion of Innovations.* New York: The Free Press, 1962.

ROMBERG, THOMAS A., AND WILSON, JAMES W. "The Development of Mathematics Achievement Tests for the National Longitudinal Study of Mathematical Abilities," *Mathematics Teacher* (May, 1968).

SAMUELSON, PAUL A. *Economics.* (7th ed.) New York: McGraw-Hill Book Company, 1967.

SAVIN, ENOCH I. *Evaluation and the Work of the Teacher.* Belmont, Calif.: Wadsworth Publishing Co., Inc., 1969.

SCHON, DONALD A. *Technology and Change, the New Heraclitus.* New York: The Delacorte Press, 1967.

SCHWEBEL, MILTON. *Who Can Be Educated?* New York: Grove Press, Inc., 1968.

SCRIVEN, MICHAEL. "The Methodology of Evaluation." In *Perspectives of Curriculum Evaluation,* by Ralph W. Tyler, Robert M. Gagné, and Michael Scriven. (*The American Educational Research Association Monograph Series on Curriculum Evaluation,* No. 1.) Chicago, Ill.: Rand McNally & Co., 1967.

SESSIONS, JOHN A. "The Bias in High School Textbooks," *The American Federationist* (January, 1967).

SIMON, ANITA, AND BOYER, E. GIL. *Mirrors for Behavior, an Anthology of Classroom Observation Instruments.* Philadelphia, Pa.: Research for Better Schools, 1967.

SIMPSON, ELIZABETH. "The Classification of Educational Objectives, Psychomotor Domain," *Illinois Teacher of Home Economics* (Winter, 1966-67).

———. "Classification of Educational Objectives, Psychomotor Domain." Mimeographed. Urbana, Ill.: Bureau of Educational Research, University of Illinois, 1969.

———. "Taxonomy of the Psychomotor Domain." Mimeographed. Urbana, Ill.: Bureau of Educational Research, 1969.

SMITH, ALFRED G. *Communication and Status: the Dynamics of a Research Center.* Eugene, Ore.: Center for the Advanced Study of Educational Administration, University of Oregon, 1966.

SOLANDT, O.M. "The Control of Technology," (an editorial). *Science* (August, 1969).

STAKE, ROBERT E. "The Countenance of Educational Evaluation," *Teachers College Record* (April, 1967).

———. "Testing in the Evaluation of Curriculum Development," *Review of Educational Research,* ch. IX (February, 1968).

STARR, CHAUNCEY. "Social Benefits versus Technological Risk," *Science* (September 19, 1969).

STEVENS, W. WILLIAM, JR. AND MORRISSETT, IRVING. "A System for Analyzing Social Science Curricula," *The EPIE Forum* (December, 1967-January, 1968).

SUCHMAN, EDWARD A. *Evaluative Research, Principles and Practices in Public Service and Social Action Programs.* New York: Russell Sage Foundation, 1967.

SYMMES, S. STOWELL. *Handbook for Developmental Economic Education Programs.* New York: Joint Council on Economic Education, 1212 Avenue of the Americas, New York, New York, 1969.

THOMSEN, DONALD R. "An Analysis of Certain Objective Measures for the Prediction of the Community's Reaction to a Principal's Behavior." Unpublished Ph.D. dissertation, University of Florida, 1956.

TYLER, RALPH W. *Basic Principles of Curriclum and Instruction: Syllabus for Education 305.* Chicago, Ill.: University of Chicago Press, 1950.

————. "New Dimensions in Curriculum Development," *Phi Delta Kappan* (September, 1966).

TYLER, RALPH W., GAGNE, ROBERT M., AND SCRIVEN, MICHAEL. *Perspectives on Curriculum Evaluation. (American Educational Research Association Monograph Series on Curriculum Evaluation,* No. 1.) Chicago, Ill.: Rand McNally & Co., 1967.

U.S. OFFICE OF EDUCATION. *Guidelines on Authorizing Limited Copyright Protection for Materials Developed Under Project Grants and Contracts.* U.S. Office of Education, July 24, 1968.

U.S. PUBLIC HEALTH SERVICE. *Evaluation in Mental Health.* (U.S. Department of Health, Education, and Welfare, Public Health Service, Publication No. 413.) Washington, D.C.: Government Printing Office, 1955.

WALLEN, NORMAN E., AND TRAVERS, ROBERT M.W. "Analysis and Investigation of Teaching Methods." In *Handbook of Research on Teaching,* edited by N.L. Gage, ch.10. Chicago, Ill.: Rand McNally & Co., 1963.

WALSH, JOHN. "Curriculum Reform: Success Hasn't Spoiled NSF Program, but Biology Study's Status Reflects Problems," *Science* (July 16, 1965).

WEBB, EUGENE J., CAMPBELL, DONALD T., SCHWARTZ, RICHARD D., AND SECHREST, LEE. *Unobtrusive Measures: Nonreactive Research in the Social Sciences.* Chicago, Ill.: Rand McNally & Co., 1966.

WILLEMS, EDWIN P., AND RAUSH, HAROLD L. (ed.). *Naturalistic Viewpoints in Psychological Research.* New York: Holt, Rinehart & Winston, Inc., 1969.

WITTROCK, M.C. "The Evaluation of Instruction: Cause and Effect Relations in Naturalistic Data." In *The Evaluation of Instruction: Issues and Problems,* edited by M.C. Wittrock and D.E. Wiley. New York: Holt, Rinehart & Winston, Inc., in press.

WOLFLE, DAEL. "Control by Accountants," (an editorial). *Science,* Vol. 156 (May 19, 1967).

WOOTON, WILLIAM. *SMSG: the Making of a Curriculum.* New Haven, Conn.: Yale University Press, 1965.

ZIGLER, EDWARD. "Training the Intellect versus Development of the Child." Paper presented at The American Educational Research Association Meeting, Los Angeles, Calif., February, 1969.

INDEX

AAAS Science Inquiry Project, 91, 99
  target audience, 121
  tests, 193
  tryouts, 143
Abbreviations and acronyms, 231-232
Acceptance of existing structure and
  media, 119-120
Accomplishment and potential, 222-224
Adaptation, 243
Affective domain, 92-96, 111, 235
Age and lifespan of the organization,
  48-55
Aiken, Wilford M., 32n
Aims, long-run, intermediate and
  immediate, 96-104
American Chemical Society, 4n
American Economy, The (JCEE film
  series), 161-162
American Geological Institute, 55
American Institute of Biological
  Sciences, 7
American Sociological Association, 55,
  59
American Textbook Publishers
  Institute, 212, 213
Analysis, 89, 111, 233, 234, 235
Anderson, Florence, 148n
Anderson, Richard C., 201, 218n
Antecedents, 172, 185
Application, 89, 233, 234
Area Consultant Program, 13
Ashenfelter, John W., 179n, 184n
Assessment of Men, 193n
Association of American Geographers,
  59
Assumptions underlying the curriculum,
  104-110
Atkin, Myron, 100
Audio material, 154
Automatic performance, 242

Auxiliary staff, 136-137
Awareness, 236
Babbott, David, 192, 193n
Background of developmental
  curriculum projects, 1-6
Balzer, Le Von, 218
Beberman, Max, 63, 140, 178
Begle, Edward, 63
Benne, Kenneth D., 44, 209
Bennis, Warren G., 2, 44, 66, 109, 209
Biological Sciences Curriculum Study,
  3, 5, 7-15
  checklist, 186, 188
  continuity of projects, 51-53
  copyrights, 150
  decentralization, 5, 63
  decision-making, 63, 138-139
  developmental approach, 114, 119
  director, 69-70
  distribution of materials, 149-150
  evaluation, 179, 203, 215-219
  funding, 39, 41, 42
  IME, 24-25, 29
  programmed discussions, 117-118
  salaries, 82-83
  sponsorship, 56
  staff rotation, 79, 80
  target audience, 121-124, 126, 128
  teacher-training, 44, 160, 162, 207
  tryouts, 144, 191
  writing conference, 131-134
Blau, Peter M., 196, 200
Bloom, Benjamin S., 89n, 93n, 102,
  227, 228, 233n, 235
Blum, Hendrick L., 205
Bobbitt, F., 108
Bode, Boyd, 108
Boffey, Philip M., 38n
Bond, Guy L., 222n
Boocock, Sarane S., 157n